Let's Talk

An Introduction to Interpersonal Communication

Third Edition

Let's Talk

An Introduction to Interpersonal Communication

Third Edition

Freda S. Sathré-Eldon
Orange Coast College

Ray W. Olson
Clinical Psychologist

Clarissa I. Whitney
Santa Ana College

Scott, Foresman and Company   **Glenview, Illinois**

Dallas, Tex.   Oakland, N.J.   Palo Alto, Cal.
Tucker, Ga.   London, England

All internal cartoons and cover art by Brian Berley.

Library of Congress Cataloging in Publication Data

Sathré-Eldon, Freda S
  Let's talk.

  Includes bibliographies and index.
    1. Communication—Psychological aspects. 2. Inter-
personal communication. I. Olson, Ray W., joint
author. II. Whitney, Clarissa I., joint author.
III. Title.
BF637.C45S27   1980   302.2   80-21212
ISBN 0-673-15376-2

45678-VHJ-9089888786

About This Book

The purpose of *Let's Talk* is to help students learn the skills and techniques essential to effective intrapersonal and interpersonal communication, and to show them how to apply these skills and techniques in their daily lives. Speech is an extension of the personality, and by learning to extend their personalities, students can develop as people and experience rewarding interpersonal relationships.

Sound relationships are based on sound communication. Unfortunately, students generally are not taught effective principles and techniques of communication. Whatever they learn about intrapersonal and interpersonal relationships is learned by chance, by observation, by intuition, or whatever. Is it any wonder they often fail to communicate effectively? Such haphazard development is not permitted in math, science, or even sports. Why, then, is it tolerated in such a crucial area as effective communication with others?

Let's Talk and the Activities Supplement for *Let's Talk* (available from the publisher) are based on the following principles:

1. The formula for developing lasting, rewarding relationships is association + aspiration + appreciation. By "association" we mean that individuals must work and play together. They must spend time with each other. By "aspiration" we mean that individuals must establish common goals and values, and then cooperate with each other to accomplish their goals and maintain their values. "Appreciation" means that we express our feelings about each other by paying sincere compliments and showing interest through telephone calls, letters, gifts, and so on. Such acts require warmth, openness, and the willingness to take risks, and they are necessary for personal growth and meaningful exchanges.

2. Every individual has a unique personality and a valuable contribution to make to others. We must learn to accept our uniqueness positively.

3. Most of us experience a sense of loneliness at times. Loneliness is a valuable catalyst or incentive for interpersonal relationships.

4. Few of us develop our full potential. We must work to do so.

5. All relationships have emotional, physical, and financial limitations. We cannot be all things to all people.

6. Handling conflict in our relationships with others requires special skills and techniques. Learning and applying these skills will enhance our relationships and enrich our lives.

7. Finding a place in the profession or vocation of our choice requires knowledge, understanding and application of communicative skills and techniques.

8. An understanding of and appreciation for other cultures and mores are vital to all of us.

9. Communicating with others requires skills as well as desire. The development of these skills increases our ability to share ideas and feelings, and thus find more meaningful relationships.

Let's Talk has been written specifically for lower-division college students, though others may well find it meaningful and useful. It has been designed to serve as an introduction to speech communication theory, dealing with a wider range of communication areas than other texts. It contains a minimum of technical or complex terminology, and areas of study are limited to those most relevant and meaningful to students in their everyday experiences.

The authors are grateful to Professor Brian R. Betz, Communications Studies Department, State University of New York at Oswego, who read the chapter on conflict reduction and contributed to its revision. Conflict is a part of daily life, whether between individuals, groups, or nations. This is not necessarily bad. Out of conflict may come growth, improvement, progress. We may not be able, personally, to resolve international conflicts, but the guidelines in the chapter on conflict reduction can help us to deal more effectively with the interpersonal conflicts we have in our everyday lives. Whether as international travelers or here in our own country, many of us come in contact with those from other cultures. We can find such contacts enriching and rewarding, if we deal effectively with the special communication problems they present. These are dealt with, and guidelines given, in the chapter on communication with other cultures. Of particular interest in this edition of *Let's Talk* is the new chapter: The Job Interview-"Communicate You." Also, each chapter contains new information, skills and techniques for the reader to learn and develop.

The activities in *Let's Talk* and the Activities Supplement are designed both to stimulate interest and to reinforce points made in the chapters. All have been classroom tested. The structure is flexible, so individual instructors can use the materials in any order that suits them or their students' needs. A combination of examples and illustrations with practical suggestions and techniques enables students to use the text unaided, if necessary. However the text is used, it is designed to help students understand their own communication problems, overcome or prevent communication breakdowns, and improve their relationships with others. We, the authors, welcome your involvement with us as we all strive to grow personally, to become more effective communicators, and to develop more rewarding interpersonal relationships.

F.S.–E.   R.W.O.   C.I.W.

Using This Book

Should help you to:

1. Develop an awareness and appreciation of the complexities of the communication process.
2. Increase your knowledge and understanding of intrapersonal and interpersonal communication.
3. Identify and overcome barriers in communication.
4. Seek out solutions to personal communication problems.
5. Develop new listening habits and a systematic method of listening behavior.
6. Become pleasantly assertive.
7. Become aware of the individual personality traits of self and others.
8. Enjoy healthy personal adjustment and better personal relationships.
9. Overcome self-consciousness and physical tension, and come to understand the importance of the proper use and coordination of both body and voice in the expression of thought.
10. Develop skill in interpreting and in conveying nonverbal cues that are consistent and congruent with the verbal message.
11. Recognize semantic problems in communication.
12. Become word-conscious in order to improve vocabulary and pronunciation.
13. Develop an easy use of language, a clear organization of ideas, and a sound analysis of problems.
14. Develop leadership skills and techniques.
15. Learn the skills and techniques involved in group process and role-playing.
16. Resolve conflicts in communication.
17. Learn the steps in critical thinking: (a) awareness of problem, (b) definition of problem, (c) formulation of possible solutions to problem, (d) choice of proper solution, (e) test of solution.
18. Learn how to "fight fair" in dealing with conflict situations, in order to bring about a resolution to the problem.
19. Learn the methods of persuasion in order to be able to change the attitudes and opinions of others.
20. Obtain speaking skills important to obtaining employment and job advancement.
21. Become acquainted with, and practice, those fundamental principles of good speech necessary for effective democratic living.
22. Learn the organizational structures in business and industry, and the role of the individual within the organization.
23. Develop an appreciation for those from other cultures, recognizing our similarities while allowing for cultural differences in our communications.

Contents

Let's Talk

1

The Nature of the Communication Process

FOR PREVIEW AND REVIEW

1. Communicating with others requires information about the speaker's and listener's backgrounds, attitudes, skills, knowledge, and physical, psychological, and emotional states.
2. An understanding of intrapersonal and interpersonal communication is vital.
3. The basic elements of communication include a person to originate an idea, the idea itself, a medium for expressing the idea, and someone to receive and interpret the idea.
4. Modes of communication include speaking, listening, reading, writing, and nonverbal communication.
5. Communication models have been constructed which illustrate the various elements in the communication process, and their relationships.
6. Techniques to prevent distortion and breakdown in communication include paraphrasing or repeating what has just been said and learning how different types of statements affect the openness of communication.
7. Twelve common problems in developing trust or in overcoming barriers, distortions, or breakdown in communication may be recognized and corrected by the use of suggested techniques.

INSTRUCTIONAL OBJECTIVES

After studying this chapter, you should be able to:
1. List the basic elements involved in communication.
2. Explain the significance of the concept of "process" as it relates to all communication factors.
3. Formulate a definition of communication, and to construct a communication model.
4. Correct distortions and breakdowns in communications with others.
5. Improve communications by practicing the echo feedback technique.
6. Learn about barriers and levels in communication and to understand the many different types of communication.
7. Learn and use statements and responses which foster open communication and to apply them in accordance with the immediate circumstances.

"That's Not What I Meant!"

"I feel like I've known you for years." Have you said that to someone—or has someone said that to you? On the other hand, have you experienced a feeling that "I know that you believe you understand what you think I said, but I am not sure you realize that what you heard is not what I meant"?

What causes these situations to occur and what can be done to enhance or change them?

Imagine two students, Trent and David, as communicators. Trent is a first semester college student and David is a fourth semester student. Trent is enthusiastic about his classes and his professors. He is anticipating meeting new people, and being exposed to new ideas. He has been working instead of going to school and has discovered a lack of knowledge in some areas of his job. He has found a real need for theoretical training to balance his practical experience. David, on the other hand, is in school because his parents want him to attend. He has followed a course prescribed by a counselor. Because he hasn't worked (other than part-time jobs) he isn't really sure what he needs or wants to learn. He has "sat through" a few classes taught by professors he didn't "like." He has survived as a student but isn't really sure he wants to finish his last semester.

Trent and David find themselves seated next to each other in a class room. The communication process begins when Trent says, "My name is Trent. How are you?" David responds with "Hi. My name is David." Let's suppose that David answers the question "How are you?" by saying, "O.K." Chances are that Trent would assume that David is looking forward to the class . . . and David might assume that Trent is as bored as he is with the prospects! Actually, very little successful communication would have taken place because Trent probably could not comprehend David's circumstances. David would also have a difficult time trying to understand Trent's circumstances.

Each individual is a unique person. There is no other person in the world just like Trent, or David, or you. Each person is extremely complex. Most of us find it difficult, and at times impossible, to express what we think and feel.

When Trent asks David, "How are you?" he probably is asking just to be polite. If David answers with the usual "Fine," they have communicated as fully as possible within the limitations of the situation at that moment. Until both of them share information with each other about their backgrounds, attitudes, skills, knowledge, and experience, David's "O.K." will have little meaning.

In the past few years much time and effort have gone into investigation of the communication process. There are no easy answers to communication problems, but there can be a more satisfying way to involve ourselves in the communication process. It must begin with each of us saying, "Each person I talk with has had different experiences than I have had. If I am to understand the other person and, indeed, even share ideas, I must concentrate on becoming aware of the other person. I must involve myself with that person. Instead of being self-conscious, I must try to interpret everything that may be a part of the communication process."

To involve myself in that total process I must first realize that all of us sometimes talk to (and answer) ourselves. When we first wake up in the morning we may say "Time to get up." We may agree and get up. On the other hand we may say "Later!" and go back to sleep. Sometimes we do this silently. Other times we vocalize it. Talking to and responding to ourselves in this way is *intrapersonal* communication. *Interpersonal* communication takes place when we extend our conversation, our world, to one or more persons. We share our ideas and feelings and receive reactions to them. Sometimes our ideas and feelings are accepted by others and sometimes they are rejected. There are many reasons why all of us act and react as we do. Some of us refuse to share with others because we fear rejection or contradiction. Or if we have been hurt, we say "Never again," and we build fences around ourselves. Being open and trusting with others represents to some of us a dependency on the person we share with. "I'd rather do it myself" is a good philosophy, but it can be overworked. Still others of us live in a private world where we feel secure. If we invited anyone into our dream world, it would no longer be our own and safe. People who feel this way might consider the saying "Two heads are better than one," especially when trying to solve a problem.

An understanding of *why* we or others act or react as we do is important, but *why*'s are reasons, not excuses. Most of us would probably be happier if we went on to develop interpersonal communication skills and techniques. We shall discuss these later in the chapter.

Some of our thoughts and feelings are so personal and private that we share them with only a few people. In our process of trusting and sharing we can and should use judgment as to when and to whom we express ourselves. We can begin at a shallow level with our acquaintances and proceed to a deeper level when we experience the trust and understanding necessary for admittance to the "sacred door" of our inner selves. Ordinarily, discussions of issues about which we have strong personal feelings are reserved for our deeper relationships. While we cannot hope to have deep and total relationships with everyone we meet every day, most of us find we decide to be open and trusting, depending of course on the people and the circumstances. In other words, we don't say everything we think and feel to just anyone or everyone, but what we do say to anyone and everyone should be honest and genuine. The old cliché "Familiarity breeds contempt" holds true only when we reveal ideas and feelings to another person who is either unwilling or incapable of handling our trust.

It is important to remember that some of our greatest poetry, music, art, and inventions are the result of *intrapersonal* communication. The greatest love affairs and the most rewarding and enduring friendships are a result of *interpersonal* communication. We can see that a knowledge of intrapersonal and interpersonal communication is vital to us.

Definitions of Communication

What is communication? There are almost as many definitions as there are people to define it. One of the simplest is that given by Lee O. Thayer. "In its broadest perspective," he says, "communication occurs whenever an individual assigns significance or meaning to an internal or external stimulus."[1] A definition you will find especially helpful in your course of study is that given by Jurgen Ruesch and Gregory Bateson:

> *Communication does not refer to verbal, explicit, and intentional transmissions of messages alone. . . . The concept of communication would include all those processes by which people influence one another. . . . This definition is based upon the premise that all actions and events have communicative aspects, as soon as they are perceived by a human being; it implies, furthermore, that such perception changes the information which an individual possesses and therefore influences him.*[2]

"So what?" we might ask. Knowing this or any other *definition* of communication (we can devise our own) won't help us understand or get along any better with our parents, spouse, friends, boss, co-workers, and the multitude of other people we all come in contact with every day. And most of us could certainly use some tips on improving our relationships with others. But before we can do anything about our communications problems—and successful relationships with others are based on communication—we need to have some understanding of the nature of communication.

Basic Elements of Communication

Obviously, there are many kinds of communication. The actor, the artist, the musician, the architect—all are communicators. All convey to others some attitude, thought, or emotion. Whatever the medium, though, there are four elements basic to all communication:

---

[1] *Administrative Communication* (Homewood, Ill.: Richard D. Irwin, Inc., 1961), p. 43.

[2] *Communication: The Social Matrix of Psychiatry* (New York: W. W. Norton & Co., Inc., 1951), pp. 5–6.

1. A person to originate a thought or idea;
2. The idea itself, as it is expressed;
3. A medium or channel for expressing the idea;
4. Someone to receive and interpret the idea.

If we take away any one of the four basic elements, effective communication cannot take place. Perhaps someday we'll have a more effective means of conveying our thoughts and emotions to others than by words, tone of voice, facial expression, gestures, and so on. (Maybe we'll even use telepathy—who knows?) But until such a time arrives—if it ever does—we're stuck with the conventional communication process.

Communication: Modes and Process

Each day as we communicate with other people and they with us, we use the different modes of speaking, listening, writing, reading, and nonverbal communication. The three modes most pertinent to our everyday exchanges with others are speaking, listening, and nonverbal communication.

On the simplest level, communication may be thought of as the sending of messages. As pictured below, the sender, *A,* communicates a message to the receiver, *B.*

Sender *A* ———————→ Message ———————→ Receiver *B*

Unfortunately, this popular notion of communication is an oversimplification that tends to confuse us and limit our understanding of what actually happens when *A* and *B* communicate. For one thing, it overemphasizes the verbal message and tends to obscure two essential factors of communication, the behavior of *A* and *B,* and the process itself (sending and receiving).

To understand the complexity of the communication process, let's go through all the steps involved. First *A,* the sender, must have an idea or emotion to express. What it is and how *A* expresses it will be governed by his or her age, status, background, education, cultural heritage, mental and physical health, environment, attitude toward the person spoken to, and a host of many other *variables* in the speaker's *field of experience.* (Even these variables may vary from day to day.) He or she must then put the thought or emotion into *words,* the word choice to be determined by vocabulary, knowledge, situation, emotional state, person communicated with, and so on. And *these* factors, too, may vary at any time. The speaker must next decide whether to transmit the message orally, in writing, or nonverbally. If orally, tone of voice and body language may say more than the words themselves. The selected *channel* of communication may be affected by various types of *interference*—smudged ink, external noises which obscure the verbal message, and interruptions, to name but a few.

Therefore, what *B,* the receiver, hears or reads or sees could be quite different from the message that *A* had in mind. The process is further complicated by the fact that what *B* receives he or she immediately "edits" according to his or her own vocabulary level, background, cultural factors, education, temperament, status, situation, attitude toward the speaker, environment, mental and physical state, prejudices, etc.—in other words, *B*'s own *field of experience* with all its variables. *B* will then usually give some sort of *feedback* to *A*, verbal or nonverbal. All of these factors in the communication process interrelate with one another, and this *interaction* can in turn alter one or more of the factors at any time. Hence the use of the term *process,* which means a phenomenon undergoing constant changes. And that certainly applies to our communications with others! The miracle is that we communicate as well as we *do,* all things considered.

So now we begin to understand the complexity of a process we take largely for granted. An awareness of all these factors and their ever changing variability should help us realize how easy it is to have a breakdown in communications, and make us more careful in our own efforts to communicate and more patient with the efforts of others.

Communication Models

The factors in the communication process are pictured in Figure 1. Obviously, the *most* effective communication will take place in areas where there is an *overlap* in the fields of experience of the two communicators. By including *fewer* variables, you could come up with a simpler model of a communication system, similar to Schramm's Human Communication Transaction model:[3]

Figure 1

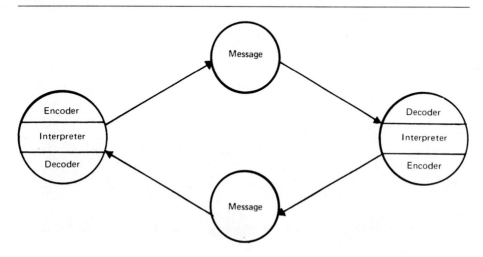

[3] Adapted from W. L. Schramm's *The Processes and Effects of Mass Communications* (Urbana: University of Illinois Press, 1954), p. 8. Copyright © 1954 by the Board of Trustees of the University of Illinois. Adapted by permission.

Or you might choose to elaborate upon the variables used, by explaining the elements of each, as in Berlo's SMCR model:[4]

Source	*Message*	*Channel*	*Receiver*
1. Communication Skills	1. Elements	1. Seeing	1. Communication Skills
2. Attitudes	2. Structure	2. Hearing	2. Attitudes
3. Knowledge Level	3. Content	3. Touching	3. Knowledge Level
4. Position in Social-Cultural System	4. Treatment	4. Tasting	4. Position in Social-Cultural System
	5. Code	5. Smelling	

—————————— *Feedback* ——————————

Let's see how the SMCR model works by adding Trent and David. The simple model becomes very complicated when we add the Fields of Experience of our communicators:

Communicating can be a very complex process.

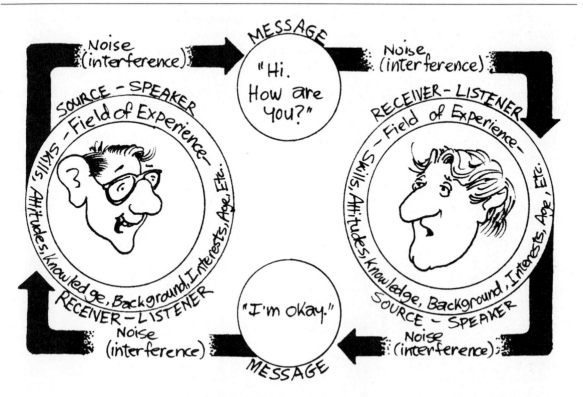

[4] From *The Process of Communication: An Introduction to Theory and Practice*, by David K. Berlo. Copyright © 1960 by Holt, Rinehart and Winston, Inc. Reprinted by permission of Holt, Rinehart and Winston, Inc.

When the speaker (Trent) sends a message to the listener (David), Trent must draw on *his* field of experience (both verbal and nonverbal) to express the idea. David, in turn, must draw on *his* field of experience to decode, or interpret and understand, what Trent *means* by what he says. Since their fields of experience are so different, it's easy to see why their communication might well be inaccurate or inadequate. Instead of concluding their communication experience with the "I feel like I've known you for years" attitude, they may ignore or avoid each other the next class period. If this is the case we could say there was "noise" in the communication process. Anything that interferes in the process (whether it be differences in fields of experience, *or* something in the "message" or "channel") is explained and defined by one word: *noise.* Trent and David have "noise" in their process because they have differences in attitudes and knowledge; there *may* be other differences or variables. It is important to understand that Trent and David can, through continuing the process, identify the variables in their communication and find it possible to eliminate the "noise." They *could* find it helpful to know each other! Trent can learn much of what he needs to know from David and David can learn a great deal from Trent. In every area of our personal lives, and in our vocational or professional lives, we will find that our satisfaction and success is in direct correlation with our ability and willingness to communicate effectively. Some of us may enjoy gratifying social or professional relationships. Whatever the circumstances, when:

   a. fields of experience overlap,
   b. individuals care enough about each other to allow and accept differences and diversities (*accepting* another person without having to *agree* with the person), and
   c. individuals are willing to learn—and use—skills and techniques to clear up the "noise" in the communication channel, then effective and rewarding communication is possible.

For some of us these things may sound simple. There are complexities! It is important to remember communication is a *circular* process. Both of the individuals involved in the process alternately *send → receive → interpret* (or *decode*) *→ give "feedback"* (or *send*). Thus the *"speaker"* becomes the *"listener,"* then the *"listener"* becomes the *"speaker"*! Because there are *numerous* variables we need to consider them and remember that they are *never static.* By their very nature—the fact that they are part of a process—variables will change. So we must learn to expect inconsistency and variability in the communication efforts of ourselves and others. Although we are not always able to control disruptive factors, such as poor self-image or a particular physical environment, just being aware of their presence and influence can help us achieve better interaction.

Distortion and Breakdown in Communication

As we have noted, a distortion often develops between what a speaker (*A*) intends to say and what a listener (*B*) understands. This problem is diagrammed in Figure 2. Notice that *A* has actually communicated something

10

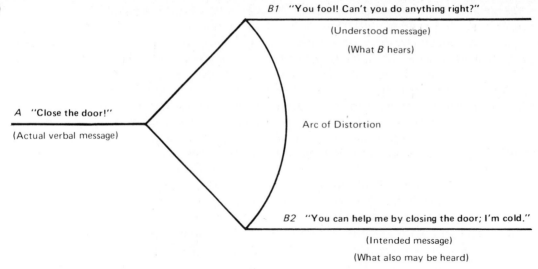

B1 "You fool! Can't you do anything right?"

(Understood message)

(What *B* hears)

A "Close the door!"

(Actual verbal message)

Arc of Distortion

B2 "You can help me by closing the door; I'm cold."

(Intended message)

(What also may be heard)

Figure 2 *What is meant is not always what is heard.*

different from the message intended. This distortion may be the result of voice tone, body movement or gestures, or any of the other factors involved in communication. Perhaps *B* has not listened carefully or perceived accurately, but it does little good to establish where the blame lies. The point is that the intended message, for one reason or another, has not been received. The real question is not who is to blame, but what can be done.

Techniques to Improve Communication—the Echo Technique

The echo, or "I hear you saying," technique can sometimes help clear up arcs of distortion. This involves having the listener repeat the message as he or she understands it. In this way the listener checks with the speaker to see whether the message the speaker intended was received. For example:

A. "Can't you see how stupid it is to vote for Dr. Green? She lacks all the qualifications and has been convicted twice for unethical practices."

B. "I hear you saying that because I believe Dr. Green is the better qualified of the two candidates, I am stupid and shouldn't be allowed to vote. Is that what you meant?"

A. "Not at all. What I meant was that I think you're wrong—that she is not the better candidate."

This example is deliberately obvious and is simplified for the purpose of clarity. However, by thinking of examples from our own experiences when communication broke down because of distortion between intention and understanding, especially in encounters that were strained emotionally, we can see how saying simply, "I hear you saying. . . . Is that what you intend?" could help avoid misunderstandings. This method often seems mechanical and awkward at first. Certainly we do not need to check out every message this way. But the technique is helpful, especially when we suspect that there is a breakdown in communication because of emotional or awkward social factors. Variations of the technique might be:

1. "I heard you say . . . . Am I right?"
2. "Do I understand you correctly? Are you saying that . . . ?"
3. "Did you mean to say . . . ?"
4. "What I think you mean is . . . . Is that what you meant?"
5. "The way I understand what you're saying is . . . . Am I right?"
6. "I'm not sure I understand you; did you say . . . ?"

Some potential advantages of using the echo technique are as follows:

1. The *receiver* is assured he or she received the message accurately.
2. The *sender* is assured the message was received accurately.
3. Any misunderstanding can be cleared up immediately.
4. The receiver is forced to "tune in" and maintain attention.
5. Both sender and receiver *share* the responsibility for effective communication.
6. The sender can "hear" what she or he said.
7. The sender can edit/change/alter the message, if desired.
8. The sender might take more care to say what she or he means.
9. Relationships with others are enhanced.
10. Could help expand the overlap in the fields of experience.
11. Tends to help "cool down" conflict situations.

The Echo Technique

Something else which might help us become more effective communicators is to develop an awareness of how different *types* of statements—different *ways* of saying things—affect the openness of communication.[6] Of course, there are no hard-and-fast rules, but the following are generally true:

1. Speaking in the third person—using such words as "people," "things," "they," "he/she," "everyone," as well as abstract ideas, general terms, any words that make the topic of discussion seem remote from the here and now—tends to create *distance* between communicators.
2. Speaking in the second person—saying "you are" or "you should" do or think or say this or that, especially if the statement is negative or critical—tends to erect barriers between those who are communicating, to put the listener on the defensive.
3. Speaking in the first person—using "I" or "we," especially if relating personal feelings of the moment, such as "I feel very warm toward you"—fosters open communication.

Here are some other factors that can lead to distortion and breakdown in communication.

Barriers to Communication

Previous experience affects most of us. We often let personal bias or prejudice interfere with present and future communication. To correct the problem, we must allow for the growth of others as well as ourselves. Instead of saying, "We worked together on a committee, and Richard wasn't dependable," it would be better to go into the new communication experience with an attitude of "Maybe Richard has learned dependability since we worked together, so I'm willing to work with him again. And maybe I've changed, too." Our friends, our parents, our employers, and we ourselves are all, it is hoped, changing and learning new, better methods of communicating, so we should be prepared to respond in a way that allows for that change and growth.

A second closely related problem might be labeled *functioning out of focus.* If Diane and I have a problem to solve or a job to do, I must keep my mind on the problem or the job to be done. I must not start thinking, "Diane had a party last month and she didn't invite me." I cannot see or handle the present situation while focusing my attention on the past. If we work for a friend or a parent, we are functioning out of focus if we expect special privileges and opportunities.

Third, we need to become aware of circumstances where *we respond to an anticipated message with a preconceived idea,* such as "Mr. Christopher is a teacher, so what he is saying is theoretical. It isn't practical." This statement probably isn't true. Teachers generally are, or should be, theoretical *and*

---

[6] Communication problems related to language are discussed more fully in Chapter 4.

One common problem is the use of trite or empty phrases.

practical. The point is, although it is great to anticipate ideas, we certainly need to openly receive them, analyze them, and then decode them.

All-ness terms or closed words also present a real barrier. When we say "everyone does this," or "people never do this," a defensive response may be expected. Better to say "many people do this," or "people seldom do this."

Another technique to practice before sending a message is to ask yourself, "If I use these words, what meaning will my listener add in decoding the message?" Conversely, when decoding a message I must ask myself, "What meaning am I adding to the message as a result of the words used?" Although this process is extremely difficult, we can begin by eliminating words and phrases which tend to result in negative responses. Most of us have strong negative responses to words and phrases such as "you know" and "when I was your age."

A fifth communication problem is *the use of trite or empty phrases.* Suppose your friend has been ill. Instead of saying "If I can do anything for you, let me know," suggest something concrete, such as "Could I check with your instructors and get your homework assignments?" or "I'd be happy to stop for you until you can drive again." Another example of a trite phrase is "Let's get together sometime." For better, more effective communication we could say, "I know you're busy, but if you are free at twelve, let's have lunch together," or "Let's have lunch together next Wednesday."

Judging instead of describing or reporting something is a sixth problem. In describing or reporting, we concentrate on facts, although we may include opinions. In judging we usually say it was good or bad, right or wrong. When we place a value judgment on something, the listener usually becomes defensive. A wise teacher might say, "The median score on this test was sixty-eight," rather than "The class did poorly on the test."

A serious barrier to communication is *attacking the person instead of the behavior.* Usually we mean "I don't like what LeAnn is doing" rather than "I don't like LeAnn," but our statement may imply the latter. Solving this problem requires a willingness to correct ourselves on the spot. If you have said angrily, "Ruth, you're stupid," correct yourself immediately by saying, "I really mean that what you are doing makes me angry even though I like you."

Instant evaluation, forming an opinion that may be inaccurate, is an eighth communication problem. One student told an instructor, "When you first walked into the classroom, I thought you were snobbish, and my first inclination was to drop the class." Instead, this student stayed and changed his attitude after hearing the instructor and observing her other nonverbal behavior. He could very well have deprived himself of some worthwhile experiences with other class members and lost some valuable time by dropping the class.

"All Indians walk in single file. At least the one I saw did." This statement may help us to identify a ninth problem. Many of us want *to learn only from our own individual experiences* and will not consider the ideas and opinions of others, especially if they clash with our own. The educational process should provide an opportunity for all of us to learn vicariously before drawing conclusions and making decisions. Chapter 6 suggests methods and techniques to help us overcome this problem.

Overloading is a term that describes another problem we may find in the classroom. As a student you may feel that some lectures are beyond comprehension, or that textbooks are written by scholars for scholars. You may feel you must read too much complex material before you can understand the concepts. We hope we, the authors of this text, have clarified the complicated process of communication by relating it in simple terms to experiences and ideas with which you can identify.

When to speak and when to be silent is a final problem. Learning to be sensitive and responsive to others is a lifetime process, and there is no set formula for success. One way we can cope with the problem is to remind ourselves that we are both speaker *and* listener in any communication process and to be effective communicators we allow time for both.

Levels of Communication

Neil Flinders points out that all of us communicate on various levels.[7] We communicate *emotionally, factually, theoretically,* and *philosophically.* One

---

[7] *Personal Communication: How to Understand and Be Understood* (Salt Lake City: Deseret Book Co., 1966).

level is not necessarily better than another, but when someone tries to communicate with us, we should try to discover what level that person is on and respond accordingly. When people communicate at an emotional level, perhaps in discussing a problem, they often want a listening ear rather than advice. If a person is angry and is expressing it in an abusive way, we might find it valuable to listen with emotion but the emotion could be empathy, sympathy, or love. Anger in response to anger often causes an "explosion" which brings about "hurt feelings" or even physical fighting. If the listener can accept the verbal abuse it is possible to prevent the physical abuse. Then, after the anger has subsided we may be able to communicate factually, theoretically, or philosophically. It's not necessary to be a "garbage can" for another person but the old adage that a fight starts with the second blow is really advocating what we have suggested. Further suggestions for handling emotional conflict are discussed in the chapter on conflict reduction. Other emotions that require emotional responses are: Grief, sorrow, pain, and joy. Obviously there are others but there is a great need for all of us at one time or another to express the above. Losing a loved one in death, missing a great opportunity, breaking a leg, or burning a hand—all of these are familiar to most of us and we remember how we needed to express the emotion. Winning a trophy, getting an A on an exam, having a baby are joyous experiences and we feel the need to express these emotions. How wonderful to find a listening ear and an expression of sharing!

If a person is communicating at a *factual* level and we are uninformed on the subject, it seems that being silent would be best. How many times has someone in your class interrupted the instructor to ask a question when, if the student had remained silent, the question would have been answered in the lecture? When we communicate at a theoretical or philosophical level, we can agree or disagree, but we should try to do so without moving to the emotional level, if possible. Many of the techniques we have discussed here can help us in this. Chapter 7 suggests ways to help us improve our communication in most "agree-disagree" situations.

Types of Communication

Each day of our life we find ourselves assuming different roles which require different *types* of communication. For example, in the classroom you, the reader, are a student. When you leave the campus you may go home, where you become a son or a daughter, or a roommate. You may be married, so you assume the role of husband or wife. You may work, where you become an employer or employee. Each role requires a different type of communication (this is discussed again in Chapter 6. It is important for us to consider at this point that each role requires some adjusting. A communicative skill may be a strength in one role—yet prove to be a limitation in another role. A graphic example is the attorney. The very skills that make a lawyer successful in court may cause communication problems at home! A police officer's ability to exercise authority on the job may be "too dictatorial" at home. Adjusting to different circumstances is difficult, but the rewards are tremendous. They warrant our dedicated efforts toward learning communicative skills and techniques, and untiring efforts in practicing them.

All of these techniques will help us be more effective in our relationships and communications with others. Much research has been done in the field of communication. We hope you will investigate the references given at the end of each chapter and continue to learn and practice better ways to communicate.

Certainly most of us want our communication with others to be open and honest. We also want warm, close relationships with others. But we must realize that to achieve these ends, *we* must be open and honest with others, and that involves risking possible hurt or rejection. Nevertheless, the chance to develop meaningful relationships is usually well worth any risk involved.

FOR FURTHER INSIGHT

1. Write an explanation of a recent incident, preferably personal, in which a communicator failed to communicate what was intended. Analyze why this happened and how it could have been avoided. Discuss the incident with your instructor.
2. Choose a person with whom you have had difficulty communicating and practice the "I hear you saying" technique. Evaluate advantages and disadvantages of this method.
3. Plan and conduct a panel discussion on a controversial topic and list factors which will probably hinder successful communication.
4. Try to recall a communication situation in which you failed because you had not established a common ground with your listener. What could you have done to prevent this?
5. List some of the physical and cultural factors which can interfere with the communication process.
6. Keep a record of *effective* communication experiences. Identify the reasons. Reinforce positive skills and techniques by repetition.
7. Ask your parents, friends, wife, husband, or boss to assist you in identifying problem areas in the communication process (barriers, levels, or types of communication).

REFERENCES

Berlo, David. *The Process of Communication*. New York: Holt, Rinehart & Winston, Inc., 1960.

Bois, J. Samuel. *The Art of Awareness*. Dubuque, Iowa: William C. Brown Co., Publishers, 1966.

Carr, Jacquelyn B. *Communicating and Relating*. Menlo Park, Ca.: The Benjamin/ Cummings Publishing Company, Inc., 1979.

Cherry, Colin. *On Human Communication*. 2nd ed. Cambridge: M.I.T. Press, 1968.

Coates, John. "Syllabus for Communication." Orange Coast College, unpublished syllabus, 1969.

Dance, Frank E. X., and Carl E. Larson. *Speech Communication Concepts and Behavior*. New York: Holt, Rinehart & Winston, Inc., 1972.

Faules, D. "The Relation of Communicator Skill to the Ability to Elicit and Interpret Feedback Under Four Conditions." *Journal of Communication*, 17 (1967), 362–71.

Flinders, Neil J. *Personal Communication: How to Understand and Be Understood.* Salt Lake City, Utah: Deseret Book Co., 1966.

Gruner, Charles R., Cal M. Logue, Dwight L. Freshley, and Richard C. Huseman. *Speech Communication in Society.* Boston: Allyn & Bacon, Inc., 1972.

Hawes, Leonard C. "Elements of a Model for Communication Processes." *The Quarterly Journal of Speech*, 59 (February 1973), 11–21.

Heun, Linda R., and Richard E. Heun. *Developing Skills for Human Interaction.* Columbus, Ohio: Charles E. Merrill Publishing Co., 1975.

Hopper, Robert, and Jack L. Whitehead, Jr. *Communication Concepts and Skills.* New York: Harper & Row, 1979.

Kelly, C. M. "Listening: Complex of Activities—and a Unitary Skill?" *Speech Monographs*, 34 (1967), 464.

Rothwell, J. Dan, and James I. Costigan. *Interpersonal Communication Influences and Alternatives.* Columbus, Ohio: Charles E. Merrill Publishing Co., 1975.

Scheidel, Thomas M. *Speech Communication and Human Interaction.* 2nd ed. Glenview, Illinois: Scott, Foresman and Co., 1976.

Sereno, Kenneth K., and Edward M. Bodaken. *Trans-Per; Understanding Human Communication.* Boston: Houghton Mifflin Co., 1975.

Stewart, John, and Gary D'Angelo. *Together; Communicating Interpersonally.* Reading, Mass.: Addison-Wesley Publishing Co., 1975.

Tubbs, Stewart L., and Sylvia Moss. *Interpersonal Communication.* New York: Random House, 1978.

Verderber, Rudolph F., and Kathleen S. Verderber. *Inter-Act.* Belmont, Ca.: Wadsworth Publishing Co., 1980.

Weinberg, Sanford, ed. *Messages: A Reader in Human Communication.* New York: Random House, 1980.

2 Listening Skills

FOR PREVIEW AND REVIEW

1. Listening, the communication skill we use most, is the one for which we are given the least training.
2. Two general types of listening are *serious* and *social*. Serious listening includes listening to understand and remember, and listening to analyze and make judgments. Social listening includes listening for enjoyment and listening out of courtesy or respect.
3. The most common listening problems consist primarily of failing to pay attention, or paying attention to the wrong things.
4. Learning to listen effectively involves developing the ability to concentrate, learning how to handle distractions from within or without, becoming active and empathetic listeners, and making sure we understand completely.
5. Good listeners share the responsibility for effective communication by giving clear and appropriate feedback to the speaker.
6. Ultimately, good listening is not only a vital basic skill, but can be a creative art.

INSTRUCTIONAL OBJECTIVES

After studying this chapter, you should be able to:
1. Differentiate between serious and social listening, identifying the skills needed by each one, and the skills common to both.
2. Identify your own bad listening habits.
3. Correct the most common listening problems by developing good listening skills.
4. Demonstrate good listener feedback techniques.
5. Become a creative listener.

"What Did You Say?"

Nothing is more flattering than to have someone pay rapt attention to every word we utter. It makes us feel (sometimes erroneously) that what we are saying is really important, and that our listener really cares about us and/or our message. This is to be expected when two sweethearts are sharing confidences and "sweet nothings," and perhaps in a few other instances. But a good share of the time most of us listen with only half an ear, while our minds are busy with any number of other thoughts and personal concerns. We may *hear*, but we don't really *listen*. Have you ever been in a conversation in which the other person was talking and your mind wandered, only to be brought abruptly back to attention as the other person asked you a question—and you had no idea what had been said or asked? Embarrassing, isn't it? Hardly the way to make friends, or to communicate effectively! Yet this has happened to most of us more than once, and it is only one situation of any number which illustrates our need to improve our listening skills.

Approximately 70 percent of an adult's waking day is spent in some form of verbal communication—reading, writing, speaking, or listening. From the standpoint of time spent using each of the communication forms, we should receive the most training in listening, for we spend about 45 percent of our time listening. Yet not more than one or two out of thirty entering college freshmen have had any instruction in listening skills. It has been said that we hear half of what is said, we listen to half of that, we understand half of that, we believe half of that, and we remember half of that. Keep in mind, then, that listening is a combination of what we *hear*, what we *understand*, and what we *remember*.

Reasons for Listening

Not only will you spend 45 percent or more of your time in college listening, but you will also be expected to remember most of what you hear in lectures for exams and discussions. Yet the average student forgets most of what he or she has heard within a week or two, retaining only 20 to 25 percent of the original material. That's a pretty poor level of learning efficiency, leading to correspondingly discouraging educational results. Anyone doing business on that level of efficiency would soon go bankrupt!

Are there other reasons for listening? Socially, the reasons are self-evident, unless you want to become a hermit or an outcast. But perhaps a few more reasons will provide some incentive for improving your listening skills. One reason is that if you listen in class, you will do better on exams. Another is that if you stay alert, you will be better able to answer questions, and this will improve your self-confidence. A third reason is that, as you listen to others speak, you can improve your own vocabulary and language ability. Fourth, listening can be a shortcut to knowledge, for it is faster, and often more efficient, to hear someone explain a new concept, idea, or technique than to dig out the information for yourself from several different sources—assuming you know where to look. Another reason is that listening can help you save time and gain financial benefits as you learn more efficient ways to do things, pick up tips on how to save money, etc. Sixth, listening can help make you a better conversationalist, which could improve your personality.

Good listening can also be of great benefit on the job. Supervisors need to listen to their employees (see Chapter 10 on Communication in Organiza-

We often hear without listening.

tions); and employees need to listen more carefully to their employers in order to follow directions accurately and completely. Good listening is also essential in any interview situation (see Chapter 9 on The Employment Interview). So you can see that there are many reasons why it would be advantageous to improve your listening skills, not the least of which is to enable you to gain a better education, get a better job, or have more rewarding relationships.

Misconceptions About Listening

Before we go into specific listening problems and how to correct them, it might be a good idea to clear up a few misconceptions about listening. One is that a poor listener is lacking in intelligence. This is not necessarily true; people may *appear* stupid because they did not listen. Another misconception is that listening ability is directly related to hearing ability. Once again, this is not necessarily true; people who say they did not hear what we said might not have been listening or paying attention. A third misconception is that we cannot improve our listening ability. By practicing good listening habits, we *can* improve our listening ability. A fourth misconception is that learning to read will automatically teach us to listen, but a moment's thought should make evident the error of this assumption. Listening is a social activity, whereas reading is done alone; when we listen we must adjust to the rate of the speaker, but when we read we set our own rate.

Serious and Social Listening

Every day we engage in different types of listening: *serious* listening in classes, lectures, and such, and *social* listening in conversations, at concerts, plays, and movies, and so on.

Serious Listening

Serious listening involves listening with a specific purpose, to comprehend, understand, remember, evaluate, or criticize, and it includes both critical listening and discriminative listening. *Critical listening* attempts to analyze evidence or ideas and to make critical judgments about the validity and quality of materials presented. If we are going to be effective critical listeners, we need the ability to do the following: distinguish between fact and opinion; distinguish between emotional and logical arguments; detect bias and prejudice; evaluate the speaker's arguments; recognize propaganda; draw inferences; make judgments; and evaluate "sales gimmicks." These skills will be discussed in more detail in Chapters 5 (Language) and 8 (Persuasion).

Discriminative listening, or listening for the purpose of understanding and remembering, is the type of listening most often done in the classroom, and involves several related skills. We must have the ability to: understand the meanings of words from context; understand the relationship of details to main points; follow steps in directions; follow the sequence of a message; listen for supporting materials; listen to questions with the intent to answer; recognize the speaker's purpose; recognize the repetition of the same idea in different words; repeat what was heard; and take notes effectively.

The rewards for serious listening—both critical and discriminative—are many, but a few of them may be mentioned again. Serious listening helps us expand our knowledge, develop language facility and vocabulary, evaluate strong and weak points in a message, pass exams, save time and money, and acquire knowledge.

Social Listening

Social listening involves listening for entertainment or enjoyment, and includes appreciative listening, conversational listening, courteous listening, and listening to indicate love or respect. *Appreciative listening* is listening to anything which pleases us—concerts, radio, plays, stories, poetry, television, records, and so on. *Conversational listening* is just what it says—listening to family, friends, acquaintances, in a conversational situation. *Courteous listening* is somewhat similar, except that we do less talking and more listening, as when we listen to guests expound on their views, even though we may not really be interested. *Listening to indicate love or respect* is related to courteous listening, only we are closer to the speaker, or care more, as when a mother listens to her child tell about the day at school, or about the caterpillar the class saw. Even though she may not be interested in the topic, she is interested in the speaker.

But more important than any labeling of types of social listening are the rewards to be gained. Social listening can increase our enjoyment of aural stimuli, as well as help us enlarge our experience, expand our interests, decrease tension, expand our awareness of cultural and ethnic influences, mature socially, improve our personalities or the "images" of us held by other people, and improve our self-confidence.

Differences Between Men's and Women's Listening Habits

Researchers have found differences in the listening habits of men and women. These differences are probably due in great part to differences in the training and demands society provides for boys and girls. Because men and women have different perceptual habits or attentional styles, they pay attention to *different* aspects of the stimuli they receive every day. This selective attention will affect what types of things our listeners will tune in to: men and women may hear something different in the same message. If we are aware of this difference, we can take it into consideration and compensate for it in our communications. (It might even help explain some of the misunderstandings we have with the opposite sex!) Carl Weaver discusses the differences in his book *Human Listening: Processes and Behavior.*

In Chinese, the basic symbol for the word "ear" is:

The basic symbol for the word "gate" is:

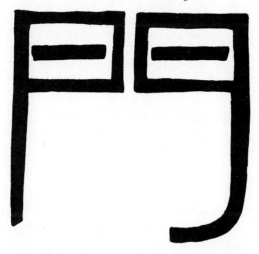

Put them both together, and you have:

which is the basic symbol for the word "listen."

Figure 3 *The ear is a gateway to the mind.*

The female is more easily distracted by competing details, whereas the male finds segments of configurations . . . and ignores much of the message that the female hears quite well. The male is less aware of subtle differences between parts of a configuration because he ignores most parts. He tends to restructure the configuration in the light of his goal, whereas the female tends to accept the pattern as it is in order to perceive relations, including social relations. This would tend to allow the female to hear more of the data in a message because she rejects less of it. It would also tend to cause the male to make more coherent sense of a message—that is, hear more general ideas and conclusions—because building general structure is his main interest. . . . Finally, the female attentional style allows emotions and unclear impressions to govern selective attention more than the male.

. . . as a result of these differences men are not going to hear the same meanings when you talk as women will. Women will probably hear the details better and the social relational data. They may not fit what you say into what they already know as well as men will. They may be more emotional and more easily persuaded and will probably select data on the basis of humanistic values more than men will. In short, they will hear different data in your message. But that does not make men poor listeners, nor does it make women poor listeners. It only makes them somewhat different. You should realize this and correct your talking for it as much as you can.[1]

Does Weaver seem to describe differences you have observed in men and women?

Common Listening Problems

In the following discussion of some of the most common listening problems, or bad listening habits, try to identify which ones you may need to work on. These problems can exist at any time, but they are particularly evident when we listen to sustained discourse, as in lectures.

One of the most common problems is *viewing a topic as uninteresting*. If our immediate reaction to a subject is that it's dull or boring, that we couldn't care less, that we've already heard it, that we just don't feel like listening, then we're licked before we start. Chances are we'll get exactly what we thought we would from the speech, sermon, or lecture—*nothing*—because we tuned out before we even gave the speaker a chance. It might be well to consider the words of G. K. Chesterton: "In all this world there is no such thing as an uninteresting subject; there are only uninterested people."

A second listening problem is *criticizing a speaker's delivery or appearance*, instead of the message. We sometimes get hung up on the speaker's voice quality, mannerisms, dress, or any of the external factors which really have nothing to do with the worth of what is said, to the extent that we do not even *try* to listen to the message. This is obviously foolish and self-defeating, as what is *in* the message is much more important than the package it comes in.

A third problem is *getting overstimulated* by something the speaker says to the extent that we start thinking of our own rebuttals and fail to hear the

[1] From *Human Listening: Processes and Behavior* by Carl H. Weaver, copyright © 1972 by The Bobbs-Merrill Company, Inc., reprinted by permission of the publisher.

Recognize your listening problem and make a conscious effort to correct it.

rest of what is said. More than likely we will miss any evidence or qualifying statements the speaker may go on to give; so when we jump in to counter what was said, we will probably end up feeling rather foolish.

Another problem is *listening only for facts.* Studies conducted at several colleges and universities revealed that poor listeners had one thing in common—they all said they listened primarily for facts. They spent so much time making notes of names, dates, and other details that they often missed the main points which gave the facts significance. Obviously, facts are important, but only when they can be related to some general concept or principle or idea.

The next listening problem is *trying to outline every speech or lecture* we hear. Some people become so involved with the mechanics of outlining— the use of letters, numbers, margins, etc.—that they don't have time to listen to what is being said. This wouldn't be such a big problem if all speakers were well organized, but we know only too well that they are not. Some speakers use a pattern of organization that requires some type of note-taking other than outlining. In any case, trying to outline *every* speech or lecture is a losing proposition.

Another problem is *tolerating, creating, or failing to adjust to distractions.* Gum chewing, pen clicking, and paper rattling are a few of the things that can distract listeners. Proper room temperature, lighting, ventilation, and seating arrangements promote good listening. Being able to see and hear the speaker without straining is of primary importance. If distractions exist, and we fail either to correct them or to adjust to them, listening will be less effective.

One listening problem which most of us are guilty of at one time or another is *faking attention,* or looking at the speaker and pretending to listen while we are really thinking of something else. This is self-deceptive. We think that, since we are paying the apparent courtesy of listening, we are free to pursue any mental tangent we wish. But sooner or later we get caught with a direct question from a speaker who wants some immediate feedback, and we don't even know what the question was, let alone what was said that led to it.

Another bad listening habit is *listening only to easy material.* This problem is common with inexperienced listeners, whose most challenging listening is an adventure series or variety show on television. Such programs are great for relaxation and entertainment, but they hardly prepare us to listen with understanding to a lecture on a complex and difficult subject such as physics, biology, geology, or any other college course which we may have to take.

The next problem is *letting emotion-laden words interfere with listening.* Almost all of us have one or more words or phrases that trigger emotional responses in us, get us uptight. Some such words might be "hippie," "radical," "establishment," "Bircher"—we can each think of our own "trigger" words. If we hear a speaker use one of these words or phrases, we react immediately, and we might as well not be there for all we'll hear of the rest the speaker has to say.

Another problem is *permitting personal prejudice or deep-seated convictions to impair comprehension.* This bad habit is akin to having a closed mind, and is usually triggered by a threat to deeply held opinions or attitudes, or by situations in which there is strong ego-involvement. Regardless of the reason, little real listening takes place.

A final listening problem is *wasting the differential between speech rate and thought speed.* The approximate rate at which we speak is 125 to 175 words per minute, and the approximate rate at which we think (if thoughts could be measured in words per minute) is over 1000 words per minute. Is it any wonder we can think circles around what a speaker is saying, take in everything else in our environment, decide what to do about our most pressing problem, go out for a mental coffee break, and still keep general track of what is being said? This differential can be our greatest problem or our biggest asset, depending on how we use it.

Improving Listening Skills

Which brings us to the next topic of discussion—what we can do about these listening problems. Before we can do anything, we must realize that our attitude is of the utmost importance. We must recognize which problems we have, admit that they are problems, and really want to do something about them. Good listening is not easy—it is hard work. It requires heightened tension, increased alertness, and intense concentration. Perhaps one of the first things to do, if we would become good listeners, is to develop our ability to concentrate. Good listening requires that we be *active* listeners

Listen between the lines.

who listen with all our senses, immerse ourselves in the act of listening, attempt to screen out distractions, and listen with a purpose.

Here, then, are some suggestions for improving listening skills. These are applicable to any communication situation. You might check those that would be most helpful to you.

1. Be Prepared to Listen. This means getting ready to listen. *Stop talking* (you can't listen while you are talking). *Put other thoughts and concerns out of your mind.* Try to put your worries, your fears, and your problems aside, as they may prevent you from listening well. *Assume a listening posture;* focus your full attention on the speaker; maintain eye contact (if possible in the situation). *Think about the topic in advance,* when possible; mental previewing, anticipating, or speculating about the topic for even a minute or two before the speaker begins will help you tune in to what is said. *Develop a desire to listen,* as half the battle is won if you can learn to listen because you really want to.

2. Start Listening Immediately. Don't wait even a minute or two before tuning in on a speaker. Begin active listening as soon as the speaker begins. He or she will often give the main idea in the first few sentences.

3. Listen for Something You Can Use. You can usually learn something from every person you listen to; so find something you can use from what is said.

4. *When Possible, Eliminate Distractions to Improve Your Listening Environment.* Take the initiative in controlling room lighting and ventilation, if necessary. Sit where you can see and hear well. Ask the speaker to speak louder, if you have to. Don't create distractions by tapping a finger, clicking a pen, chewing gum loudly, and so on. If others are doing these things, ask them politely to stop.

5. *Concentrate on the Message, Instead of Judging the Speaker.* Don't let your reaction to the speaker's dress, appearance, mannerisms, voice, or other such factors influence your reception of what is said. The ideas and information may be of value even if you don't particularly like something about the speaker. Also, *avoid classifying the speaker.* Classifying may have some value, but beware! All too often we classify someone as a particular type of person, then try to fit everything he or she says into our idea of what a person like that thinks or believes. Also, our perceptions of what is said will be colored by whether we like or dislike the classification we have put the person into! At times it may help us to understand people to know their politics, their religious beliefs, their jobs, and so on, but people have a way of being unpredictable, of not always fitting these classifications.

6. *Listen for Main Ideas, Principles, Concepts.* They are usually the most important things to remember. They are the pegs on which to hang all other pieces of information. Also, *try to determine the speaker's intent or purpose.* This will help you give focus to what you hear.

7. *Identify and Evaluate the Facts, Evidence, and Reasoning.* As you listen, try to identify how significant and relevant the facts and evidence presented are in supporting the main points. *Identify the type of reasoning used.* Is it valid or faulty? Though often difficult to determine, the effort itself will help you concentrate.

8. *Listen Between the Lines.* *Listen for what is not said.* Sometimes you can learn just as much by determining what the speaker leaves out or avoids as by what is actually said. *Listen with empathy.* Take the speaker's point of view; try to put yourself in the speaker's place so that you can see what she or he is trying to get at. Actively focus your attention on the words, ideas, and feelings related to the subject. *Listen to* how *something is said.* We frequently concentrate so hard on what is said that we miss the importance of the emotions and attitudes related to what is said. The speaker's attitudes and emotional reactions may be more important than what is said in so many words.

9. *Hear the Speaker Out.* Make sure you understand the complete message fully before you evaluate it. Don't let yourself get involved in a mental argument on something the speaker says, as you will then fail to listen to the rest of what is said and can't possibly have a full understanding of the message. *Be courteous.* Don't interrupt; give the speaker time to finish what he or she has to say. Ask questions when you don't understand or need further clarification, but be tactful. Don't ask questions that will embarrass or show up the other person. *Be flexible in your views.* Be willing to entertain new ideas. It will help you to understand them better, even if you ultimately decide not to accept them as your own.

10. *Do Not Relax and Fake Attention.* Do not pretend to be listening when you are not. Remember that good listening requires your full attention.

11. *Use Varied Note-taking Techniques.* Do not try to outline every speech or lecture you hear. Listen to the speaker for a minute or two, and if she or he is well-organized, go ahead and outline; if not, try listing principles and facts, summarizing, or some other type of note-taking. Also, keep in mind that some types of information simply do not lend themselves to outlining, no matter how well-organized the speaker is.

12. *Expand Your Listening Ability. Practice listening to difficult expository material.* Your listening ability will grow and develop only as you are willing to challenge yourself with more difficult and different types of material than you usually listen to. *Build your vocabulary.* The more words you know and use, the more likely it is that you will understand what you hear.

13. *Control Your Emotions. Control your reaction to emotion-laden words; stay tuned in.* Be aware of the words or phrases that trigger your emotions; if you can't eliminate such reactions, at least try to keep from tuning the speaker out. *Compensate for ideas which are contrary to your prejudices or convictions.* Become aware of your own biases, and allow for them (put them aside, if possible) as you listen. Try not to get angry if something is said contrary to your convictions; your anger may prevent understanding.

14. *Learn to Concentrate.* Instead of letting your thoughts wander, use the differential between the speaker's rate of speech and your thought speed to improve your listening ability. You can do so by practicing the following *keys to concentration:* 1. Identify the developmental techniques used by the speaker (the pattern of organization). 2. Anticipate the next main point. 3. Review the previous points. 4. Identify the supporting materials. 5. Every five minutes or so, review all that has been said. 6. Search for deeper meanings than you received upon first hearing the message.

Compressed Speech

A relatively new technique that has significant possibilities for students is *compressed speech*. Compressed speech involves the taped speed-up of normal verbalization to make better use of time. Any lecture or speech taped at normal speaking rates can be put on a special machine which eliminates or reduces pauses and speeds up the speaking to any one of a number of compression ratios, without distorting the voice quality. Compressed speech can help us make use of the differential between any speaker's speech rate and our thought speed (time which we often waste by taking various mental holidays). Remember, people speak from 125 to 175 words per minute, whereas we can think several times faster than this. So if we can speed up the speech or lecture, we will have less free time to let our minds wander. Studies indicate that we can listen to compressed speech at rates up to 400–450 words per minute, but that after this point comprehension and retention drop off rapidly. Teachers who employ this technique can tape their lectures, compress them into two thirds or one half the time (compress a one-hour lecture into thirty or forty minutes), and make them available in a listening lab or library for student use. Students can then listen to the tapes at their convenience, instead of at just one class period. It takes less time to go through the material, and students can listen more than once if they wish. Additionally, they probably retain more of what they hear, as the compressed rate forces the listener to concentrate harder. By denying the listener time for mind-wandering, compressed speech can help eliminate perhaps the biggest problem we have in learning to listen effectively.

Guidelines for Listener Feedback

One final consideration in discussing listening skills is the manner in which the listener gives *feedback,* both verbal and nonverbal, to the speaker. As speakers we are influenced considerably by both the amount and the nature of the feedback we receive. If we get absolutely no response at all (which is in itself a type of feedback), we get a decidedly negative impression and are likely either to get angry or to stop trying to communicate. If we perceive what we consider to be negative feedback, such as a frown or an impatient tapping of the foot, we are apt to alter what we were going to say in midsentence, or not say at all what we originally intended to say, in order to get a more positive response, such as a smile or nod of the head.

These examples should serve to illustrate the fact that feedback is important in communication, and that the good listener tries to follow certain guidelines in the feedback he or she sends. Many of our communication problems arise from failure to observe these guidelines.

Listen openly and empathetically. Focus your total attention on the person talking to you. Listen with as much interest as you possibly can. Follow the other person's train of thought. Do not be concerned about what your response should be: don't try to think out answers in advance. Forget yourself and hear what the other person is saying; try as much as possible to feel along with him or her.

Show your genuine interest and caring. Give congruent nonverbal cues that show your interest and attention. Face the other person; establish eye contact. Indicate your acceptance of the other person, even if you don't accept his or her behavior or ideas.

Send feedback that is appropriate. Consider who the *speaker* is (age, sex, relationship, emotional state, etc.), the nature of the *message,* and the *situation* you are in to guide the feedback you give.

Be certain the speaker perceived the feedback. If there is any question, send it again to insure proper understanding.

Make certain the feedback is clear. Whether verbal or nonverbal, feedback can be misunderstood. Check it out.

Encourage the other person to express himself or herself by asking open questions. Open questions cannot be answered yes or no, but rather invite a true expression of opinion and feelings. For example: "What do you think about . . . ?" or "How do you feel about . . . ?"

Avoid responding verbally until the other person has completely finished. Allow for pauses that the speaker needs in order to get in touch with his or her feelings and thoughts.

Nonverbal feedback may be given during the message. While the other person is speaking, maintain eye contact, give appropriate nods, smiles, facial expressions, etc.

Listen to find out what the other person really thinks and feels. As the speaker is expressing his or her views, try not to evaluate, judge, approve, or disapprove. Look at the ideas and feelings in terms of his or her values, not yours. Understand *with* the other person, not *about* the other person.

Occasionally restate or summarize the speaker's ideas and feelings. Do this especially when you are not sure you understand what the other person intends. (See the Echo Technique, Chapter 1.) This assures that you interpreted the message correctly. It also satisfies the speaker that you are really listening and want to understand, and it helps the other person to clarify his or her own thinking.

Don't overload the system. Beware of sending too much feedback in too short a time. Time your responses at appropriate intervals.

Delay in performing any activity that might create an effect you did not intend. There are many possible ways for this kind of situation to occur. If someone is in the midst of discussing a serious problem, for instance, try not to let yourself yawn or glance at your watch.

Send the feedback quickly, once the speaker has asked a question or completed the message. Delayed response or silence may be misinterpreted as ambiguous or negative feedback. If you need time to think about your answer, say so. Don't leave the speaker hanging.

Keep feedback to the message separate from your personal evaluation. Use neutral, noncritical feedback to assure the speaker that you understand the message, feelings, point of view. *Do not give your evaluation of the speaker or the message unless and until he or she asks for it.*

Make sure you understand the message before you respond with any critical or judgmental feedback. Even when we are asked to be honest, people are touchy about receiving criticism, evaluation, judgments. Don't compound the problem by responding before you have checked out your understanding of the message itself. Even then, use tact.

Early attempts at giving more effective feedback may seem unnatural at first, but will improve with practice. The dividends in improved relationships make the effort well worth your while.

A Listening Program

There are many possible approaches to improving your listening skills, once the basic problems are identified. Awareness of the problems, and concentrated effort to correct them, are essential if any progress is to be made. Needless to say, it will require more than one week's time! We cannot eliminate bad habits we have had for many years in just a few days or weeks. But with time and effort, we can become better listeners.

If a course in listening skills is offered at your school or in your area, by all means take it! This is one of the best ways of assuring the consistent, long-term effort necessary to develop new, better listening habits.

However, you can do a great deal on your own. What are your listening problems? Write them down. Then choose the one that seems to be the biggest problem. Resolve to correct it! (Your attitude and desire are of primary importance.) Perhaps you have the habit of faking attention, while your mind is really on other things. For a week (or more), concentrate on correcting that problem. Don't permit yourself to relax too much in class. If you usually slump down in your seat in the back of the room, move to the front if possible. Sit up, take notes, force yourself to remain alert and active. If you find your mind wandering, force yourself to tune back in. It helps to jot down at the end of each day how successful you were that day in correcting the problem. Note when you were not successful, and try to determine why. Keep working on the problem until you feel you have mastered, or at least substantially improved, the problem. Then start working on another problem on your list and repeat the process.

Sometimes it helps to have a friend who is also interested in improving listening skills. Then you can periodically compare notes, check each other's progress, discuss difficulties, etc. Many of us put forth more effort, more consistently, when we have made a verbal commitment in front of someone else that we are going to do something, and then check in with that person on a regular basis. This type of sharing and reinforcement can be mutually productive.

You can also use the group approach, in which several people or a whole class work on their listening skills, and have regular sharing sessions. You can help encourage each other over a period of time. One advantage in this approach is that you can often find someone else in the group who is working on the same problem you are, so you will have common experiences. Another advantage is that if your friend drops out or quits trying, there are others you can share with.

However, it is important to keep in mind that listening improvement is ultimately an individual matter, as is developing any skill. No one else can learn to play an instrument for you; nor can anyone improve your skill in listening except *you*. Regardless of what approach you use, the important thing is to do *something*. If you are consistent and persistent in your efforts, you will see improvement not only in your listening skills, but also in your relationships with others.

Some final thoughts. Hearing is not listening. Effective listening involves skills that can be developed by practicing good listening habits. But listening can also be an art. This creative listening can bring the ultimate rewards.

Further suggestions you might find helpful in developing listening as an art have been offered by Wilfred A. Peterson.[2]

The key to the art of listening is selectivity. You stand guard at the ear-gateway to your mind, heart, and spirit. You decide what you will accept.

Listen to the good. Tune your ears to love, hope, and courage. Tune out gossip, fear, and resentment.

Listen to the beautiful. Relax to the music of the masters; listen to the symphony of nature—hum of the wind in the treetops, bird songs, thundering surf.

Listen with your eyes. Imaginatively listen to the sounds in a poem, a novel, a picture.

Listen critically. Mentally challenge assertions, ideas, philosophies. Seek truth with an open mind.

Listen with patience. Do not hurry the other person. Show him the courtesy of listening to what he has to say, no matter how much you may disagree. You may learn something.

Listen with your heart. Practice empathy when you listen; put yourself in the other person's place and try to hear his problem in your heart.

Listen for growth. Be an inquisitive listener. Ask questions. Everyone has something to say which will help you to grow.

Listen creatively. Listen carefully for ideas or the germs of ideas. Listen for hints or clues which will spark creative projects.

Listen to yourself. Listen to your deepest yearnings, your highest aspirations, your noblest impulses. Listen to the better man within you.

Listen with depth. Be still and meditate. Listen with the ear of intuition for the inspiration of the Infinite.

And finally, some thoughts on creative listening by an unidentified author:[3]

Listening creatively can be a powerful thing. It is often much more effective than glib talk because it relaxes the other person's defenses. I am not referring to the impatient listening of someone in an argument, acidly awaiting an opportunity to reassert his own ideas with renewed vigor. I am not referring to the inquisitive listening of the gossip, eager to acquire some new bit of information to be whispered with relish, nor to the critical listening of one who waits to pounce on some misstatement of fact or flaw in logic. I am not talking about the empty listening of someone who merely keeps quiet but hears nothing, nor about the sapless and mechanical listening of someone who wants only to be analytical. All of these create emotional distance. They separate because they threaten.

Creative listening is something else again. With no flaw of impatience, no insincerity, no stupidity, no mere mechanics, no attempt at imposing one's own ideas, it sets about honestly trying to find out what the other person is feeling. With quiet com-

---

[2] From *The New Book of the Art of Living* by Wilfred A. Peterson copyright © 1962, 1963 Reprinted by permission of Simon & Schuster, a division of Gulf and Western Corporation.

[3] The authors regret that they are unable to locate the source of this material despite having made every effort to determine authorship.

prehension it attempts to discover the real nature of the intellectual soil and the emotional climate which the other requires in order to flourish; it tries to sense his underlying motives, his standards of value, his emotional hungers.

So an individual listens. At first all that comes may be superficial, obvious, even rebellious. But by being skillful enough, sincere enough, patient enough, by asking the right questions in the right way; by avoiding any attempt to impress by being brilliant, or witty, or superior; by encouraging the other person to talk, it is possible to create the conditions in which he can express his real self. At first he may be suspicious, uneasy, self-conscious. But wait. Soon he will demobilize his emotions, cast off his personality armor, crawl out of the dust bowl of despair, and allow his inner self to come alive. He will analyze his own feelings as he pours them out, discriminate between what he has done and what he more honestly could have wanted to do. Through the miracle of someone listening creatively, he will at last listen to himself.

FOR FURTHER INSIGHT

1. List the types of physical distractions that most bother you as a listener. What could you do about them? If there *is* something you could do, the next time the distraction occurs, challenge yourself to *do* it. If it is something you cannot do something about, see if you can control your reaction and *stay tuned in,* despite the distraction. Discuss the results with someone.

2. Go to a lecture given by a person you do want to listen to, and to another lecture given by a person you don't want to listen to. Evaluate each of the lectures and your reactions to each of them. Can we get important information even when we don't want to listen? How important is the desire to listen in determining how much we get out of any listening situation?

3. Go to a lecture and *just listen;* don't take any notes. *Immediately* after the lecture, write down as much as you can of the lecture. (Enlist the help of a classmate before the lecture, and arrange to borrow the classmate's notes). Then compare your notes with those of the classmate who was writing during the lecture. Is there a significant difference? Did you hear, and remember, more than you thought you would? We can learn to rely more upon our ears, if we give them the opportunity.

4. List the kinds of emotional factors which most affect your listening. What can you do about them? Next time emotions interfere with your listening, really try to overcome the interference and stay tuned in. How successful were you in doing so?

5. Choose one of your listening problems (other than distractions or emotions) and work on it for at least one week. Each time the problem occurs, work at overcoming it. At the end of a week, share your successes or failures with someone, and set a new goal for the next week.

6. What types of work or activities require more than average listening skill? Identify as many as you can, and comment on the role listening plays in each one.

7. Practice effective feedback techniques for at least one day. What were the results? Did you notice an improvement in communication?

Banville, Thomas G. *How to Listen—How to Be Heard*. Chicago: Nelson-Hall, 1978.

Barbara, Dominick A. *The Art of Listening*. Springfield, Ill. : Charles C Thomas, Publisher, 1974.

Barbara, Dominick A. *How to Make People Listen to You*. (American Lec. Comm. Series), Springfield, Illinois: Charles C Thomas, Publisher, 1971.

————. "Listening with a Modest Ear." *Today's Speech*, 9 (February 1961), 1–3.

DeVito, Joseph A. *Communication: Concepts and Processes*. Englewood Cliffs, N.J.: Prentice-Hall, Inc., 1976.

Education, 75 (January 1955). Complete issue deals with listening and listening behavior.

Faber, Carl A. *On Listening*. Perseus Press, 1976.

Fessenden, Seth A. et al. *Speech for the Creative Teacher*. 2nd ed. Dubuque, Iowa: William C. Brown Co., Publishers, 1973.

Geeting, Baxter, and Corinne Geeting. *How to Listen Assertively*. New York: Monarch Press, 1978.

Girzaitis, Loretta. *Listening: A Response Ability*. Winona, Minn.: St. Mary's Press, 1972.

Hayakawa, S. I. "The Language of Social Control." In *Language in Thought and Action*. 4th ed. New York: Harcourt Brace Jovanovich, Inc., 1978.

Hayakawa, S. I. *Two-Way Communication: Speaking, Listening, Understanding*. Arthur Chandler, ed. New York: Harper & Row, Publishers, 1979.

Johnson, Wendell. *Your Most Enchanted Listener*. New York: Harper & Row, Publishers, 1972.

Kelly, Charles M. "Mental Ability and Personality Factors in Listening." *The Quarterly Journal of Speech*, 49 (April 1963), 152–56.

Keltner, John W. *Interpersonal Speech-Communication: Elements and Structures*. Belmont, Calif.: Wadsworth Publishing Co., Inc., 1970.

Koile, Earl. *Listening As a Way of Becoming*. Waco, Texas: Word Books, 1977.

Langs, Robert. *The Listening Process*. New York: Aronson Press, 1978.

Lee, Irving J. "They Talk Past Each Other." In *How to Talk with People*. New York: Harper & Row, Publishers, 1952. Pp. 11–26.

Lieb, Barbara. "How to Be Influenced Discriminatingly." *Today's Speech*, 8 (April 1960) 24–26.

Mills, Ernest P. *Listening: Key to Communication*. New York: Van Nostrand Reinhold, 1974.

Nichols, Ralph G. "Do We Know How to Listen? Practical Helps in a Modern Age." *The Speech Teacher*, 10 (March 1961), 118–24.

Nichols, R. G., and L. A. Stevens. *Are You Listening?* New York: McGraw-Hill Book Company, 1957.

Perls, F., R. F. Hefferline, and P. Goodman. *Gestalt Therapy, Excitement and Growth in the Human Personality*. New York: Crown Publishing Co., 1977.

Weaver, Carl H. *Human Listening: Processes and Behavior*. New York: The Bobbs-Merrill Company, Inc., 1972.

Weintraub, Daniel J., and E. L. Walker. *Perception*. Monterey, Calif.: Brooks/Cole Publishing Co., 1966.

Wiseman, Gordon, and Larry Barker. *Speech—Interpersonal Communication*, 2nd edition. Scranton, Pennsylvania: Harper & Row, Publishers, 1974.

3 Self-Awareness

FOR PREVIEW AND REVIEW

1. Our self-concept includes all the beliefs we have about our own behavior.
2. The ideal self refers to the person we would like to be, or feel we should be. It is derived from the values instilled in us by authoritative figures and is resistant to change. When we fail to live up to it we often feel guilty or worthless.
3. Conflicts between our public self, or how we want others to view us, and our self-concept and ideal self can cause great stress.
4. Our real self is our real inner nature, the source of our authentic interests and energies, which is constantly changing and unfolding. We should try to keep our self-concept and ideal and public selves compatible with this.
5. Learning to read the communications of others can help free us of patterns of controlling them and being controlled ourselves.
6. To develop positively, we should cultivate self-acceptance and acceptance of others. This is made possible by good communication.

INSTRUCTIONAL OBJECTIVES

After studying this chapter, you should be able to:
1. List the factors influential in the development of the self-concept.
2. Complete a self-analysis as one important step to better understanding yourself, how you relate to others and they to you, and how this understanding can help in communicating more effectively with others.
3. Determine the sources of your individual values, and to recognize their significance in personal growth.
4. Explain the possible differences among your ideal, public, and real selves, and the causes of such differences, as well as their relationships to your self-concept.
5. Practice positive self-acceptance behavior.

"Who Am I?"

Most of us share Robert Burns' famous wish for the gift "to see oursels as ithers see us." We never see ourselves with complete objectivity, and often the image we present to others is quite different from our self-image. What happens when we see ourselves as honest, but find ourselves cheating on an examination or lying to our parents about our whereabouts the previous night? Why do we try to show off our good points and conceal our inadequacies? Why are we inordinately modest at times and flagrantly immodest at others? What happens when we "freeze" on a test, but know the material? Why do people behave as they do?

There are various ways to view personality that can help us understand the fascinating yet confusing individual differences in people and the interpersonal dilemmas which bother all of us. One way to get a perspective on such confusing, contradictory behavior is to look at our self-structures, our various selves, because how we see ourselves is a very important determiner of our behavior and life-style. We all try to behave in ways which are consistent with our self-structures, and we attempt to avoid actions, feelings, thoughts, and attitudes which are contrary to them. Awareness of our various selves and of the ways in which we defend and communicate our self-structures is critical to personality development.

While quite elusive, our self-structures can best be perceived and evaluated by describing ourselves as we believe we are (self-concept), as we would like to be (ideal self), and as we want other people to see us (public self).

The Self-Concept

The *self-concept* refers to all the beliefs a person has with respect to his or her own behavior. This is sometimes called the *perceived self* because people are never totally objective about themselves. Many times we find inconsistencies between how we view ourselves and how other people see us. Among those who know us, there will be many different perceptions of what kind of person we are. Each person sees us a little—or even a lot—differently from the way the others do. Some awareness of these differing perceptions can help us communicate more effectively.

Others' perceptions of us influence the way they perceive our actions. If, for example, a teacher shouted at a student for misbehaving, a classmate who didn't like the student would probably perceive the teacher as firm but just, while a friend of the reprimanded student might consider his friend "picked on" by the teacher and unlucky for having been caught.

Most of the attitudes, expectancies, demands, and beliefs we have are acquired from our interactions with others. Early home experiences with our immediate family are critical in the development of our selves and our personalities. Relatives and other significant people (persons who are important to us) observe our behavior, respond physically and verbally, and thus convey their beliefs to us. We then adopt their beliefs and tend to perpetuate and live up to them. If the adults in a family are happy, resourceful, and enthusiastic, these traits will often be developed in younger family members.

Many of the beliefs people hold about themselves are based on others' value judgments and abstractions which are implanted early in life. These beliefs are unconsciously assumed, and we often have little awareness of

Each person sees us a little differently. . . .

their source. Favorable treatment by significant persons, such as parents and friends, is likely to engender feelings of self-esteem and self-worth. The more favorable our parents' attitudes toward us, the more positive is our self-concept.

Very early in childhood we learn that we must act in specific ways to be acceptable to our parents. After consistent performance in these acceptable ways, we come to believe that we are acceptable to our parents, and we gain attention, love, and security from behaving in ways that please them. The behavior and the belief in the self-concept are thus constantly rewarded and reinforced.

Because we are always around others who are important to us, most of us continually modify our self-concepts so that our beliefs agree with the values of these respected people. Conflict occurs when these people are hostile, or when contradictory beliefs clash. It is unfortunately true that unhappy, hostile teachers generally teach students to be hostile toward the subject matter, as well as toward the teacher. Frustration and apathy are common in classes taught by such a teacher, and both the teacher and the subject matter may be quickly forgotten, or remembered unfavorably.

Many of us become angry when we are prevented from reaching our goals, when others withhold things we need or oppose our standards and ideals. It is important to realize that everyone gets hostile and that anger is acceptable and can be tolerated and handled. We need to recognize when we are angry, and then must learn to direct our anger appropriately so that it can be satisfactorily released, not built up to be released against the wrong person, or in an overly intense way. If we react angrily toward our friends and families, a matter-of-fact, open expression and mutual acceptance of such feelings may help clear the way for honest talk and better relations. Understanding the source of anger and improving personal skills in expressing and accepting it can aid in our interpersonal relationships and lead to greater self-awareness. Psychological research, while not conclusive, indicates that people who possess accurate, relatively objective self-concepts are not as defensive as people who do not see themselves accurately. It is thus important to learn to accept all of our feelings, even the threatening, "unacceptable" ones.

The Ideal Self

The *ideal self* refers to the person we would *like* to be. We all have certain expectations and self-demands which develop quite early in life, typically based on moral principles imparted by our families. If there is a discrepancy between our self-concepts and these ideal-self expectancies, we may experience guilt, anxiety, and self-hatred. Many demands are made on the child by parents and other adults, and conformity to these expectations results in approval and happiness. Punishment and rejection are received for failure to conform. Children eventually adopt, or internalize, these demands and expect the same behavior from themselves. Parents often demand obedience, hard work, honesty, etc., and if these expectancies are not met, children learn to question themselves and to feel bad until they are met. The ideal self is fairly well formed by middle childhood, when it becomes an internalized standard by which we evaluate ourselves. Violations of this standard usually result in strong self-judgments and negative self-evaluations.

The ideal self is related to our values, to our sense of right and wrong, and it is often resistant to change. Because our values usually come from parents, teachers, and other authoritative figures, we often dread the idea of rejecting them. Most of us just obey these imposed values without question. We typically try to avoid thinking about them. The fear of rejection and other anxieties keep our ideal selves and our consciences firm, unyielding, and even self-punishing. We often unwittingly deceive ourselves with justifications for our ideal selves, rationalize our conduct and beliefs, and anesthetize ourselves when our ideals and our behavior conflict.

We also appeal to authorities to support and reaffirm our beliefs. It is difficult for many college students to leave the protection and security of home for college and new adventures. One way to handle this threat might be to perceive and treat teachers as if they were parents. This may be temporarily satisfying, but it will lead to conflict and puzzlement when the teacher does not behave in the expected parental manner. Tests and evaluations by the teacher may reactivate feelings associated with parental judgments, and confusion, "freezing," and other behaviors which are not appropriate to the student role may result.

Students who have overly high standards for college performance and grades and do not get these high grades often end up feeling worthless. They may find it difficult to change their standards, and it then seems easier to change or distort the facts and environment, blame others, and miss the chance for personal growth.

The Public Self

The *public self* refers to the image we prefer others to have about us. Our reputation results from the ways in which others view us. If we can make others believe certain things about us, we can manipulate them, get them to like us, or otherwise reach our social goals. If, on the other hand, others believe the wrong things about us, we can be rejected, hurt, ignored, or punished by them. Most people are aware that there is often a difference between their self-concepts and their public selves, and this conflict must be resolved.

We often consciously and unconsciously set the scene to create a preferred image in our interaction with others. We select the mood, place, and communications to influence others. We then listen to the feedback and modify or continue our efforts to project the preferred image. Once convinced that the recipient has understood our message, we continue the same operations to maintain that public self.

Because we may have many public selves, we may sometimes forget which role we are currently playing, behave inappropriately, alienate others, and destroy the image. If we lie to a person to whom honesty was publicly projected, guilt or embarrassment results. Most of us are very much concerned with making the right impression, and we work hard to maintain our public image. It is ironic that many public figures create distorted, false images by consciously using public relations techniques, and then are rewarded for this manipulative, dishonest communication. One of the obvious problems with conflicting public selves is that they must constantly be switched, denied, or defensively justified, to remain effective. This defensiveness uses up energy and time which might be more positively used in establishing honest relations with others.

The extent to which our public selves agree with our self-concepts and our ideal selves is crucial to our personality cohesiveness and mental health. The social structure demands that we be concerned with the opinions of people around us. We learn to behave as others expect us to behave, sometimes in contradiction with our own feelings and desires. We defend and maintain our public selves by lying, wearing masks, and denying some of our feelings and inconsistencies. Secrecy is also used to defend our public selves. If our families don't know when we have behaved badly away from them, we feel more comfortable and secure. If our friends behave badly, we often will deny this to our families, and publicly lie about them to save face for both of us and to preserve the friendship.

One source of difficulty arises when we are in groups in which different members have different images of us. Which self should we use? If we are idealistic and proper with one member, seductive with another, competitive with a third, it may be impossible to reconcile these different images. Each of these roles and perceptions may be a part of our selves, but we seldom let everyone know all about us. The more consistent and honest our public selves are, the less we have to play games and maintain partial roles, and the more integrated and appropriate our behavior will seem to others.

The Real Self

Our *real self* includes those subjective thoughts, feelings, and needs which are our potent, alive center as we strive for self-expression. It is our real inner nature, which is constantly in the process of becoming and unfolding—the source of our authentic, spontaneous interests and energies.

One goal of communication is to liberate, understand, accept, and experience the real self. This process is called *self-actualization*. Self-actualization is achieved through acceptance of the self and through relating meaningfully with others. Effective interpersonal relationships are the foundation for self-actualization, and these relationships are dependent upon good communication. Whether we are eighteen or eighty, the number of effective interpersonal relationships we have and the adequacy of our communication skills largely determine how effective and happy we are.

The real self is continually changing, and the healthy personality strives honestly for self-knowledge and to relate the inner self to the realities of the outside world. According to many psychologists, a common drive exists in all of us to actualize and experience the real self—"I want to be me." Because the real self is a flowing process, not a static thing, it is elusive and can never be completely known or experienced. A happy, healthy personality can communicate much of that real self to others when it is appropriate to do so. Insecure, fearful people with poorly integrated self-concepts generally are not able to experience the real self and relate honestly, but are overly defensive and have conflicting feelings and needs. When people hide or repress their real selves, alienation occurs, with resultant unhealthy personality development, anxiety, and the excessive use of adjustive defense mechanisms.

Our self-structures are like valued theories, and even in the face of contradictory evidence we strongly maintain our theories about ourselves. Thus, we are all subject to inaccurate beliefs, perceptions, and conflicts among our various selves. Experience of ourselves on the level of self-awareness and self-knowledge depends upon acceptance of our real selves, acceptance of others, and nondefensive, open communication.

Anxiety is the result of a conflict between the real self and the other self-structures. When a feeling, thought, motive, or memory conflicts with our beliefs about ourselves, we feel threatened. We defend our self-structures by distorting, denying, and ignoring the experiences which induce the threat. When our defenses are effective, the threat is eliminated, but we have missed a chance to grow, to experience new events. For example, if you develop headaches each time a test or term paper is required, few will fail to sympathize with you for staying home and avoiding the demanding situation, but you will miss growth opportunities and tend to repeat this essentially self-defeating escape behavior.

Sometimes we don't want to reveal ourselves as we truly are, as we have fears about ourselves and about revealing what we feel are our inadequacies to other people. We feel vulnerable when we are "too open."

Insights from psychotherapy sessions and research indicate that our inner secrets and fears are associated with three main themes: (1) a feeling of personal inadequacy, (2) a feeling of interpersonal alienation, and (3) a sexual secret or fear. These feelings are prevalent in our culture, and most of us try to conceal fears in these areas and are reluctant to admit our personal inadequacies, distance from others, and sexual problems. We should all be careful about probing and prying in these areas, as inquisitiveness may lead others to distrust and interact poorly with us.

Self-Perception

We all differ in the extent to which we can see ourselves as others see us. Adequate self-judgment requires insight, or the ability to view the self objectively, and acceptance of the self.

According to the theory of transactional analysis, which Thomas A. Harris discusses in his book *I'm OK—You're OK*, we all have within us three different facets of our personalities—*parent, adult,* and *child*—each of which serves an important function in contributing to our sense of well-being.[1]

---

[1] Adapted from pp. 43, 46, 48, 50 in *I'm OK—You're OK* by Thomas A. Harris. Copyright © 1967, 1968, 1969 by Thomas A. Harris, M.D. By permission of Harper & Row, Publishers, Inc.

The *parent* within us, derived from our upbringing, reflects how we perceived our own parents when we were children, with the accompanying "do's" and "don't's." Our inner parent is the part of us that tells us we should or should not do this or that, the part that criticizes, judges, and punishes our actions and behavior.

The way in which the *child* within us reacts to the inner parent depends on how we as children perceived our relationship with our parents. Our inner child arises from our spontaneous needs of the moment, thinks only of its immediate gratification, can be impulsive and do things with no regard for the consequences, and says, "I want to do it, so I will." It is also the source of our emotions and our creativity.

The third facet of personality we have within us, the *adult,* serves as an arbiter or referee in the struggle between the parent and child. The adult within us makes more rational, objective decisions than the child, and is less judgmental and punishing than the parent. If we let our parent or our child control us all the time, we will obviously have problems. If our adult is in control most of the time, it may *choose* to allow either the parent or the child to dominate in any given situation, knowing full well the consequences, but choosing to accept them. Such reflective choices on the part of our inner adult are indicative of the more mature, actualizing person.

Depending on our own individual balance among these three facets of our personalities, we may find ourselves adopting any one of four basic positions with respect to ourselves and others.

We constantly relate from one of these basic positions.

1. *I'm Not OK, You're OK.* Caught in this position, people feel at the mercy of others. They need much support, acceptance, and recognition from others. They hope that others who are OK will supply their needs, and they worry about what they have to do to get others to give them the reassurance and support they need. They communicate to others that they are self-rejecting, without much value, and desperately need the acceptance and support of others. People who play the "wooden leg" game are examples—"I can't do it because I'm sick . . . . I'm tired . . . . It won't work . . . . We're all lost . . . ." Take your pick. Any alibi will do, but alibis do not solve problems.

2. *I'm Not OK, You're Not OK.* In this unfortunate position there is no source of acceptance and support, not from one's self or from others. People in this position give up hope of being happy and may withdraw from others. Even when others try to give support, people with this attitude cannot accept help because they feel that others also are bad, weak, and "not OK." They end up communicating to others rejection both of themselves and of others. Many "loners" play this game, and they do not interact easily with others.

3. *I'm OK, You're Not OK.* People with this attitude reject support from others, but provide their own support. They feel that they will more than likely be fine if others leave them alone. They are very independent and don't want to get close to or involved with others. They reject the support and acceptance of others because they are "not OK." They communicate that they are fine, but that they feel others are not. Such people may be correct and sure of themselves, but they will communicate that they need much elbowroom for themselves and will keep a distance from others.

4. *I'm OK, You're OK.* In this most mature position, people decide that they are worthwhile and valuable and that others are also valuable and worthwhile. They accept themselves and can accept others. They are free to get involved in happy, meaningful relationships. This is the position which facilitates close, happy interpersonal relationships. We should all strive for this appreciation of others and the self, and the resultant conclusion that life is a meaningful, worthwhile experience.

We consistently relate from one of these basic positions, and it is important to make the conscious decision that we are going to adopt the *I'm OK, You're OK* attitude. The self-accepting person views the world as a happier, more congenial place than does the self-rejecting person. A high level of self-acceptance is reflected in a high level of personal adjustment, and good mental health depends upon good feelings about the self. Healthy individuals see themselves as wanted, liked, capable, worthy, and acceptable to others. People who feel inadequate, unliked, unwanted, unacceptable, and inferior are more likely to be in prisons, mental hospitals, and custodial institutions. To grow and develop positively, we must actively cultivate self-acceptance. If we think well of ourselves, we are also likely to think well of others.

A good sense of identity, adequate self-esteem, and happy relationships with others are developed by consistent behavior that is congruent with our self-structures. If there is a large discrepancy between selves, there will be anxiety and threat, with resultant attempts to defend and maintain the status quo, and little personality growth will occur. The signs of integrated, adequate self-structures are:

1. A self-concept that is closely related to the person's real self. An integrated person can accept his or her feelings, thoughts, needs, and hopes and can appropriately communicate these to others;

2. An ideal self that is workable, accepting societal values without strain, and congruent with the real self. Comfortable, relaxed feelings with others, as well as a clear conscience and sense of being worthwhile, are indications of a good, functioning ideal self;

3. Public selves that are relatively honest, consistent, and compatible with the real self.

While no perfect self-structures exist, the ability to communicate honestly and effectively is one important criterion for the happy, healthy person. Mutual knowledge and understanding are enhanced by open communication. Mistrust, poor relationships, and ignorance cause poor communication. Through interaction we influence one another, alter beliefs, values, and even life-styles. Acceptance of the self and of others is an important characteristic of well-adjusted people and is also indicative of good communication.

Many people want to change their thinking, feelings, or life-style, but change is often difficult to achieve, despite good intentions. Positive change and personal growth were once left to religious experience, but more recently mental health and social science practitioners have become influential agents of change. Many experts accept the notion that self-awareness causes change, but exactly what it is we need to be aware of, and the conditions which foster awareness, are currently the subject of much controversy. It is generally accepted that our ways of perceiving and behaving are related to our past developmental history, to our personalities, and to our unconscious here-and-now processes. When we understand our past, our motives and needs, and achieve a better understanding of these factors, we usually grow and change in a positive way.

Lately there have been major theoretical shifts as more emphasis has been placed upon social values and interpersonal relationships. Many of the interpersonal theories of human interaction and gamesmanship define mental illness as a disturbed communication. Maladjusted people thus do not send clear messages, or they have difficulty perceiving and understanding communications and related interpersonal activities.

Ernst Beier and Evans Valens develop well the theme that we control each other, and are, in turn, controlled, by all sorts of very subtle communications.[2] Our dress, gestures, eating and drinking habits, words, even our jobs, and, in fact, everything we do is a communication to others and to ourselves of what we need and want from them and of what we are willing to give. Most of the time we are not even aware that we control others and are,

[2] *People-Reading* (New York: Stein and Day, Publishers, 1975).

likewise, controlled by them. Most of our acts and life choices thus are made blindly and automatically. We stay in old patterns and ruts, locked in self-made prisons.

To achieve freedom and choice we can learn the art of communicating and people-reading. We can learn to listen for what is really being communicated, for how what is being said truly affects us in significant ways.

Learning to listen to communications in our own and others' behaviors can give us the knowledge we need to choose what we want, not what others want for or from us, and can help us break out of patterns of controlling others and also being controlled ourselves. The importance of open, accurate communication in our daily lives can hardly be over-emphasized.

The Johari Window

There are things that we know about ourselves and things that we don't know. There are also things that others know about us and things that they don't know. A way of representing these levels of awareness is pictured in what is called the Johari Window.

Things about myself that I . . .[3]

		know	do not know
Things about myself that others . . .	know	Common knowledge. Things that others and I both know.	My blind spots; things my best friends haven't told me about yet.
	do not know	My secrets, and things I haven't had a chance to tell yet.	My hidden potentials; things I never dreamed I could do or be.

As you develop a good relationship with another person, in which each of you helps the other grow, the secret areas ("blind spots") become smaller as more information is shared between you. As the sharing increases and grows, a trust develops that allows us to tentatively explore and thus discover new abilities in our areas of undeveloped potentials. This growth can be accomplished through effective communication techniques, including active listening and giving and receiving accurate feedback with others. It often seems risky to share with others and to participate in self-disclosure but, as in life generally, you have to give in order to get. If the self-disclosure is appropriate to the relationship, the feelings and growth will be rewarding and the relationship will grow in a positive way.

[3] Reprinted from *Group Processes: An Introduction to Group Dynamics* by Joseph Luft, by permission of Mayfield Publishing Company (formerly National Press Books), and the author. Copyright © 1963, 1970 Joseph Luft.

Defense Mechanisms

We all use defense mechanisms to maintain our self-structures unchanged and unthreatened. Under stress and conflict we feel a need to protect our present status and self-concepts, so our defense mechanisms help us deal temporarily with threat and anxiety. These mechanisms are dynamic and automatic, mostly unconscious, and they generally avoid basic problems, dealing only with anxiety and the feelings related to the perceived threat. Our defenses do not usually deal with basic problems. Most basic problems are internalized self-conflicts, or are related to external, environmental pressures and problems, often perpetuated by and associated with poor communication.

If we forget a class assignment, we may be using the defense mechanism of repression to avoid the feelings we have about the class, the teacher, or the assignment, but obviously this does not help us complete the assignment. It is reported that Darwin constantly forgot criticisms of his theory of evolution. He was able to remedy his defensiveness, however, by writing down the criticisms immediately, and then including the criticisms in his theory. This was a practical way to circumvent his repressive forgetting of the painful criticisms. Similarly, if we have a value conflict with two or more differing internalized influences frustrating us, we may rationalize, or avoid and ignore this problem. If we need to feel that we are our brother's keeper,

Our defense mechanisms help us deal temporarily with threat and anxiety.

for example, and are very cooperative people, we may not be able to compete openly for grades or other symbols of success. This conflict may lead to escape, anxiety, illness, or other nonproductive, self-defeating behavior. The processes of repression and denial are used by just about all of us. These two mechanisms help us avoid and remain unaware of conflicts. Much of our forgetting is repressive. Alcoholics and drug addicts who refuse to admit that they have a problem are often using denial and are not likely to solve that problem until they honestly admit it exists.

Most of us *rationalize* our behavior at times, and this allows us to look good and justify our motives to others. If you come up with good reasons or alibis for always being late for appointments, you likely are rationalizing and also setting yourself up for further future conflict.

Another common defense mechanism in college classes is the *question-and-answer game:* the student is obedient, subservient, questioning, and childlike, while the teacher is dominant and authoritative, with answers for all questions. Little real communication or growth is experienced by either participant in this type of ritualized game, and perceptive teachers and students will avoid it.

Regression is shown when we retreat into the past to solve our problems. If a person avoids a problem by becoming childlike and sleeping or eating excessively as perhaps he or she did as a child, regression to an earlier stage of development may be shown. This will not handle problems well over a period of time.

Substitution or *compensation* is used when we reject goals or rewards involved in a conflict and substitute other goals which are not a part of the present conflict. This type of problem resolution is a compromise and sometimes is shown in vocational selection when desired career goals are blocked by our feelings or by harsh realities. This kind of behavior can be realistic in some situations.

Identification means that we take on or internalize the characteristics of other people, especially our parents. Most of us have at least a few of our parents' characteristics, but we often deny these characteristics that we don't like and are surprised that others see them in us.

Interpersonal conflicts constitute both problems and opportunities which require solution in order for a relationship to get started and grow. Accepting, recognizing, and understanding the conflicts and the problems, as well as the opportunity they present, is necessary for a satisfactory resolution. In poor relationships communication is fragmentary and restricted, which leads to restricted and constricted interpersonal behavior. In good relationships a high degree and quality of empathy, commitment, warmth, understanding, trust, genuineness, reciprocity, common goals, and freedom for self-disclosure are vital.

There are now important changes in societal perceptions and reactions which have resulted in what currently is being called The Age of Melancholy, which was preceded by The Age of Anxiety. It appears that depression and despair have recently become the dominant cultural moods because there is a gap between our expectations and cruel reality. Depression often occurs when we have given up hope, which suggests that our defensive and coping mechanisms have not been working very well. We have traditionally relied on the family, church, and immediate neighborhood for psychological support, but all of these sources appear to have broken down, with resultant emotional disruption and feelings of being alone, worthless, and melancholy.

Depression appears to be a consequence of the absence of a social repertoire and positive social reinforcement. These threats to the sense of self, the lack of attachments to family, friends, church, and community all can be helped by close relationships and good feelings with others. Accurate, effective communication plays a crucial role in understanding ourselves, in relating happily with others, and may be critical in our handling The Age of Melancholy.[4]

Positive Self-Acceptance Behaviors

D. E. Hamachek states that a person who has positive self-acceptance:

1. Has a strong belief in certain values and principles and will defend them to others. He/she is secure enough, though, to modify these beliefs when new experiences and evidence are presented;
2. Does not react with excessive guilt if others disapprove of his/her actions, and can act upon his/her own best judgment;
3. Does not worry unduly about the past, the future, or what is taking place right now;
4. Has confidence in his/her own abilities to handle problems, even in the face of failures;
5. Feels equal to others as a person and not superior or inferior, despite differences in abilities, backgrounds, and attitudes;
6. Can take for granted that he/she is a person of value and interest to others, at least to friends and associates;
7. Can accept praise without pretense and false modesty, and can compliment others sincerely;
8. Can resist the efforts of others to dominate him/her;
9. Is able to feel and accept a wide range of feelings and impulses, ranging from anger to love, from sorrow to joy, from deep acceptance to deep resentment;
10. Can genuinely enjoy himself/herself in many activities involving work, creative self-expression, play, companionship, or simply relaxation;
11. Is sensitive to the needs of others, accepts social customs, and does not enjoy himself/herself continuously at the expense of others.[5]

Communication is involved in these subtly intricate, critical interactions. Each person in good relationships respects the autonomy and the individuality of the other. Personal adjustments are continuous and involve being able to change one's mind when the evidence supports the change.

---

[4]Elerman, G., "The Age of Melancholy," *Psychology Today*, April, 1979, p. 37.

[5] Adapted with permission from *Encounters with the Self* (New York: Holt, Rinehart & Winston, Inc., 1971).

Some practical rules for promoting better communication and self-perception, as well as more successful relationships, are:

1. Learn to accept yourself and others;
2. Listen actively, with undivided attention, to all messages;
3. Try to perceive issues from others' points of view, without immediately judging and stereotyping them;
4. Be sensitive to unspoken, unconscious issues. Often what is being discussed verbally may not be the true problem;
5. Think of the needs of others;
6. Try to help others, and yourself, learn from failures;
7. Lead, don't just obstruct;
8. Accept evidence which is contrary to your point of view, when valid;
9. Communicate openly, and actualize your feelings in a nondefensive way.

FOR FURTHER INSIGHT

1. Analyze yourself, describing your self-concept, ideal self, and as many public selves as you are aware of.
2. Make a list of your good points and your weak points, and ask your best friend to do so also. How do the lists differ? Are some of the differences due to a communication problem? If so, does a discussion of these differences lead to a better understanding of yourself and your friend?
3. Have your long-range goals changed since you entered college? If so, how?
4. Interview two people whom you believe to be successful. Ask them for their definition of and "recipe" for success. Do *they* believe they are successful?
5. Select a person whom you believe relates and communicates with others very well. Through observation and interview, try to discover the characteristics this person possesses which enable him or her to communicate so well. Are these characteristics you could develop?
6. Agree or disagree with the following: "One's personality is formed by the time one is eight years old. After that it is difficult, if not impossible, to change."
7. List your social groups and organizations which are helpful to your personal worth and identity.

REFERENCES

Beier, Ernst G., and Evans G. Valens. *People-Reading*. New York: Stein and Day, Publishers, 1975.

Berne, Eric. *Games People Play*. New York: Grove Press, Inc., 1964.

Borgatta, Edgar F., and William W. Lambert, eds. *Handbook of Personality Theory and Research*. Chicago: Rand McNally & Co., 1967.

Elerman, G. "The Age of Melancholy." *Psychology Today*, April 1979, p. 37.

Freud, Sigmund. *An Outline of Psychoanalysis*. New York: W. W. Norton & Co., Inc., 1949.

Fromm, Erich. *The Sane Society*. New York: Holt, Rinehart & Winston, Inc., 1955.

Hamachek, D. E. *Encounters with the Self*. New York: Holt, Rinehart & Winston, Inc., 1971.

Harris, Thomas A. *I'm OK—You're OK*. New York: Harper & Row, Publishers, 1967.

Johnson, Wendell. *People in Quandaries*. New York: Harper & Row, Publishers, 1946.

Luft, Joseph. *Group Processes: An Introduction to Group Dynamics*. Palo Alto: Mayfield Publishing Co., 1970.

Maslow, Abraham. *Motivation and Personality*. New York: Harper & Row, Publishers, 1954.

Perls, Frederick. *Gestalt Therapy Verbatim*. New York: Bantam Books, Inc., 1969.

Rogers, Carl. *On Becoming a Person*. Boston: Houghton Mifflin Co., 1961.

Ruesch, Jurgen. *Therapeutic Communication*. New York: W. W. Norton & Co., Inc., 1961.

Zurcher, Louis A., Jr. *The Mutable Self: A Self-Concept for Social Change*. Beverly Hills, Calif.: Sage, 1977.

Nonverbal Communication

FOR PREVIEW AND REVIEW

1. Although nonverbal communication is usually more powerful than verbal, it is also more ambiguous and difficult to interpret.
2. The ability to send congruent nonverbal messages, and to interpret the nonverbal messages of others, can help us establish more solid relationships.
3. Just like other animals, we humans maintain various individual, personal territories. Invasion of these territories by people with whom we are not sufficiently intimate can result in either discomfort and withdrawal or strong opposition.
4. Various positions, expressions, and gestures, while suggestive of various emotions or attitudes, are completely understandable only in terms of the situation, the cultural background, and the particular individual's behavior patterns.

INSTRUCTIONAL OBJECTIVES

After studying this chapter, you should be able to:
1. Develop skills in using and interpreting nonverbal communication.
2. Demonstrate that nonverbal communication, whether deliberate or unconscious, is more powerful than verbal.
3. Use and interpret nonverbal messages of space, position, facial expression, and gesture.
4. Identify personal territorial areas, and to experience their effects on relationships with others.

"It's Not What You Say, But . . ."

Although the study of verbal communication has a lengthy history, only recently has the systematic study of nonverbal communication been explored. *Kinesics* is the study of body language, with an emphasis on the physical behavioral patterns of nonverbal communication. It may seem surprising, but nonverbal messages are usually more powerful in communicating feelings than are verbal messages; however, they are often more difficult to interpret, as well. We should try to understand how we communicate through our postures, physical appearance, facial expressions, gestures, spatial distance, and tone of voice, as well as by the words we use. In order to communicate effectively, we must be sure that all our verbal and nonverbal messages agree, that they do not contradict each other.

Sigmund Freud, a perceptive observer of human behavior, once noted that while a patient was verbally expressing happiness with her marriage, she was unconsciously slipping her wedding ring on and off her finger. It did not surprise him when the problems in her marriage began to surface, as he was already aware of the unconscious, symbolic significance of her gesture. If we can learn to understand body language, we can communicate more effectively and enhance our social interactions, as well as our self-understanding.

The study of kinesics includes all of our expressive movements, from deliberate acts to unconscious communications. Communications experts believe that many of our gestures are remnants of earlier conflicts and feelings, and that some hand-to-mouth movements, for example, might be remnants of earlier thumb-sucking behavior. Many of our gestures and physical mannerisms are learned very early in life and are well established by the time we are two or three years old.

Body Language and Communication

People are generally unaware of much of their own body language, but they continuously communicate attitudes and feelings which can accurately be

Nonverbal messages can be more powerful than verbal messages.

read by the sensitive observer. If the verbal responses are consistent with the gestures, then it is likely that real basic feelings are being expressed. Consistency between body language and words is one way to check our observations and help correctly evaluate our interpersonal relationships, thereby improving our social skills. Inconsistent messages require more careful evaluation and observation.

How do we know if someone is tuned in, or is tuning us out? Knowledge of types of feedback and the impression others have of us is critical in determining how our messages are being received. In attempting to penetrate the fronts people maintain, many of the gestures discussed in this chapter reliably indicate openness and receptivity, and a readiness to accept us and our ideas.

Watching people can be fun and informative, as well as valuable and interesting. The variety of nonverbal cues is almost limitless, but some of the principles and gestures discussed only briefly here may help us perceive others' nonverbal cues and our own expressive behavior in a new, insightful way.

We could all profitably share these insights with friends and family in a mutually helpful fashion, as an understanding of nonverbal communication can help us anticipate or interpret verbal statements, thus increasing the depth and quality of our relationships. Body language is often used by therapists in psychotherapy to help people become aware of their feelings, clarify their hangups, and relate more openly and honestly. These basic kinesic principles may help us enhance our interactions and open up communications with others, with a corresponding lessening of manipulative gamesmanship, psychological distance, and misunderstanding.

Mannerisms Affecting Communications

We are all continually involved in the complex process of interpreting the gestures of others. Mannerisms will change from individual to individual and from culture to culture. Anyone who has traveled in a foreign country will recognize the importance of gestures in communication when there is a language difference, and will appreciate the frustrations connected with this type of communication. Observations of those who are blind and deaf dramatically emphasize the importance of nonverbal communication, without which the sensory-handicapped person would be even more seriously impaired and isolated.

Gestures are an important means of communication in all cultures. In some cases, such as the American Indian system of sign language, they may permit entire conversations to be carried on without the use of speech, an advantage when members of different tribes meet. Among people who speak the same language, gestures are a means of reinforcing, or substituting for, the spoken word. Affection is displayed by the Eskimos by rubbing noses, while the Mongols smell heads. Europeans and Americans show approval by back slapping. Turks and Persians indicate humility by throwing themselves on their backs, rolling from side to side, and slapping the outsides of their thighs; these gestures convey the message: "I'm subdued already. You need not subdue me." Satisfaction is expressed by some North American Indians by massaging the stomach. Surprise is indicated by the people of Tibet by pinching the cheek.

Skill in perceiving and interpreting nonverbal communication can be learned, and can lead to more effective understanding and improved relationships. We differ in our self-understanding and in our ability to read and evaluate others. We must continually check our observations and assessments with others and not assume that all our personal judgments are accurate. Misinterpretations and misperceptions may arise from personal needs and from cultural, class, and sex differences, as well as from other general communication problems.

Just as with verbal communication, more than the solitary, individual nonverbal message must be attended to; the context, feelings, and consistency of the message must also be evaluated. We sometimes react too quickly to single, isolated messages, not recognizing the ongoing, continuous nature of the communication process. Often one gesture is countermanded by verbal messages, or it may be filtered, amplified, or confused by further ongoing expressive messages.

In fact, Bateson, et al.[1] have formulated the *double-bind hypothesis,* which states that the pairing of mutually contradictory messages in family communications is the basis of serious mental illness. The double-bind often occurs when a mother typically says to her child "I love you," but her nonverbal actions mean the opposite; after many repetitions, the child often withdraws from reality, feeling she or he can't win because of the way the dilemma is structured. An accurate reader of behavior will resist jumping to conclusions based upon single, out-of-context gestures. For example, tears may indicate only an allergic condition and not a significant communication.

Message Congruency

The ability to send and interpret harmonious, congruent messages can make the behavior process more meaningful to us and help us establish solid relationships. The total experience is important, not merely the small bits which make up the whole. When a teacher talks with a student, several behaviors may simultaneously take place: to maintain status, a space may separate them, and their chairs may be different; the hand-to-face "thinker" (problem-solving) posture may be assumed by the teacher; the teacher may nod in a friendly way to encourage the student, who will usually assume the submissive, compliant "I understand" role; the teacher may take notes, indicating interest and suggesting subtle status differences. Such interaction is rather common, but this teacher behavior with another teacher would be seen as a put-down and lead to awkwardness and bad feelings. Nonverbal behavior signaling equal status would be more appropriate in a teacher-to-teacher or student-to-student relationship.

It is important to realize that we are constantly sending nonverbal messages, and that we are often unaware of the messages we send. Even the "poker face" conveys discernible messages, if the complete context and the total body language are considered. Are the fingers being tapped impatiently, the arms crossed to block out messages, the posture slumped, or are the vocal characteristics conveying contradictory messages? A. Mehrabian believes that the total impact of a message is about 7 percent verbal (words only), 38 percent vocal, and 55 percent facial. These percentages stress the importance of nonverbal factors and the relative lack of importance of words alone in ordinary communication.[2] What we *do* and *how* we do it speak more loudly than what we *say!* Differing tones of voice clearly communicate excitement, fear, love, and other strong emotions. For example, you might note the tone and quality of your voice the next time you address the class, as contrasted with your voice at the next football game when you are excited.

Long silences can be another means of communication. They may reflect strong anxiety, fear of disclosure, intimacy, or they may mask other feelings.

[1] Bateson, G., Jackson, D., Haley, J., and Weakland, J. "Toward a Theory of Schizophrenia," *Behavioral Science,* 1956.

[2] "Communication Without Words," *Psychology Today,* September 1968, p. 52.

Despite the lack of verbal output, nonverbal cues can help us interpret the silent person's behavior accurately. The silent person is constantly sending nonverbal messages, and the silences should be dealt with as a series of communications, like other behaviors. If teachers could be trained to be aware of the communications of quiet students and to interpret the students' nonverbal cues, the educational process could be made more exciting, effective, and valuable for many students who are not being reached now. If words are only 7 percent of the message, let's learn to "listen" to the other 93 percent and become more effective communicators.

Physical Characteristics Affecting Communications

The most immediate and obvious information that we obtain about others comes from their observable physical appearance. Certain physical characteristics are often associated with psychological variables. However, it is difficult to know how much the characteristics themselves influence personality and how much personality is affected by stereotyped beliefs people have about these characteristics. Are fat people really more talkative, good-natured, dependent, and trusting, while thin people are more ambitious, tense, stubborn, pessimistic, and quiet? Are muscular people really more adventurous and more mature?[3] We should avoid jumping to conclusions about people on the basis of physical characteristics.

Skin color and hair length also affect the way some people are viewed in our society. The existence of racial prejudice is widely known, but this prejudice may vary with the individual's appearance. For example, a light-colored black often arouses less fear and/or resentment among whites than does a darker black. Men with long hair frequently attract hostility where people make judgments about their character on the basis of their hair.

According to Knapp,[4] much evidence supports the idea that we respond initially to others much more favorably when we perceive them as being physically attractive. Many studies indicate that physically attractive people rate higher than unattractive individuals on such socially desirable characteristics as success, sociability, sexuality, personality, and general happiness. Teachers and peers both appear to interact less, and less positively, with unattractive schoolchildren. Many studies have shown that there are high levels of agreement in identifying handsome and beautiful people.

The body image is one important aspect of self-image (see Chapter 3). Studies suggest that males are most satisfied with their bodies when they are somewhat taller and larger than normal. Females are most satisfied when their bodies are smaller than normal, but when their bustline is larger than average.[5]

---

[3] W. Wells and B. Siegel, "Stereotyped Somatypes," *Psychological Reports*, 8 (1961), pp. 77–78.

[4] Knapp, Mark L. *Nonverbal Communication in Human Interaction.* N.Y.: Holt, Rinehart and Winston, 1978.

[5] Jourard, S. M. and Secord, P. F. *British Journal of Psychology.* 46, 1955.

Clothing and Communication

Clothes are also important in communicating to others, and they fulfill various functions in our society.

Clothes protect us, and are used for decoration, self-assertion, sexual attraction, concealment, show our status or vocational role, as well as our group identification. The way we wear our clothes, and their style, type, and colors, often inform people of the wearer's knowledge of cultural roles.

New, stylish clothes usually help the wearer to feel more confident and assured, and most people are embarrassed when wearing clothes which are different. Clothes or shoes which don't fit well also typically make the wearer feel "out of it," or uncomfortable. Much current work is being done on the relationship of clothing to personality, and the early results appear promising in helping us learn to communicate more positively and effectively with each other.

Clothes can influence the way we perceive others, especially people we don't know very well. Clothes can communicate economic status, occupation, personality, and values. They can also affect our self-image. A new outfit usually makes us happy, but if we turn out to be overdressed we may become very self-conscious.[6] Many school boards believe they can control student behavior by controlling the way students dress, but they frequently succeed only in demonstrating the importance they place on superficial appearances.

Territoriality

An important concept in nonverbal communication is that of *territoriality*. We know that birds have a particular nesting and feeding territory, and will fight off any intruders of their own species. This holds true for many other animals, including humans. Today, however, the individual city-dweller can usually claim no more territory than his or her own home.

Each of us also has a type of personal territory, or comfortable distance when communicating with others. It is interesting to note what happens when personal space is threatened or occupied by an intruder. An angry, aggressive intruder who comes too close to a person may provoke a quick physical retreat. If the aggressor pursues, however, the victim may stand firm and fight to protect his or her territory. How we handle our personal territorial zones and how we approach other people's zones is a very important part of how we relate with others. All of us have our favorite place, a preferred seat or space at home, in class, or in a car. Many authorities prefer to keep a desk or podium between themselves and their subordinates, keeping them "at arm's length." Putting feet on a chair or desk, or putting a leg over the arm of a chair, is a sign of assertion of territorial rights and ownership.

---

[6] For more on the relationship between physical appearance and human communication, see Mark Knapp, *Nonverbal Communication in Human Interaction* (New York: Holt, Rinehart & Winston, Inc., 1972), pp. 63–90.

Some people place personal articles or clothes over a neighboring chair to signify occupancy and territorial rights. Notice how some students spread out books, paper, and other personal gear while studying in the library to insure the integrity of their territory.

The behavior of some people driving a car indicates that their driving body language is different from their other typical social behavior. A car may be used like a dangerous weapon to cut in front of others, inducing anger in the person whose space on the road has been invaded. The territorial zones of privacy seem to expand in cars, and this expansion changes our body limits, controls, and inhibitions. The car may give us a sense of power and invulnerability that we don't ordinarily possess. The car gives some people the feeling that their personal territory is greatly enlarged; others feel that they are in a protected cocoon. Thus we act and react differently in the car, as our own private space contracts or expands.

We often encourage intrusions into our personal space by people of whom we are fond, and we resent intrusions by strangers or people we dislike. We generally maintain a rather stable set of distances between ourselves and others, and rather precise, measurable distances for different types of interactions have been noted. Close, intimate personal interactions often involve a distance between participants of only six to eighteen inches, with actual physical contact in the case of close relatives and loved ones. More casual interpersonal exchanges with friends and acquaintances involve distances of from twenty-four to forty inches, and our public interactions take place at even greater physical distances.

At a close, intimate distance, we are strikingly aware of the other person. This closeness is most acceptable in our culture between a man and woman. It can cause embarrassment or awkwardness if it occurs between strangers. At a distance of eighteen to thirty inches we can hold our partner's hand, and this is generally the comfortable distance at cocktail parties and with friends. Close friends and married partners can comfortably operate within this range, but if strangers invade this intimate space we often react with discomfort, withdrawal, or subtle maneuverings to increase the distance between us. A wife, for example, will often become concerned when another woman approaches her husband at this close, too intimate a distance. We often signal to others that we wish to be close to them by first approaching them physically with friendly gestures and observing their response to our approach. Many inferences about feelings, status, intentions, and attitudes can be drawn from the distances we maintain in our interactions with others.

We should be careful not to make naive, hasty, or overly simplified interpretations of nonverbal cues. Neither nonverbal cues nor words alone give us the full meaning of what a person is communicating; both types of communication must be listened to carefully if we are to understand one another.

It is important to understand that no single body position or movement has an unquestionable, precise meaning. Frowning may indicate disgust, lack of interest, or concentration, or it may convey other subtle meanings. Communications are understandable only in the context of an individual's total behavior patterns, as well as the particular social context.

Postures and Positions Affecting Communications

Just about everyone has an individualized walk which is recognizable to friends. Body size and structure are important, but body posture, pace, and length of stride also vary, depending on the environment and the mood. The sad person shuffles along, head down, hands in pockets, moving slowly. The brisk precision of the military walk often trumpets strong, uncompromising authority. Preoccupied people may walk with hands behind the back, meditatively unconcerned with their surroundings. The pompous boss may walk with a deliberate step, exaggerated arm swing, raised head, and out-thrust chin, movements designed to impress observers. The happy, achieving, successful person may show enthusiasm and energy with free-swinging arm movements and a rapid, purposeful walk.

Our state of mind can be revealed without our even moving. A strong indicator of openness is an open position with the legs and body facing us directly. The crossed-leg and/or crossed-arm positions are frequently seen in a closed, competitive, or adversary relationship. If the person moves closer, has an open, direct body posture, unbuttoned clothes, or loosened tie, and looks at us directly and attentively, then openness and cooperation are likely. If these cues are accompanied by agreeable verbal communications, the openness is genuine and consistent with the total positive approach. The act of moving closer to a person suggests acceptance and a willingness to relate.

Resist jumping to conclusions based on out-of-context gestures.

An additional communication, if the body is turned away from others, is that this conversation is closed to outsiders. The hand placed upon the chest may suggest closeness, friendliness, and often devotion, sincerity, and honesty. In taking oaths and paying deep formal respect, as in saluting the flag, the hand is placed over the heart. Sex differences may be shown here, however, as a woman may show surprise or astonishment by raising her hands to her breasts.

If arms are crossed on the chest, a defensive, closed attitude is usually being shown. This symbolic stance is easy to recognize and understand, as it seems to be used throughout the world. The hands also may give important cues, as the tight fist or nervous arm grip in the defensive crossed-arms stance can indicate anger and tension, emphasizing a closed, rejecting attitude. Similarly, people who cross their legs are often indicating nonacceptance, opposition, or competition. If the crossed leg is moving slightly in a kicking motion, boredom, irritation, or impatience is probably being expressed. People who are not accepting what we are communicating may fold their arms, move away, put a hand up or cross their legs. More subtle gestures are modifications of these behaviors, with a slight turning of the body and the arms partly crossed to express mildly negative feelings. The sideways glance is similar to the sideways posture, suggesting possible rejection and a tentative "no." The nose-rubbing gesture, especially a side-to-side motion with the index finger, could also be expressing disagreement or doubt.

The "leg up" position might seem to be open and cooperative, but such a position is more often associated with territorial dominance and superiority feelings. Placing the feet on top of a desk or straddling a chair with the arms resting on the back of the chair usually demonstrates a superior attitude in spite of the apparent casual, disarming appearance. Sitting in a higher position or standing over a seated person often conveys an "I'm bigger than you are" message, and creates a feeling in the listener of being "talked down to." Desks, tables, and other barriers separate people, maintain a comfortable distance, and perpetuate a status difference, preventing too much closeness. Another typically American position indicating one-upmanship, and a superior, rather relaxed, aggressive attitude, involves lacing the hands behind the head and leaning the body back as far as the chair allows.

Facial Expressions Affecting Communication

Studies indicate that most people focus their eyes on the face more than on any other part of the body, and facial expressions are rapidly and readily interpreted. The raised eyebrow, the come-hither look, the disinterested glance, the fisheye look, the "look that could kill," and the narrow-lidded, suspicious glance are all rather easily recognized; but the eyes are also capable of many subtle nuances. We tend to maintain more eye contact when we listen than when we are talking. Eye contact is avoided when we are asked questions that make us feel uncomfortable or guilty. Often, when reacting in a defensive or aggressive manner we increase eye contact dramatically, and our pupils often dilate when we are emotionally aroused and excited. In an "eyeball-to-eyeball" confrontation, both individuals attempt to maintain eye contact. During such confrontations the concentration is usually very intense. Intense eye contact is awkward, and it is generally considered impolite, suggestive, or hostile to stare too long at others. This basic rule in our culture sometimes presents problems, however, as it is also impolite to ignore others and avoid looking at them. It is acceptable, however, to stare at animals and other objects, and, under special conditions, to stare at some people, as in a long, intimate look between lovers.

It is interesting—and often important in our relations with people from other cultures—to note differences in cultural patterns of eye contact. For instance, many English people gaze intently at the speaker all the time they are listening, their glance never wavering. We Americans would consider this behavior rude; conversely, they would consider us rude and inattentive if we did not maintain such intense eye contact with them while they were speaking. It's easy to see how misunderstandings can occur. It is considered polite, an indication of respect, among Spanish-speaking cultures for young people to lower their eyes when being addressed by an adult. Yet Americans expect young people to have a straightforward gaze, to "look us in the eye." This caused a problem in one school when several girls were caught smoking in the restroom and were taken to the dean's office. One girl, a Spanish-American, had just happened to be in the restroom and was innocent, but when the dean questioned her she lowered her gaze. The dean took this to be a sign of guilt and expelled her from school with the other girls. He later learned of his error and reinstated the innocent girl, but many such errors are never corrected. We would be wise not to read our own interpretation into others' nonverbal behavior.

Positive attitudes between people are associated with greater eye contact. Contact is greater when addressing a moderately high-status person, and lower when addressing a low-status person. Intense eye contact, accompanied by lowered eyebrows and outthrust lips and chin, is often maintained during a quarrel. Neither person wants to lose eye contact first, because this might be interpreted as admitting defeat or giving in.

Many shy or fearful people minimize and avoid eye contact. By so doing they frequently communicate doubt, hesitation, and possible shiftiness or dishonesty. Many people cannot face an accusing police officer or other questioning government official, and they usually will look away guiltily when gazed at by someone with an accusing, authoritative stare.

Displeasure or thoughtfulness may be shown by a frown, and antagonism conveyed through squinting of the eyes and tightened jaw muscles. Disbelief is often expressed by the raised eyebrow. In expressing surprise the mouth is wide open, and the chin drops. Occasionally an open mouth signifies concentration, and biting the lips or protruding the tongue may reflect deep involvement.

Many types of smiles have been noted and studied, and three types are quite common. The *simple* smile is a mild upward curve of the lips with the teeth unexposed, and is usually made when we are relatively uninvolved and not participating in socially active interchange. It may be seen when we are feeling thoughtful, introspective, or happy. This smile is often a noncommittal smiling to ourselves. The *upper* smile reveals the upper teeth, and is usually accompanied by eye contact with others. We often use it in greeting others, especially friends and relatives. The *broad* smile is usually seen during play and joyful laughter. Both the upper and lower teeth are exposed, but eye contact is generally fleeting and sporadic.

Smiles are not always related to happy experiences, but frequently serve as masks to avoid close contact and keep others at a distance. For example, an *oblong* smile, a forced or phony smile, might be seen on the face of a person who is receiving unwanted attention from a drunk at a party, or who has just heard an off-color story or unappreciated remark. Many people who feel angry or annoyed attempt to hide behind a vacant smile indicating that they don't want to be a threat or don't want to intrude or hurt others. Often the campus "Mr. Cool" hides behind a stolid exterior and variety of nonexpressive gestures or simple smiles, but it is often easy to see behind this deliberately noncommunicative facade if other body cues are accurately observed and evaluated.

Remember that facial expressions must be examined in context—a frown may be a sign of annoyance at home, deep concentration in the classroom, or puzzlement in another situation. We need to know what is going on inside the frowner, because looking at the face alone won't tell us the exact meaning of the frown.

Gestures Affecting Communications

The hands are expressive instruments, and all actors are coached in the proper use of hands to communicate a feeling or mood. Tightly clenched hands may reflect tension or anger. The pointing index finger is often used like a sword or dagger to reprimand, instruct, or put down an opponent. This gesture is frequently offensive in individual conversations, but it is often used effectively in public talks. With large groups the pointing finger is innocuous, forceful, and acceptable. Touching the nose or the eye with the index finger may show doubt, and rubbing near the ear frequently indicates hesitation, but the whole complex of behaviors must be evaluated in order for us to be confident about these conclusions.

Placing the hands on the hips is a frequent gesture seen in confident, goal-oriented people who are competitive and ready to take on a job. In the seated position, this readiness to engage is shown by placing one hand on one knee and resting the other arm on the other knee with a forward-leaning, alert posture. Another common gesture which expresses confidence is placing the hands together so as to touch the fingertips. This steepling gesture indicates that the person may be proud, self-confident, and often talks down to listeners. Members of the clergy, teachers, and business executives often use this gesture. If this message agrees with other body language, be careful not to humiliate or embarrass the person using it. If your teacher employs it, wait until the lecture is over (and the hands are open) before questioning or challenging.

People often use their hands to interrupt others when they want to speak. This behavior may derive from the child's reaching out to get comfort from adults; the adult gesture is an upward movement of the hand. Interrupting gestures may range from a hand placed on the speaker's arm to a tug of the earlobe, or just a subtle upward hand movement of a few inches, with the hand then falling back to the original position. Accurate assessment of interrupting gestures will assure better interaction, make us more aware of others, and prevent us from dominating conversations and boring our listeners.

Many gestures indicate anxiety, apprehension, and tension, and accurate perception of these movements can help avoid arguments and confrontations. The anxious, pacing father-to-be who cannot sit down and the seated, fidgeting, constantly-in-motion person reveal strong tensions by their physical motions. A white face and frequent deep sighs signal apprehension, and the audible expelling of air is an attempt to ease the uptight feelings. Nearly all students have experienced anxiety at the thought of speaking before a group and have been embarrassed by the tight feeling in the throat which they cannot clear. This throat clearing, stuttering, and repetitive use of words like "well . . . uh . . ." are outward signs of the strong feelings the person is experiencing. Nervous hand gestures, adjusting of clothing, tugging at the ear, or rubbing the face are other typical body language cues of tension. Recognition of these signals can help us put another person at ease, or help us be more accepting, understanding, and patient until the tension leaves and smoother relations are possible.

Touching others is a common form of nonverbal communication designed to express affection, to calm, or to interrupt, depending upon the context. Touching may show possessiveness or reassurance, and is universally prominent in love relationships. Many touchers are outwardly demonstrative and may show their feelings quickly, but they also may withdraw quickly.

Preening gestures are associated with actions designed to call attention to the body, and are typically aimed at the opposite sex, emphasizing and pointing to desirable physical attributes. Rearranging the clothing, smoothing the hair, crossing the legs, glancing sensually, and looking in mirrors are quite common courtship gestures. The fingering of hair and sideways headshaking to show off long hair also may be attempts to signify desirability, beauty, and availability. These gestures are thought to be related to the constant grooming and careful fur-rubbing gestures noted in monkeys and other primates. Availability is also communicated by facial expressions, strict conformity to in-group clothing and personal hygiene standards, and intense interest in the communications of an acceptable partner. Flirting glances, blushing, body posturing and demure, subtle gestures, with increased touching and intimate glances, usually accompany deepening courtship development.

To indicate receptivity, expressive people often show open hands with the palms facing upward or toward the other person. Actors often use this gesture to indicate openness and, conversely, hands hidden behind the back or in pockets may indicate defensiveness, avoidance, or a closed mind. Loosening a shirt or unbuttoning a coat also communicates receptivity and relaxed friendliness. Many animals lie on their backs, exposing their throats openly to a dominant animal, to show submission and openness. A person who opens up to us by loosening or unbuttoning clothing is trying to show a receptive attitude.

Our present-day greeting, the handshake, is an action which many people feel is indicative of a person's character and personality. The weak, clammy handshake is universally disliked, while the firm, positive grip is thought to be characteristic of a genuine, sincere person. It may be difficult to reserve judgment and not jump to conclusions about handshaking. The wide range of individual differences and the large variation from culture to culture should suggest caution. Some people consider handshaking to be in poor taste, while the French shake hands often, usually upon entering and leaving a room.

Women frequently don't shake hands in our culture. They may, instead, gently hold both hands and exchange pleasant and concerned facial expressions. Often an embrace or hug is also exchanged, but these intimate gestures are seldom used by men. Many people with sensitive or especially valuable hands, such as dentists, physicians, artists, and musicians, will reluctantly and defensively shake hands. A common "sincere" handshake is the politician's two-handed handshake. Needless to say, this is often merely an ingratiating public relations gesture designed simply to get votes. Dominance is often expressed by the handshake. If someone holds another's hand tightly, turning it so that his or her own hand is on top, the physical domination may signal an attempt to control. When the hand is offered palm up, this signifies cooperation and a willingness to be subordinate.

The skillful use of props can also effectively communicate attitudes and show strong feelings. Pipe smokers get involved in the ritual of preparing the pipe for smoking, cleaning it, and keeping it lit; these maneuvers often give an impression of patience and deep thought. Many pipe smokers are deliberate and tend to delay decision making. Cigarette smokers often communicate nervousness and impulsiveness. When they are very anxious they let the cigarette burn without puffing, or they may put it out forcefully, in an agitated fashion. After the pressure is released the cigarette smoker lights up, and the smoke seems to be a tranquilizer. Cigar smokers often give an impression of self-assurance and superior status, and generally hold the cigar possessively for long periods of time, often flicking it in a debonair fashion like a baton to emphasize verbal points.

People who wear glasses may stall for time—something pipe smokers often do—by slowly removing the glasses and carefully inspecting them or by putting the earpiece of the frame in their mouth. A person who can't see a point being made may remove his or her glasses to signify the fact. In an

Look for feedback from others about their perceptions of you.

argument in which this behavior occurs, the other person had best wait until the glasses are back on and both are seeing the issue in a more congruent way.

Integration of Communications

Does your nonverbal behavior agree with or contradict what you say? While most of us are defensive and at least somewhat resistant to change, here are some suggestions for improving communication and integrating verbal with nonverbal behavior:

1. Know thyself. A life-long project (see Chapter 3)
2. Develop active listening skills.
3. In group discussions, be aware of and look for feedback from others about their perceptions of you.
4. Focus on the attempts of others to influence you.
5. Consciously pursue an understanding of what roles, values, and attitudes you are conveying to others, as the interactions occur.
6. Ask for clarification when you do not understand others' comments about yourself.
7. When you become aware of an important feeling or insight about yourself, check it out with others.

8. When you find yourself saying one thing and feeling another, look objectively and honestly at the discrepancy. Feedback from friends may help clarify the differences and aid in problem solving.

9. Look for patterns in your life-style and check whether all of your behaviors are consistent with promoting a given pattern.

10. Be honest with others. They, in turn, will be more likely to level with you, with mutual benefits and insights.

11. Actively search for open, two-way communication. Accept closeness as well as criticism.

12. Don't be afraid to consult an accredited psychologist or psychiatrist if you are serious about self-integration, or if you have continuing deep concern about your happiness and interpersonal relationships.

1. List at least four different types of occupations in which nonverbal communication is vital.

2. Place yourself somewhere, perhaps in a parked car or on a park bench, where you can watch people without hearing them. Make note of the types of nonverbal communication you observe.

3. Watch a professional production on stage, on television, or in a movie theatre, and pay special attention to the nonverbal communication the actors employ. To increase your awareness of the actors' body language, you might try going to a foreign-language movie and ignoring the subtitles for a while, or watching a television program with the volume off.

4. Compare professional use of body language with nonprofessional by going to an amateur theatre production or watching some of your teachers carefully for a few days. Do the nonprofessionals employ nonverbal communication as much or as well as the professionals? Can you generalize?

5. List as many positive nonverbal ways of communicating as you can think of, and practice five for a week. Evaluate the results.

6. Watch your behavior in trying to persuade a friend to do something. What nonverbal communications did you use? Were they helpful?

7. Observe the nonverbal behaviors of a friend who wants you to do something with him/her. What nonverbal cues were you aware of? Were the cues helpful, congruent, or non-effective?

8. Carefully note the clothing and physical attractiveness (to you) of a friend. Do you also attribute other positive psychological traits to your friend? On what basis?

9. Are you able to see positive traits and characteristics in relatively unattractive people?

10. Do you believe that beauty is more than skin deep? Why?

FOR FURTHER INSIGHT

Aiken, L. "Relationships of Dress to Selected Measures of Personality in Undergraduate Women." *Journal of Social Psychology*, 59 (1963), 119–28.

Allport, G. W., and P. L. Vernon. *Studies in Expressive Behavior.* 2nd ed. New York: Hafner Publishing Co., 1967.

REFERENCES

Ardey, Robert. *The Territorial Imperative*. New York: Atheneum House, Inc., 1970.

Argyle, M., and J. Dean. "Eye Contact, Distance, and Affiliation." *Sociometry*, 28 (1965), 289–304.

Bateson, G.; D. Jackson; J. Haley; and J. Weakland. "Toward a Theory of Schizophrenia." *Behavioral Science*, 1956.

Birdwhistell, Ray. *Kinesics and Context*. Philadelphia: University of Pennsylvania Press, 1970.

Darwin, Charles. *The Expression of Emotion in Man and Animals*. London: Appleton-Century-Crofts, 1872.

Fast, Julius. *Body Language*. New York: M. Evans & Co., Inc., 1970.

Harper, Robert G., Wiens, Arthur N., and Matarazzo, Joseph D. *Nonverbal Communication: The State of the Art*. New York: Wiley-Interscience, 1978.

Knapp, Mark L. *Nonverbal Communication in Human Interaction*. New York: Holt, Rinehart & Winston, Inc., 1978.

Jourard, S. M. and Secord, P. F. *British Journal of Psychology*, (1955).

Mehrabian, Albert. "Communication Without Words." *Psychology Today*, September 1968, pp. 52–55.

——. *Silent Messages*. Belmont, California: Wadsworth Publishing Company, Inc., 1971.

Morris, Desmond. *The Human Zoo*. New York: McGraw-Hill Book Co., 1969.

Nierenberg, Gerard. *The Art of Negotiating*. New York: Hawthorn Books, Inc., 1968.

Nierenberg, Gerard, and Henry H. Calero. *How to Read a Person Like a Book*. New York: Hawthorn Books, Inc., 1971.

Reik, Theodore. *Listening with the Third Ear*. New York: Farrar, Strauss & Giroux, Inc., 1948.

5 Language and Symbolic Process

FOR PREVIEW AND REVIEW

1. Among the reasons we communicate are to transmit or receive information, to get others to do what we want, to express emotion, and to make possible or prevent further communication.
2. A word can have many different meanings, so it is essential to know what the speaker means by it.
3. Some of our problems with language come about because reality is constantly changing, but our language remains static; we perceive things selectively, through our fields of experience, and not as they actually exist; we see what we want or expect to see, rather than what is actually there; and we mistakenly believe that words correspond exactly to the things they refer to.
4. General Semantics is the study of how our language habits affect our behavior, including any semantic reactions.
5. The sentences or statements we use may describe our perceptions (*observations*), draw conclusions from what we or others have observed (*inference*), or make *value judgments* about someone or something.
6. Awareness of the ways in which words influence behavior can help us learn to use language intelligently.

INSTRUCTIONAL OBJECTIVES

After studying this chapter, you should be able to:
1. Explain the various types of communication and their significance in our interactions with others.
2. Identify the various problems which can arise when using words, and to overcome them as they occur in our everyday communications.
3. Analyze and overcome basic problems in the use of language as they relate to reality, to our selective perceptions, and to communication.
4. Demonstrate a knowledge of the differences among statements of observation, inference, and judgment, and the effect each has on our communications with others.
5. List the ways in which words influence behavior and the problems that can result, and to overcome any of these problems which we have.
6. Identify our individual communication problems relating to language, and to use the suggestions given to improve our language behavior.

"Some Words About Words"

"I didn't mean that at all!" "Why don't you *say* what you mean?" Such statements—often spoken in anger or exasperation—are familiar to us all. Who hasn't been misunderstood? It seems as if one problem with trying to communicate is that the words often get in the way. Frequently we have to rephrase what we're trying to say two or three times before our listener understands what we mean. Since it is unlikely that we will soon discover some means of instant communication, perhaps we can help improve our efforts by learning a little more about the nature of language and what it does to us—and we do to it!

Types of Communication

First, let us briefly discuss the various *kinds of communication* we engage in every day. The most common expressions are the polite social remarks and small talk, such as "Hi! How are you?" "Fine." "Great day!" "See you later." And so on. Such *phatic* communication is superficial, adding little to our knowledge and understanding of others. But it does let them know we notice them, and serves to open the door to further communication, should it be desired.

If we do not want to talk to someone, we might say, "Sorry, I'm in a rush!" and hurry away. This is *preventative* communication, the purpose of which is to make further communication impossible. Some other ways to accomplish this would be to cut someone off, make a snide remark, simply stare in silence, or dominate the conversation ourselves. There are many other effective techniques, but the purpose of them all is the prevention of communication.

A third common type of communication we can call the *recording-transmitting function*. Every time we ask how to do something, give someone directions, or answer factual questions, we are recording or transmitting information.

A fourth type of communication attempts to get others to do as we ask. The request may be direct ("Please turn down the stereo"), indirect ("I'd appreciate it if the stereo weren't so loud") or implied ("Don't you think the stereo is too loud?"). It may be polite, as above, or impolite ("Pipe down!"), but if the person does what we want, we were successful in our use of *instrumental* communication. If he or she doesn't do as we asked, then what we said was *not* instrumental in producing the desired action.

A fifth type of communication is an expression of the feelings and emotions of the speaker, or *affective* communication: "I really feel lousy today!" "I'm sorry I hurt your feelings." "You make me so mad I could scream!" "I just don't care anymore." These are all examples of affective communication. But human nature being what it is, it would be a good idea for us to listen between the lines of what is being said and try to determine if this is what the speaker really feels.

Another type of communication has to do with the idea that words have some sort of inherent power, or *magic.* "Don't talk about the plane crashing, or it will!" "If you plan a picnic, it will rain." "Don't discuss your plans for a new venture with anyone, or it will fail." These are all examples of the idea that words have some sort of magical power.

A final type of communication is to be found in various types of organizations or groups in which there are set phrases or responses, such as passwords in fraternal organizations, prayers in religious ceremonies, etc. This is the *ritual* use of language.

Problems with Words

Denotation/Connotation

So far, so good—we can understand the types of communication without too much difficulty. But what about the words themselves, and the problems they frequently cause? Let's first discuss the literal, dictionary meanings of words—the *denotations.* Surely no one would misunderstand us if we used a common, concrete word such as tree, bed, or hat. Or would they? How many times have we been misunderstood, without our ever knowing it? Think about it.

Perhaps a few facts will illuminate the problem. There are about 600,000 words in the English language today. The educated adult uses about 2,000 words in daily conversation. The 500 most frequently used words have *14,000* dictionary definitions! Is it any wonder that what *we* think of when we use a certain word is not necessarily what our *listener* will think of?

The problem is further compounded by the *connotative* definitions, or subjective *personal* interpretations and meanings, that words have. Though two people might know what is meant by *dog,* one may have warm memories of a childhood pet, giving the word positive connotations for him, while the other may, as a child, have been bitten and mauled by a dog, giving the word frightening connotations for him. It is very important that we remember this: *words* don't mean, *people* do. Words don't carry meanings like buckets carry

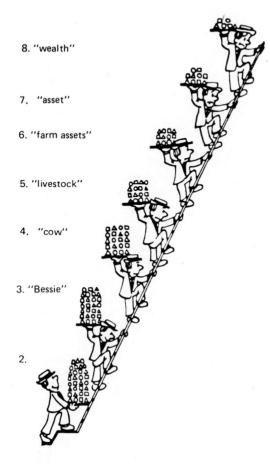

8. "wealth"

7. "asset"

6. "farm assets"

5. "livestock"

4. "cow"

3. "Bessie"

2.

8. The word "wealth" is at an extremely high level of abstraction, omitting *almost* all reference to the characteristics of Bessie.

7. When Bessie is referred to as an "asset," still more of her characteristics are left out.

6. When Bessie is included among "farm assets," reference is made only to what she has in common with all other salable items on the farm.

5. When Bessie is referred to as "livestock," only those characteristics she has in common with pigs, chickens, goats, etc., are referred to.

4. The word "cow" stands for the characteristics we have abstracted as common to cow_1, cow_2, cow_3 . . . cow_n. Characteristics peculiar to specific cows are left out.

3. The word "Bessie" (cow_1) is the name we give to the object of perception of level 2. The name is *not* the object; it merely *stands* for the object and omits reference to many of the characteristics of the object.

2. The cow we perceive is not the word, but the object of experience, that which our nervous system abstracts (selects) from the totality that constitutes the process-cow. Many of the characteristics of the process-cow are left out.

1. The cow known to science ultimately consists of atoms, electrons, etc., according to present-day scientific inference. Characteristics (represented by circles) are infinite at this level and ever-changing. This is the *process level*.

Figure 1.   The abstraction ladder.

water. Words are only symbols for something and do not have meanings in and of themselves; only *people* can have meanings for the words as they *use* them. So rather than ask, "What does it (the word) mean?" we should ask, "What does the *person* mean?" We should not assume we know what a person means when he or she uses any given word, but should check it out to avoid misunderstanding (use the Echo Technique).

Abstract/Concrete

So far we've talked primarily about problems with specific concrete words. Another problem with words is related to the varying *degrees* of concreteness of words, from concrete, specific words, like "college freshman," "bicycle," "tuna sandwich," etc., to abstract or general words, ideas, and concepts, such as "love," "knowledge," "education." Simply stated, the more *concrete* or specific a word is, the more likely it is to be understood; conversely, the more general or *abstract* a word is, the more possible interpretations it might have, thus increasing the probability that we will misunderstand, or not get the meaning the speaker intended. Hayakawa's Ladder of Abstraction[1] (Figure 1) illustrates this point. Of course, general terms or abstractions are useful; it would take forever to communicate if we had to reduce every idea to basic-level concrete terms. But we should not treat abstractions as if they were concrete terms, or act as if they had no interpretations other than the ones we give them. Such behavior can only lead to communication problems. Rather, we must be *aware* when we or others are using higher level abstractions, and be sure we *define* or *clarify* them.

Levels of Usage

We are all aware that there are different *levels of usage,* that formal English is different from the slang we use with our friends, which is in turn different from the usage of an illiterate person. We are also aware that we use one vocabulary level in a college seminar, another when talking to our friends, still another when coaxing a young brother or sister to do something. The point is that we usually adapt our communication efforts as best we can to the level of the situation and person(s) to whom we're talking. If we do not, or are not aware of a difference when there is one, problems can result.

Verbiage

Another problem is that some people carry on in their verbalizations, going around the issue, stating the same thing ten times in ten slightly different ways. They use fancy or vague words, with many generalities, and thoroughly obscure their meaning under tons of verbiage. For example:

> *A plumber wrote the U.S. Bureau of Standards about using hydrochloric acid to clean drain pipes. . . .*
>
>   *Several days later he received this reply, "The efficacy of hydrochloric acid is indisputable, but the corrosive residue is incompatible with metallic permanence."*
>
>   *Confused, he wrote again and asked if the acid "is okay to use or not."*
>
>   *A second letter advised him, "We cannot assume responsibility for the production of toxic and noxious residue, and suggest that you use an alternative procedure."*

---

[1] From *Language in Thought and Action.* 2nd ed., by S. I. Hayakawa, copyright © 1941, 1949, 1963, 1964 by Harcourt Brace Jovanovich, Inc., and reproduced with their permission. Also reprinted by permission of Allen & Unwin Ltd. (London).

Still baffled, he wrote, "Do you mean it's okay to use hydrochloric acid?"
A final letter resolved the question.
"Don't use hydrochloric acid. It eats the hell out of pipes."[2]

75

*Language and
Symbolic Process*

It takes skill to pin such a person down, or to try to get at the essence of what is meant—but if we don't, no effective communication can be achieved.

Paraphrase Problem

Most of us have the habit of putting what we hear into our own words when we repeat it to someone else, without checking to make sure we got the message right in the first place (see "Echo Technique," Chapter 1). In so doing, we frequently distort the original intent and meaning of the message according to our own understanding (or misunderstanding). This is a risky thing to do, at best, and can lead to serious communication breakdowns in which the conversation goes something like this: "Why did you tell Bob that I . . . ?" "Because you said. . . ." "No, I didn't! I said. . . ." "But I thought you said. . . ." And so it goes. This is an all-too-familiar experience for many of us! We would be wise to check with the person right away, to make sure we got the message right, before paraphrasing and repeating it to someone else.

Making Sense/Closure

This problem is increased when we don't quite catch or understand one word or phrase of the message, and can't or don't want to ask that it be clarified. The natural tendency in this case is to *try to make sense out of what we hear.* In so doing, we may substitute another word or phrase that sounds something like the original, or that we think means about the same thing (how do we know, if we didn't catch the word in the first place?)—or we may even make something up to fill in the gap! Needless to say, we should not do *any* of the above if we want to communicate accurately and effectively! Similarly, when parts of letters or words or objects are missing from something we read or see, we automatically (and often unconsciously) fill in the missing parts. This process is called *closure.*

Some Basic Problems in Perception and the Use of Language

Language (Symbolic World) and Reality (Empirical World)

The first assumption we must do away with is that language is neutral, a medium of exchange between the world and the individual that in no way affects the individual's behavior. This is just not so. When we take language for granted, we may conclude that everyone else thinks very much as we do. Again, not so. What characterizes reality at all levels is not the presence of things, but rather a *process*—something ever changing. Our language sug-

[2] From Stuart Chase, *The Power of Words* (New York: Harcourt Brace Jovanovich, Inc., 1953), p. 154.

gests permanence, yet we know that the only thing that *is* permanent is the fact that experience, people, and things *will change.* Our *dynamic* world of process is represented in words that are *static.* And this fact creates many problems.

Selective Perception (Abstracting Process) and Communication

A second factor in the use of language that we should be aware of is the process by which we apprehend the events of reality, how we arrive at our perceptions. Our only contact with the world "out there" is through our senses, which transmit *images* of reality to each of us. These images or sensory impressions are as close as we come to knowing the world. In truth, the world of events, objects, and people—the objective reality "out there"—is never touched by human beings. Instead, each of us lives in a subjective world, one of sensory images and impressions, that is a product of the perceptual process. It might be said that everything we see is an "optical illusion" that is the result of our preconceptions, training, values, goals, experiences, etc.

We are bombarded each second by numerous environmental and interpersonal stimuli. Unable to notice and remember all we experience, we engage in selective perception; that is, we see and hear (etc.) only *some* of the available stimuli that surround us. Our selective perception is significantly influenced by our fields of experience, including our *preconceptions.* We perceive, largely, what we *expect*, want, or need to perceive, dismissing or overlooking contradictory data, and anything else that is perceptible at any given moment. Also, from the countless sensory stimuli present in any given situation, we pay conscious attention only to those that are meaningful to us at the moment. We see mostly what we have learned to look at, and we look at what we think we need to look at. What seems unnecessary or threatening we ignore. We perceive what is on our mind and not always what is presented to us, and this myopia increases when we are under stress or in conflict. Yet we are often unaware that we have been selective, that we have perceived only a small part of that which was perceptible. And that small part becomes our "truth" or our "reality." Given the same situation, someone else probably perceived things differently in some respects (based on his or her own field of experience and preconceptions), and arrived at a different "truth" or "reality." Since each of us perceives reality differently, it should not be surprising that events, words, and actions can be interpreted in many ways. We behave according to what we bring to the occasion, and we constantly *abstract* (select, ignore, and rearrange) whatever we perceive. An awareness of this *abstracting process* (involving selective perception) should encourage a more cautious, less dogmatic attitude about our "knowledge," or what we "know." Until we realize that each person perceives reality differently, and accept such differences, we will continue to have communication problems and interpersonal conflicts with those who do not share our view of the world. Perhaps it is this awareness of different possibilities and limitations that best describes what we call an education.

General Semantics

This brings us from fairly common, easily understandable concepts to something which might be new to some—the basic principles of *general semantics.* Generally, semantics is the study of the meanings of words. There are many branches of such study: etymology and philology study the historical development of language; linguistics studies language families, dialects, grammars; traditional semantics studies the relationship between the word (symbol) and the thing it stands for (referent). These are all interesting areas of study, but we will be most concerned with general semantics, or the study of how our language habits affect our behavior—how we respond to words and other symbols, our attitudes toward language, reality, and human behavior. The way in which we use language influences the way in which we think, and this in turn influences the way we act or behave. General semantics is in large part concerned with improving our abilities for using language, hence thinking, hence acting.

The principles of general semantics were formulated by Count Alfred Korzybski (1877–1950), who believed that (1) language influences all of human behavior; (2) if our language habits are immature or distorted, our behavior will also be less than mature; (3) we can correct our bad language habits through retraining our nervous systems, or eliminating our negative responses to certain words or phrases.

The same word often means different things to different people.

One basic distinction we need to make before going any further is that between sign and symbol. A *sign* is an experience, object, etc., which has an unmistakable meaning. A stop sign at an intersection means all cars should stop there momentarily. A class bell means that all classes should begin or end. A sign calls for a single, definite response.

A *symbol,* on the other hand, can mean many different things, so it can call forth many different responses. Because its meaning depends on the situation and the responses of those involved, it must be studied carefully. To someone who is cold and hungry, a fire is a symbol of warmth and a way to cook food. To a forest ranger in the summer, it is more likely a symbol of potential death and destruction. Symbols also call forth different responses in different cultures. A country's flag may symbolize peace and honor to the people who live there, and aggression and dishonor to their neighbors whom they have invaded.

Because words are themselves symbols, they can stand for many different things, even among people who share the same culture. Obviously, the problem is multiplied many times when we interact with those from different cultures (see Chapter 11). Words are only labels people attach to objects, concepts, etc., and their meanings constantly change as the world they describe changes. This is one reason it is so hard to know how to respond to words, and why it can be a problem if we always respond in only one way—a way that we perhaps learned years ago.

Even though a sign has a single, unmistakable meaning, we are free to respond in any way we choose (often at our own risk). We are free because we can reason, instead of reacting automatically. Sometimes, because of our conditioning, we react to symbols as if they were signs. That is, an event or word or circumstance may trigger a particular emotional response from us. In the case of such *signal* or *semantic reactions,* we no longer exercise intelligent choice; we allow someone or something to "push our buttons" or manipulate our responses. In so doing, we abandon our right as human beings to *think* and *choose.*

The ability to symbolize also involves the ability to call up *internal* responses (emotional, biological, psychological) using only the symbols. And therein lies the danger. As children we are often conditioned to respond in certain ways to various words: "That's a naughty word!" "Don't call your brother a. . . ." "That's its name because that's what it *is*." (How wrong can we get?) In fact, as adults we often find ourselves reacting to words in the way we were taught to react as children—we respond to them as if they were signs capable of producing just the one *reaction,* instead of as symbols with many possible meanings which can elicit many possible responses.

These gut level responses are one type of irrational behavior Korzybski felt we need to overcome. Otherwise, any time someone pushes the right button by saying the right word or phrase to us, he or she can trigger such a semantic reaction. We need to be better masters of our own minds and responses. We need to learn to *act,* instead of *react!* As our culture becomes more symbol-laden, even symbol-bound, the ability to distinguish between the word-symbol and the thing itself becomes even more important. The keynote for this whole chapter might well be the following idea, expressed by John Condon: "Learning to use language intelligently begins by learning not to be used by language."[3] To do this, we must constantly remind ourselves that *the word is not the thing*—that we should not respond to words as if they were the things they describe. To be called a name does not affect what you are, *unless you let it*.

Observation, Inference, Judgment

We live in two different worlds—a world of real people, objects, and events, and a world of words and symbols. Too often we confuse the two worlds, and we respond to words as if they were things, as if they were reality. In our everyday experiences we are constantly observing things around us, describing to others what we see, hear, or experience, drawing conclusions (inferences) about these things, and frequently making judgments. And we do all this without giving it much thought. The processes involved are simply a part of our language habits, but they are not always good habits. Let's examine the problem more closely.

To begin with, we observe, and describe what we observe, on the basis of two general types of data: *sense data* reality and a *system* of other symbols. Words may be tested against either standard, whichever is appropriate. Sense data have an *extensional orientation,* extending to the world around us and experienced through our senses—what we see, hear, taste, touch, and smell. To be oriented *extensionally* is to realize the primary importance of life facts, to emphasize the roles of observation and investigation, to go to the facts first and abide by them. Sense data, if reported accurately, are the most likely to be objective—if *anything* can be said to be truly objective. Extensional orientation, then, gives primary attention to the real world, and *only then* uses words to describe it.

Yet sense data have more meaning for us as we relate them to some larger system, such as cultural mores, philosophy, religion, government, economics. We are oriented *intensionally* to such systems—that is, we put them together to make sense of them within ourselves, in our thinking. To be oriented intensionally is to order behavior in terms of our own *internalized* systems, definitions, arguments, verbal proofs, theories, etc., often disregarding what is "out there" in reality and is verifiable. This intensional orientation involves our verbalizations, which represent what goes on "inside the skin." (But how can *this* be verified?!) This includes the tendency to respond to words and labels and in the process to neglect or give only secondary attention to the real world. One of the goals of general semantics is to foster a more extensional attitude and approach—to encourage us to respond to the way things are, and not to the way they are talked about.

Neither view, in and of itself, is satisfactory. A system that disregards our daily experiences is of limited usefulness; a system based purely on inducted sense data is impossible. The way we interpret everyday experiences requires a combination of system and sense data. As we try to make our

[3] *Semantics and Communication* (London: The Macmillan Co., 1969), p. 10.

experiences meaningful, we move from one orientation to the other. All experience is a combination of immediate sense data that we give meaning within a larger system—of language, or religion, or politics, or society—by which we interpret the event.

In order to record or communicate our experiences, we reduce them to symbols (words) that can be readily understood. Because these symbols must be negotiable within the whole society that speaks our language, our expressions of experiences are necessarily loose, even sloppy. *Language is never precise;* its very nature and purpose require it to be more general than any single experience that we might describe with it. Ordinary language conveys the bulk of our symbolized experience. As we move from sense data to system experience, the degree of our personal involvement increases considerably. There are also degrees of personal involvement in the statements we make about the outside world. Whenever we say *anything,* we put something of ourselves into what we describe. And even though our ordinary language is less than precise, we can still make important distinctions among the kinds of statements we use—distinctions based on the degree of personal involvement. For example, examine the following statements: "The cat is purring." "The cat is healthy." "Cats make the best pets." Each is different, and each illustrates one of the three types of statements we'll discuss.

Stereotypes can block communication.

Statements of observation ("The cat is purring") rely solely on observable sense data reality, reporting what is observed, without attempting to interpret or evaluate. According to Welden and Ellingsworth, a statement may be said to be an observation if it:

1. *Describes phenomena in the world of objects and events (is about physical reality).*
2. *Does not appear to describe anything which was not observed. . . .*
3. *Is about a phenomenon that is capable of being observed by others (has the possibility of being tested by verification).*
4. *Does not appear to attach any values to what was observed, such as "good," "bad," "beautiful," or "undesirable."*[4]

A statement of observation tells us more about the thing being described than about the person making the statement. Even so, the words we choose to describe something help to determine our perception of it, and our behavior toward it.

Statements of inference are those which draw conclusions from what we observe. A statement may be said to be an inference if it:

1. *Relates known or observed events to unknown events (is about the reality of relationships). Relates the known to the unknown or the yet-to-be-observed.*
2. *Implies the existence of a number of observations which lead to the inference. Thus the test of an inference is:*
   a. *What statements of observation would need to be available in order to make the inference possible?*
   b. *Based on the number and kind of observations available, how probable is it that the inference can be made? What is the probable relationship between the implied statements and the inference?*
   c. *Is it dependent on the physical reality which has been observed and to a lesser extent on the social reality of the observer? Two observers might make radically different inferences from the same data, based on the social reality from which they operate.*[5] (See Figure 2.)

An example of an inference statement is "The cat is healthy." The validity of any inference depends on the availability and the truth of a set of observations. Inferences cannot be proven true or false, but they can be demonstrated to be *probable* or *improbable,* and possibly verifiable.

Probably most of human behavior operates on the basis of inference. Most of the time we just do not have the facts on which to base our behavior. Yet to make sense of what we do and to anticipate what we should do in the future, we must make assumptions, draw conclusions. Recognizing this fact, we must be especially careful when dealing with inferences, noting those that are more or less probable, recognizing the base of fact-description that supports them (or lack of it), and being willing to alter our assumptions when new information comes along. Neither type of statement is better than the

---

[4] From *Effective Speech Communication* by Terry A. Welden and Huber W. Ellingsworth, p. 57. Copyright © 1970 by Scott, Foresman and Company. Reprinted by permission.

[5] Welden and Ellingsworth, pp. 57–58.

WHAT HAPPENED	MR. "A" SAYS:		MR. "B" SAYS:	COMMENT
THE EVENT	"I see a		"I see a	No argument
THE LABEL (1st Inference)	"It is a man with a brief-case."	MAN AND BRIEFCASE	"It is a man with a brief-case."	Inference because it could be a woman dressed like a man.
2nd Inference	"He is taking some work home with him."	MAN AND BRIEFCASE	"Spies sometimes use briefcases."	Going off in different directions
3rd Inference	He must be a very dedicated man to take work home with him."	MAN AND BRIEFCASE	"I wouldn't be surprised if that man doesn't turn out to be a spy."	Where's everybody going?
4th Inference	A man that dedi-cated is bound to be a success in life and an asset to our community."	MAN AND BRIEFCASE	"This country is infested with spies and unless we do something about it we're in trouble."	Brother!
ETC.	ETC.	MAN AND BRIEFCASE	ETC.	ENDSVILLE

Figure 2. *Down the road from fact to fallacy.*[6]

other. Both are useful and necessary. Problems arise from *acting as if* our inferential statements are factual.

If we recognize the distinction between statements of fact and state-ments of inference, and learn to act on inferences as if they are inferences and not facts, we will be less dogmatic about what we say, more open to conflicting ideas and possibilities, psychologically prepared to be proven wrong, and less likely to be hurt if and when we are proven wrong.

Statements of judgment go one step further than inferences and make *value judgments* about what was observed or experienced—or merely heard about! A statement may be said to be a judgment if it:

1. *Describes phenomena in the world of objects, events, or relationships.*
2. *Is expressed in a form which reveals more about the observer than about the event being described—one which contains a word or phrase about the event's acceptability to the observer, such as "like," "dislike," "is beautiful," "is confusing," etc.*
3. *Is capable of being believed or rejected—that is, of generating a statement such as "I believe that," or "I can't accept that."*
4. *Acceptance can be tested by finding out whether others are willing to believe or reject the statement.*[7]

[6] Adapted with permission of Glencoe Publishing Co., Inc. from *Communications: The Transfer of Meaning*, by Don Fabun. Copyright © 1968 by Kaiser Aluminum & Chemical Corporation.

[7] Welden and Ellingsworth, p. 58.

An example of a judgment statement is "Cats make the best pets." This is a statement about the relationship of an individual to cats. It is based on internalized, *personal* responses, preferences, or opinions. It cannot be right or wrong, as we are all entitled to our own opinions, but we may agree or disagree. We would do well to recognize judgments for what they are, and not expect or demand uniformity of judgment. What is important is to realize when we are making judgments, to avoid stating judgments as if they were facts, and to be open to other choices. Such an attitude can only improve the climate for communication and understanding.

Ways in Which Words Influence Behavior

So far we have discussed many problems with words, with language in general, and with types of statements—ways in which we might misuse language, or let it use us. But perhaps we should be most concerned with how words can influence our behavior. We shall now apply and expand some of the principles presented earlier in order to illustrate a few of the many ways in which words influence behavior.

Inherent Bias (Classification)

We are all aware that, try as we may, we can never be totally objective in our statements about things, experience, reality. When we *group* or *classify* things, we often talk and act as if the groupings we have chosen *were* objective; but even if we consider them objective, our listeners may not find them so. The very nature of language and the process of our selection of groupings by which to classify things precludes objectivity. A classification reflects not only a purpose, but also an attitude associated with the classification. So remember: *no category or classification is neutral.* By its very nature, it involves some bias.

This principle is most important when dealing with and talking about human beings and human behavior. Many people respond to an individual not as a unique human being but as a member of a class. Many of us have preconceived notions of what characteristics are associated with what classes. When we meet a member of such a class, we are prone to respond not to the unique individual, but rather to the class to which she or he belongs and base our responses largely on those characteristics which we think apply to the whole class and hence to this individual as a member of that class. If we recognize the fact that no two things are identical, and integrate this concept into our thinking and language habits, we are less likely to fall into the trap of responding to classes rather than to individuals.

For instance, if someone were to tell you about a friend, John Jones, your attitude toward him might vary depending on whether he was described as a college graduate, an elementary schoolteacher, an art major, a songwriter, a black. It is possible that he could be described in *all* of these terms—terms not *meant* to influence your response one way or another. But your attitude might be different with each different classification. Since the meaning of any label is partly determined by the listener, the speaker has no idea how the description of Jones might affect you. Whatever your response, you are not talking about Jones; you are talking about your own responses to words (categories).

It is also important that we recognize and avoid so-called sexist words or phrases such as *chick, stud, jock,* or *broad.* They can only hinder communication, when our object is to improve or enhance it.

When we think we have somehow totally characterized or captured the essence of the nonverbal world with a name, we run into difficulty. As long as we realize that no word does this and that any classification is but one of many possible, each with different attitudes and responses involved, we need not be deluded by language.

Exclusivity of Names

We should not forget that any one thing may be given many different names. Yet we frequently make problems for ourselves when we assume that different names for the same thing are mutually exclusive. For instance, the stock comedian's joke, "That was no lady; that was my wife!" is an example of this problem. Other examples are, "That's no junk heap; that's my car!" and "It's not a pigsty; it's my room!" When we insist that *our* name for something is the right one, or the only acceptable one, to the exclusion of all others, we often find ourselves in needless conflict. A variation of the same problem occurs when we ask someone whether he or she took a class for knowledge or for a grade, . . . dated someone for his or her brains and personality or looks, . . . took a vacation for rest or for play. Such questions assume the answer has to be one or the other, when it could easily be *both!* When we find ourselves in a conflict that can be stated in the familiar pattern, "That was no _____; that was _____," and both words apply to the same thing, we should ask why it is necessary to argue.

Two-Valued Orientation (Polarization)

Another common problem is selecting two extremes as if they were the only choices or categories possible, and ignoring the frequently wide range of middle ground. This is called two-valued orientation, polarized thinking, the black-or-white fallacy—or, "There are two sides to every question!" Examples of this are, "He's either right or wrong," "Either it's good or it's bad," "If you're not for me, you must be against me." During times of stress and tension we reduce the number of possible responses and tend toward restrictive reactions. Popular persuaders of all kinds have found it effective to narrow choice in their appeals to one of two alternatives. This distorts reality, and is a semantic problem to be avoided.

Hasty Generalization

The only exercise some people get is jumping to conclusions. This problem, the hasty generalization, involves making bald statements about people, groups, or concepts as if one instance or experience were true for all ("Seen one, and you've seen 'em all!"), or as if what was true at one time were true for *all* time. Such a practice denies process-reality—the fact that everyone and everything is constantly changing.

The same type of problem occurs when, because of one experience, we label a person as a particular type. "Joe lied to me yesterday; Joe is a liar," is an example of this. Using generalized labels saves time and effort, and also makes us appear to know more, but in the process our thinking and communication are distorted. Worse, such generalizations often stick and become the basis for other inferences that compound the distortion. It is through just such generalizations that prejudices are vented and stereotypes formed—a most irrational use of language.

Korzybski suggested that we minimize the possibility of the problem occurring by mentally *indexing* each event or person: Jim_1 would be our first contact with Jim; subsequent contacts with him would be Jim_2, Jim_3, and so on. This would serve to remind us *not* to make generalizations about Jim, or to assume that because he was one way today, he'll be the same tomorrow, or next week, or next year.

Living Up to the Label

Sometimes statements we make about others, intended only as descriptions, become instrumental in changing the persons they describe. This can be harmful under any circumstances, but it can be especially damaging to children. "You're so clumsy!" "Johnny's a real troublemaker!" "Sue is just a shy child." "Bob has always been an average student." "Cathy's a real brain!" "Bill's just no good in math." Can you begin to see what happens? Often the response to such labeling is the attitude, "If they say it, it must be true," or "If I'm going to have the name, I might as well play the game." Perhaps you can think of labels applied to you as you were growing up—or even as an adult. We all have a tendency to live up to our labels, whether they have been applied by others, or have been chosen by ourselves (joker, playboy, femme fatale, and so on). Responding to such labels might give us direction, help us decide what to do and what not to do, but more often than not the choices are not the wisest, and the direction is backward.

Self-Fulfilling Prophecy

When we try to live up to a label we have given ourselves, we limit our activities to those the label prescribes. It is also possible to change the behavior of other people and institutions by labeling them and then acting on the label. If we think a class will be dull and boring, then act as if it were, influencing others around us, the lack of interest and involvement might eventually produce a dull, boring class. If we think members of a group are unfriendly, then act as if they were, they will sense our attitude and most probably *will* be unfriendly—at least to us! The self-fulfilling prophecy may range from personal, individual behavior to international politics. (What might happen if one country acted as if another were going to start a war?

Frightening!) The self-fulfilling prophecy works only in areas in which the prophecy may be *acted upon* (socially based). If I say, "I just know I'm going to flunk the test," sure enough, I probably will! Or at least I increase the possibility that I will. We would do well to avoid such behavior unless we prophesy only positive ideas.

Reacting to Words as Things

A somewhat different type of problem results from confusing word and thing, and is sometimes caused by the self-reflexive nature of language: we make words about things, then words about *words* about things. The problem is that unless we distinguish between the two kinds of relations (words-for-things, and words-for-words-for-things), we may begin to react to our own reactions. Franklin D. Roosevelt's famous statement, "We have nothing to fear but fear itself" warns of this kind of problem. It is one thing to be afraid—it might even be healthy in certain circumstances. It is quite another to be afraid of being afraid! The latter could lead to neurosis. Being in love is natural, desirable, human; being in love with the idea of being in love is something else again! This behavior is seen in the person who can't stand to talk about certain things, whether they be rats, or plane crashes, or sex.

Symbolic Strategies

Critic Kenneth Burke gave the name *symbolic strategies* to the ways in which we may manipulate symbols in lieu of altering reality. Of course, every time we impose order on the outside world through language, we are using some kind of strategy. But there are some special strategies which we may use to come to grips with things.

One such strategy involves a mild form of *self-deception.* An example is setting clocks or watches five or ten minutes ahead; people who do so claim that such manipulation of symbols helps them to be on time for work, appointments, and so on. Another example would be the students who walk out of an exam and say, "Man, I really blew it!" Although they really feel that they probably did all right, such a strategy is designed to keep them from being disappointed when grades are announced, in case they didn't do as well as they wanted to. These strategies are not necessarily harmful, because the deceptions are intentional and directed only to the individual—a manipulation of symbols in order to fool oneself in some vaguely useful or protective way.

Another symbolic strategy is *temporary identification* with others who seem to have things under control, such as a movie actor, or characters in a particular world created on film or in a book. Our identification temporarily makes us feel more important, more responsible, and the effect frequently lasts for a while after the program, film, book, or other vicarious experience has ended.

A third symbolic strategy involves *creating our own fantasies*—or daydreaming—instead of turning to books or movies or other professionally produced symbols. A classic example of this is Thurber's Walter Mitty, who either fantasized himself as a giant in a world of midgets or else cut the world down to his size in order to feel adequate, important. Other such symbolic strategies involve poking fun at someone or something through ridicule, sarcasm, and many kinds of jokes.

A final symbolic strategy is *possessing the symbol* when what the symbol represents is difficult or nearly impossible to obtain. Today's society, through the advertising media, provides symbols of almost everything for almost everybody: power, love, status, sex, culture, etc., may be represented in cars, homes, liquor, magazines, clothing, and so on. Many people are satisfied to own books on a subject—possess the symbols—in lieu of gaining the knowledge or skill involved.

When we manipulate symbols in order to deal with the world in a way that is comforting to us, we are not necessarily acting in an unhealthy manner. But when we feel we have altered something in the nonverbal world while only playing with symbols, or when we escape to symbols so often we can't face real problems, or when we confuse our imaginative world with the real world, we may find ourselves in serious trouble.

Suggestions for Improving Language Behavior

Many suggestions for improving language behavior have already been given in this chapter as the different concepts have been discussed. If we really want to know and manage ourselves better as we (and everything in the world around us) change, we can help by watching *what* we say and do, and *how* we say and do it. It will help if we can remember and practice the following suggestions.

1. Use descriptive terms and lower-order abstractions as much as possible, avoiding absolute terms, generalities, high-level abstractions, or words that imply "all-ness" (the attitude of pretending/thinking/talking/acting as if we can know or say all). Remember that we can never know or say everything about any subject.
2. Use neutral terms, terms that are as free as possible from bias or slant, instead of judgmental terms or words loaded with approval or disapproval.
3. Speak in terms of more-or-less, give consideration to degrees and shades of meaning, avoid talking in terms of opposites. Avoid either/or thinking or arguments, describing things in terms of black and white without any gray shading. Be aware of the many values involved in any issue.
4. Differentiate carefully between people, situations, and problems. Do not speak of one as "just like" another one. Remember, no two things are absolutely alike—nor is any one thing exactly the same from one time to another. Think in terms of indexing (Jim$_1$, Jim$_2$, Jim$_3$, etc.).
5. Distinguish between what is actually going on, and what we feel or understand is going on, by being able to recognize our own in-

Differentiate carefully between people, situations, and problems.

terpretations, inferences, opinions versus the verifiable facts or sense data. We must remind ourselves that our reactions are inside-our-own-skin images, and may not reflect what is "out there."

6. Keep in mind that things change. Today is different from yesterday; tomorrow will be different from today.

7. Remember that the "process" world is very complex. There are causes rather than one cause, aims rather than one aim, and methods rather than one method. There is no one answer to anything.

8. Avoid talking as if everything could be separated, such as mind-body or ends-means, etc.

9. Think with quotation marks around words in order to be reminded of the difference between the word and the object to which it refers (the referent).

10. Avoid hasty judgments and generalizations. By not judging too quickly, we can keep our opinions less rigid.

11. Try to evaluate each situation on its own merits, instead of always insisting on upholding our own viewpoint.

12. Remember to use words as mere tokens or symbols for what we wish to convey; don't quibble over the dictionary meanings of words.

Aids in Applying These Suggestions

1. Use humor whenever possible, the light touch; avoid the grim, demanding, one-upmanship way of delivering a message.
2. Operate with trust, recognizing the great difficulties that exist in trying to communicate with yourself and with others. Give your best to that task and assume that the other person involved is equally responsible.
3. Relax, remain calm and quiet, smile, and delay reactions.
4. Talk calmly, with deliberation—not too fast and/or loud.
5. Listen with genuine attention, wait your turn to speak, then begin with something like "If this is what you mean, then. . . ." Do not interrupt and/or contradict, beginning with a "Yes—but."
6. Go easy, avoid challenges and criticism. Use suggestions and questions that invite more information, to promote learning. Criticism, even implied, can cast a blight on the desire to learn. It promotes a defensiveness that blocks communication.

1. Select one of the following words and ask at least five people to define it: love, truth, peace, freedom, beauty, friendship, education, ethics, work, religion, recreation, time, courage, humility. Compare their definitions with a dictionary's. Why are there so many different definitions for each word? How can we be sure that we understand what each of us means by the words we use when we communicate?

FOR FURTHER INSIGHT

2. Each of us perceives reality just a little bit differently. To demonstrate this, go with a friend to some public place (restaurant, shopping center, park, etc.). Each of you should attempt to remember what you see, hear, smell, etc. Then leave the chosen location, and each of you should jot down your perceptions. Discuss your lists, and the reasons for the perceptual differences.
3. Write down some examples of polarization (two-valued orientation). These may be from personal experiences, newspapers, short stories, speeches, movies, television, etc. For each example explain (1) what went wrong, and (2) how the problem or misevaluation could have been avoided.
4. Select advertisements from magazines or newspapers which rely on the reader responding intensionally rather than extensionally. How widespread is this technique? Do you think it is effective? Why?
5. For one day attempt to limit your comments strictly to observational statements. What are the consequences?
6. List the "labels" that have been given to you which influence your actions and attitudes. How and why do they do so? What can you do about feelings in regard to these labels?
7. Can you think of a recent situation in which a communication problem arose between you and another person as a result of misunderstanding words? What went wrong? How might the problem have been avoided?
8. Explain what you feel are the major implications of Irving J. Lee's observation: "The more we discriminate among, the less we discriminate against."

REFERENCES

Barfield, Owen. *The Rediscovery of Meaning and Other Essays.* Middletown, Connecticut: Wesleyan University Press, 1977.

Bois, Samuel J. *The Art of Awareness.* 3rd ed. Dubuque, Iowa: William C. Brown Co., Publishers, 1978.

Condon, John C., Jr. *Semantics and Communication.* 2nd ed. London: The Macmillan Company, 1975.

Fabun, Don. *Communications: The Transfer of Meaning.* Beverly Hills, California: The Glencoe Press, 1968.

Hayakawa, S. I. *Language in Thought and Action.* 4th ed. New York: Harcourt Brace Jovanovich, Inc., 1978.

Johnson, Wendell. *Living With Change: The Semantics of Coping.* Dorothy Moeller, ed. New York: Harper & Row, Publishers, 1972.

_____. *People in Quandaries.* New York: Harper & Row,. Publishers, 1946.

Korzybski, Alfred. *Science and Sanity: An Introduction to Non-Aristotelian Systems and General Semantics.* 4th ed. Lakeville, Connecticut: Institute of General Semantics, 1962.

Lee, Irving J. *How to Talk With People.* New York: Harper & Row, Publishers, 1952.

_____. *The Language of Wisdom and Folly.* 3rd ed. San Francisco: International Society for General Semantics, 1977.

Lee, Irving, and Laura Lee. *Handling Barriers in Communication.* 2nd ed. Lakeville, Connecticut: Institute of General Semantics, 1978.

Minteer, Catherine. *Understanding in a World of Words.* Lakeville, Connecticut: Institute of General Semantics, 1970.

_____. *Words and What They Do to You.* Lakeville, Connecticut: Institute of General Semantics, 1968.

Welden, Terry A., and Huber W. Ellingsworth. *Effective Speech-Communication.* Glenview, Illinois: Scott, Foresman and Company, 1970.

Group Process and Role-Playing

FOR PREVIEW AND REVIEW

1. Knowing about and understanding various groups (social, exploratory, laboratory, and task) should create a desire to function more effectively in society.
2. Through group discussion, or the free but disciplined exchange of ideas, we can increase our ability to solve problems, improve our personalities, increase our understanding of others, and develop creative and critical thinking.
3. We all assume various membership roles in group discussions which influence how much and how well we contribute to the groups we are in. We should try to lead when appropriate, and to help others make contributions.
4. By practicing some basic problem-solving techniques and developing certain discussion skills, we can improve any group discussion.
5. Understanding and applying the rules of brainstorming benefits the individual and the group in discussion.
6. In *assuming roles* we function more effectively as an individual personality. In *role playing* we pretend to be someone else in order to obtain understanding of, and empathy for, others.
7. Thoughtful participation in, and analysis of, role-playing situations can lead to a greater understanding of ourselves and other people.

INSTRUCTIONAL OBJECTIVES

After studying this chapter, you should be able to:
1. Identify various groups and their purposes.
2. Explain the nature and function of group processes.
3. Understand and practice effective discussion skills and techniques.
4. Identify leadership and membership roles in discussion and to know the skills and techniques necessary to be a leader or a member of a group.
5. Evaluate a group discussion.
6. Understand and practice the rules for brainstorming.
7. Demonstrate techniques of effective role-playing.
8. Clarify and/or resolve interpersonal communication conflicts through role-playing.

"Let's Get Together"

From the time we get up in the morning until we go to bed at night we are making decisions. We must first decide whether to get up or stay in bed, to eat breakfast or go without, to go to school or stay home. Some of our decisions are made for us, but most of us make decisions automatically.

It is important for us to realize the value of learning to make decisions. Today is eternity! Yesterday is gone; tomorrow isn't here yet. Today is all the time we have. This does not mean that all decisions must be made today or that everything can be *done* today, but it should cause us to ask ourselves the philosophical questions: Who am I? Where did I come from? Why am I here? Where am I going? And another vital question: How can I find the answers to the first four questions, and then make decisions which are best for me?

We all talk to ourselves at times and resolve our own problems or find answers to our own questions. This is necessary and important, but it is also necessary to communicate with others. This we can do by reading what others have said or written, by writing things we'd like to say to those who aren't around, and by discussing things with others. All three processes are extremely important to us; hence we are taught at an early age to speak, read, and write.

Group Discussion

One type of group process and personal involvement which can be a real asset to each individual is group discussion. By the use of group discussion we can, in most instances, increase our ability to solve problems. In the process, we can also improve our personalities (which could be the greatest accomplishment of our lifetime). We use discussion informally every day with friends and neighbors. We discuss our schoolwork, social activities, and personal problems by making comments and asking questions.

Our consideration of human experience starts with individual human beings and their internal adjustments. Human experience can be thought of

Productive group functioning requires a free but disciplined exchange of ideas.

as a series of encounters, most of which involve two or more human beings. Effective democratic human relations consist of an encounter or a series of encounters in which a person forms a group with one or more others. Group encounter is a free but disciplined exchange of ideas. "Disciplined" means that the individual participants attempt to stay on the subject of the discussion. "Exchange" implies that we are constantly involved as either speakers or listeners. Yet very little is accomplished within a group if the members expect only an even exchange of ideas. If every member of a group brought a dollar and exchanged a dollar, there would be little reason for getting together. Many of us do this in group discussions. We bring an idea, we share it, but we refuse to accept any feedback or to give feedback to others. We sometimes defend our actions by saying, "That's the way it is," or "Everyone knows the answer." Some of us simply refuse to listen to or learn from others. As Benjamin Franklin wrote, "Experience keeps a dear school, but fools will learn in no other."

Being an understanding person and being understood by others are essential to good interpersonal communication. Effective group discussion requires all members to relate to each other honestly and openly their feelings, as well as their ideas and opinions. The result in most cases is maximum productivity. Artists, composers, writers, poets, engineers, architects—in fact, most individuals—find great joy when another person or group understands and appreciates a message they have conveyed through their creative efforts. Participants in group discussion should feel the same about their creative ideas.

Productive group functioning can be hampered when the free but disciplined interaction of ideas is blocked by prejudices and fixed ideas, or when goal-directed members are stymied by individuals insensitive to the needs of others and too concerned with personal needs, or when members relating to each other ethically and emotionally are hindered by the frustrations and hostilities of other group members. Most often these negative behaviors are protective shells that individuals use to protect their own sense of self-worth. We become more effective in our relations with others when we recognize our defenses, are willing to risk the rejection of our ideas, and learn more authentic and effective ways of relating to others.

Types of Groups

When two or more individuals communicate with each other they are involved in "group discussion." It is helpful to identify various groups and their purposes—for example, social groups, exploratory groups, laboratory groups, and task groups. By identifying such groups we can recognize what we should contribute and what we can gain from participation in them.

The *social group* is composed of individuals whose main purpose is simply to enjoy each other's company. The *exploratory group* meets to share knowledge and experiences in common interests and hobbies, such as photography, rock collecting, chess, and so on. The *laboratory group* generally meets and directs its attention toward the problem of the individual. It may study members' individual behavior as they interact with each other. The *task group* generally has a specific job or jobs to perform.

In earlier chapters we discussed qualities, techniques, and skills that can and should be developed if we are to become effective participants in all groups. If we have learned and understand the communication process and the echo feedback technique; if we have learned about communication barriers (and we are working to overcome them); if we have remembered we communicate on different levels and we assume various roles as we communicate; if we have become aware of, and are working to overcome our bad listening habits; if we are becoming more aware of our personalities—our strengths and limitations—we are beginning to function more effectively in our *social* groups and in *exploratory* groups. As a participant in a communication class we have participated to a degree in a *laboratory* group. We have talked with, listened to, and observed other class members. In so doing we have learned behavorial skills, verbal and nonverbal. Laboratory groups are usually conducted by individuals trained in human behavior. They can be helpful. They may also be harmful, depending upon the needs and capabilities of the individuals in the group and the capabilities of the group leader. Laboratory groups in communication classes are limited. Communication classes are not designed nor are they conducted to assist one who may have serious personality problems.

For these reasons we shall concentrate specifically on the task group functions in this chapter.

Thinking and sharing are tremendously important in task groups. The distinguished American philosopher John Dewey suggested that thinking on any problem goes through the following stages:

1. Becoming aware of the problem;
2. Defining the precise nature of the problem;
3. Discovering possible solutions to the problem;
4. Deciding upon the best solution;
5. Testing the decision by putting it into practice.[1]

As each of us applies these steps in group interaction, we often assume a particular role. This is not the role-playing we mean when we assume someone else's identity, which we will discuss later in this chapter. When we refer here to assuming a particular role in discussion, we mean that we call forth from our own personality the unique contributions we are capable of sharing at the time and under the given set of circumstances. For instance, the authors' roles are those of teachers and counselors, musicians, friends, and so on. We are called upon to assume different roles at different times. Obviously, in the classroom our basic role is that of teachers; at choir practice we are directors and/or vocalists. In a group discussion concerning the choice of a political candidate for a particular office, our individual role would be that of interested citizen. Our knowledge of music or speech at this time would not be as valuable as our knowledge of public affairs.

All of us, then, when participating in groups, assume "membership roles," and/or "leadership roles." Our contributions to the group depend on our knowledge and our verbal and nonverbal communicative ability.

Group Membership Roles and Functions

As a contributing member you should be ready to:

1. Research and organize information and contribute that information when it will be most helpful.
2. Help establish and clarify group goals and assist in directing the discussion toward the goals.
3. Propose new ideas and suggestions.
4. Encourage other group members by asking questions and giving positive feedback.
5. Acknowledge differing opinions and speak up when necessary to agree or disagree.
6. Attempt to bring ideas together to develop concepts.
7. Show interest and enthusiasm verbally and nonverbally.
8. Be sensitive to others. Help prevent hurt feelings within the group.
9. Allow all members to participate.
10. Show sincerity and flexibility.
11. Show courtesy and consideration.
12. Remain active until the group has reached the established goals.

[1] For further discussion, see Donald C. Bryant and Karl R. Wallace, *Oral Communication*, 3rd ed. (New York: Appleton-Century-Crofts, 1966).

Many of us assume leadership roles in discussion. We may be appointed or elected, or we may simply emerge in the group process. There are three basic types of leadership: *democratic, authoritarian,* and *laissez-faire.* Halbert E. Gulley has depicted the three leadership roles on a continuum ranging from laissez-faire at one end to authoritarian at the other, with the do-nothing leader exercising minimum control and the authoritarian insisting on maximum control. The democratic style is somewhere in the center.

Effective group leaders generally display most of the characteristics listed for model group members. Good leaders are also good followers! The knowledge of when to lead and when to follow is invaluable. The most successful leaders may use all three types of leadership. If the highest priority is efficiency, the leader will probably be more authoritarian (directive and purposeful but not demanding). If time permits, the leader will probably choose to be democratic. And on rare occasions the laissez-faire approach might be the best choice. A leader should attempt to foster a climate for critical, creative, and reflective thinking. In other words, the effective leader can identify and select the best type of leadership for the occasion. The successful group leader should:

1. Be willing to work;
2. Care about others;
3. Recognize the need for goals and assist the group in establishing them;
4. Maintain a disciplined but flexible and open atmosphere;
5. Ask questions which will stimulate group members to participate;
6. Comment on the remarks of other group members in a complimentary and encouraging manner;
7. Get maximum participation from each group member;
8. Assist in eliminating tension in the group by being pleasant and articulate;
9. Keep group members on the track;
10. Be open-minded but have a good grasp of the problem of the group;
11. Be a good listener;
12. Close the discussion effectively.

One of the greatest tests of leadership is experienced or observed when a group cannot reach a consensus but a decision must be made. This problem requires a skillful, diplomatic, authoritarian leader. He or she observes all of the above characteristics. He or she may also caucus in dyads or triads to reinforce a positive atmosphere, showing respect and appreciation for the individual member of the group. The leader may then call for a decision without consensus, letting the majority rule, *or* make the decision and ask for the support of those who may not agree. After making the latter decision the leader does everything possible to establish rapport with the individual or individuals who may not agree and/or approve the decision. In short, leaders do not manipulate; they *persuade.* The reader will be introduced to the methods of persuasion in Chapter 8.

Principles for Effective Problem-Solving Discussions

Regardless of the type of group we find ourselves in, or the type of group leader we have, there are certain important principles for any effective problem-solving discussion. Norman R. F. Maier presents them in detail in *Problem-Solving Discussions and Conferences.* [2] The following are adaptations of these principles.

Principle 1—Success in problem solving requires that effort be directed toward overcoming surmountable obstacles. This principle suggests not only that groups should define tasks which can be overcome, but that they should examine carefully several alternatives for overcoming obstacles so as not to become stymied on traditional approaches.

Principle 2—Available facts should be used even when they are inadequate. Trust facts more than tradition. Don't overgeneralize solutions.

Principle 3—The starting point of a problem is richest in solution possibilities. One never has more alternatives for trying to solve a problem than at the beginning. With each decision, we become committed to certain directions that exclude other directions.

Principle 4—Problem-mindedness should be increased while solution-mindedness is delayed. People have a penchant for solving a problem before they have even agreed what the problem they wish to solve is. A clearly defined problem is 51 percent of the solution, according to Einstein.

Principle 5—Disagreement can lead either to hard feelings or to innovation, depending on the discussion leader. People fear unfavorable judgment from leaders and group members, which tends to promote conformity and discourage innovation. Disagreement should become legitimate, valued, and nonpersonal. Encourage the constructive dissenter.

Principle 6—The idea-getting process should be separated from the idea-evaluation process because the latter inhibits the former. Creative thinking must be able to explore uncharted waters before it can sight hitherto undiscovered lands. Past learning, practical considerations, and evaluation all tend to depress flights of the imagination. Create before you criticize.

Principle 7—Choice situations should be turned into problem situations. Ordinary choices lead to ordinary solutions. Create alternatives.

Principle 8—Problem situations should be turned into choice situations. Avoid choosing automatically the obvious solution to surmounting an obstacle. Again, create alternatives.

Principle 9—Solutions suggested by the leader are often improperly evaluated and tend to be either accepted or rejected. Authority tends to be either blindly accepted or defiantly rejected.

Principles Concerning the Appropriate Use of Group Discussion

There are some basic principles which determine the appropriate use of group discussion. The following principles should help us when we are considering the process.

[2] From *Problem-Solving Discussions and Conferences* by Norman R. F. Maier, pp. 240–52. Copyright © 1963 by McGraw-Hill Book Company. Used with permission of McGraw-Hill Book Company.

1. When diverse opinions and ideas are needed (a group setting stimulates the individual in the group; the individual may not produce the idea if he or she is working alone).
2. When a decision must be made and time is "unlimited" (the diversity and stimulation of a group increases the possibility of a good decision).
3. When group pressure will not inhibit the value of an individual opinion.
4. When there is a need for information sharing or problem solving.

Problems in discussion may arise if these principles are not considered carefully. Irving Janis identifies a problem which he calls "Groupthink." It is the result of a special type of uniformity pressure. According to Janis, groupthink refers to a "mode of thinking that people engage in when they are deeply involved in a cohesive in-group, when the members' striving for unanimity overrides their motivation to realistically appraise alternative courses of action." It is characterized by an ineffective type of communication-interaction in groups that leads to defective decision making.[3]

Discussion groups, regardless of the nature of the group have three primary concerns:

1. To accomplish the goals of the group.
2. To maintain the group's identity by being concerned about morale, cohesion, and autonomy.
3. To satisfy the ego needs of the group members.

For a group to function effectively each member of the group must be sensitive to these concerns and contribute in every way possible to achieve them.

Discussion Skills

There are certain skills we all need for effective group participation. While assuming various roles in group discussions, we can develop both pleasant and productive skills as participants and/or observers. *Pleasant skills* are listening and hearing, being respectful, being congenial, sensing the level of sophistication of the group, discouraging the verbal person from dominating the conversation, actively encouraging participation without putting an individual on the spot, and relieving tension. *Productive skills* are being vocal and active, keeping to the topic of discussion, appreciating the significance of the discussion, helping develop the ideas of others, synthesizing what has been said, developing functional procedures, getting the group to act, sensing the need for evaluation, mediating when necessary, and realizing outside factors, such as members' backgrounds, which may influence the group.

We stated in Chapter 1 that the process of communication is extremely complex. We would not wish to imply that group discussion as we are defin-

---

[3] For further discussion see I. L. Janis, *Victims of Groupthink: A Psychological Study of Foreign-Policy Decisions and Fiascoes* (Boston: Houghton Mifflin Company, 1972).

ing it is an easy answer or a simple way to solve problems, but we do believe that the group process can assist any individual and any group in learning to solve problems. Hopefully the reader will be motivated to review and further investigate the theory and practices of group discussion, and to recognize the potential personal improvement to be gained.

Preparation for Group Discussion

For groups to function at their best it is necessary to consider the steps in preparation. They include:

1. Choosing participants and either choosing a leader or dividing the leadership among the members.
2. Determining the type of discussion and specifying the situation.
3. Selecting and wording an appropriate question.
4. Collecting information and resource materials.
5. An outline or agenda.
6. Planning the physical arrangements.
7. Establishing a time schedule.
8. Plans for getting the discussion underway.
9. Plans for evaluating the discussion.
10. Studying the structure, processes, and dynamics of the small group and learning effective discussion skills.

Brainstorming—Rules and Values

Among the many skills and techniques in group discussion, the brainstorming session is one of the most often used and abused! Quite often a person will say, "Let's brainstorm." Then, as soon as someone offers an idea, it is criticized or "killed." Brainstorming is a valuable tool if the following rules are applied:

1. *Quantity* of ideas, not *quality,* is the goal.
2. All contributions are accepted. No idea is too wild to be expressed.
3. No idea is criticized.
4. Development of an idea is encouraged.
5. Every contribution is recorded.
6. At the end of the session all of the ideas are either combined and improved—or discarded.

Brainstorming is valuable in all groups and applies to almost any situation from helping an individual (a student getting poor grades) to a group (a family with financial problems). Understanding the rules makes it possible for almost anyone to conduct, or participate in, the process.

Role-Playing

A technique that has a wide variety of uses in group discussion is role-playing. Few workshops, seminars, or human relations training programs

Role-playing brings to the surface many important emotional currents.

take place today without some use of role-playing. This technique can serve as a valuable tool in learning how to participate in discussions, and in assuming leadership roles at school, at work, or in our personal lives.

Most of us at one time or another have pretended we were someone else. As children we said, "Let's pretend," then assumed the role of fire fighter, nurse, astronaut, or whoever we wanted to be, and acted the way we thought that person would act. Most of what we did we learned from observation of someone who really was the person we wanted to be for the moment.

In recent years people have learned the value for adults of pretending in the technique known as role-playing. However, *role-playing is not a game.* This is the first and most important fact we must remember if the experience is to be of utmost value to us. Role-playing refers to a technique of personal and group involvement in which individuals act out real-life problems. The participants and observers then analyze their actions and reactions. The technique of role-playing engages the *whole* individual. Whether a participant or an observer, the person sees, hears, describes, and experiences real actions and reactions. In this way role-playing brings to the surface many important emotional currents that each individual experiences. How individuals feel about something is as important as what they think. By assuming a role, the individual begins to understand how *another* person feels and thinks in a given situation. The result is often a greater understanding of, and appreciation for, the other person.

Role-playing usually involves:

1. A real-life situation which has meaning for the participants and observers;
2. A clearly defined plot, simply stated;
3. A clear mental picture for the participants of the roles they are to play;
4. Instructions for players and observers as to the problem and the purposes;
5. Termination of the role-playing when the purpose has been accomplished;
6. An analysis of the role-playing for further understanding and suggested behavior modification.

There are several ways to select and construct a meaningful problem situation for role-playing. First, the director or teacher may plan the problem and characterize the problem for role-playing. Second, the members of the group may assist in creating a problem, structuring the stages, suggesting the behavior of the characters, and giving the characters instructions for the roles they will play. Third, a selected group, under the direction of a trainer, may plan a role-playing situation and perform for the others. Fourth, the director or members of the class may select a prepared case problem. (There are prepared cases available in the books listed at the end of this chapter.)

Once we have chosen the problems to role-play, the next step is to choose the players. The instructor or director may ask for volunteers or choose the individuals for each role. Some directors know the participants well enough to place them in roles they can assume effectively. However, if such knowledge is limited, the director's responsibility is to stress to the participants that members who participate should play their roles seriously and sincerely. An individual should not be forced to play a role, nor should any individual be deeply involved emotionally.

Instructions given to *role-players* should be brief, with simple explanations of the roles to be portrayed. Staging instructions for the role-playing should also be concise.

Instructions to *observers* are very important. Observers should note what takes place, try to determine the feelings of the role-players as they participate, watch for actions that either resolve or block the resolution of the problem, determine the motivations for the actions of the role-players, try to think of other ways the role-players could have resolved the problem, and notice the similarities to other problems the participants may have experienced.

Finally, everyone should evaluate the role-playing experience. This is very important because observers and participants can develop a greater understanding of problems in human relations by analyzing the performances. They can also develop skills in handling their own individual problems. Therefore, the analysis of the performance should include a discussion of the following questions:

1. What took place during the role-playing?
2. How did the role-players feel as they participated?
3. How could the players have brought about a better or quicker resolution?

4. Were the situations similar to problems in other areas of life?

5. As a result of this experience, have we gained insight to aid us in solving other problems in our lives?

There are many variations of role-playing. The director should consider the group and the observers in determining the techniques and procedure. A multiple role-playing situation is described a little later in this chapter, as well as scenes which require only two participants. Role-playing scenes are frequently replayed. It is also possible to use scripts for role-playing, especially for more complex situations.

The purpose of this material is to introduce you to the basic concepts involved in role-playing, and to provide experiences through which you can develop an understanding of yourself and others. Role-playing can and should be a rewarding and satisfying experience in improving communication skills. To insure the proper use of role-playing, you should remember and observe the following suggestions:

1. The problem should be meaningful to everyone in the group, both players and observers.

2. Individuals should not be forced to participate.

3. Role-playing should not be used as entertainment. The purpose should be to gain insight and understanding of oneself and others.

4. The problems to be role-played should be clearly defined.

5. The problems to be role-played should be practical.

6. Successful role-playing takes *time.* Allow for the time needed.

7. *Analyzing* the role-playing is more important than *perfecting* the role-playing.

8. Role-playing for therapeutic purposes should be done only under the supervision of professionally trained group therapists. Teachers and observers, in most instances, do not have enough training and experience, or understanding of a particular individual or problem, to handle therapeutic role-playing and the problems that could arise.

A Role-Playing Situation

A description of a fairly typical role-playing situation follows.

General Situation

Four college students have decided to rent a three-bedroom house, sharing expenses and responsibilities. They have signed a lease for one year. The expenses are to be divided equally and the responsibilities have been defined and agreed upon. Each student has agreed to rotate the responsibilities. After three months each student finds the arrangement unsatisfactory but the lease cannot be broken. The group has met to see if they can resolve their differences.

Specific Instructions

In acting out your part in the role-playing, assume the attitude suggested by your specific role. Accept the facts as given, and let your feelings develop with whatever transpires in the role-playing process. If facts or events arise which are not covered by your role or the roles of others, try to make up things which are consistent with the way it might be in a real-life situation.

Role for Dorothy

You look upon housework and cooking as tasks to do with the least amount of effort. You are concerned about getting good grades. You believe the others should excuse you from your responsibilities if you have some heavy class assignments.

Role for Linda

You are a Family and Consumer Studies major. You plan a profession as a wife and mother. You want to practice what you are learning. Having a clean house and well-planned meals are very important to you.

Role for Nancy

You are going to school to have a good time. As far as you are concerned, everyone should accept whatever happens. Your parents are sending you a monthly check so money is not a problem. You can always eat out if you want to and you don't mind clutter and confusion.

Role for Darlene

You are on a limited income and you require good food and undisturbed sleep. You really want to get along with everyone but you think everyone should eat health foods and get at least 8 hours of uninterrupted sleep each night.

If we role-played this situation, the director would note when the key issues had been pointed out and when all members had participated to some extent. The role-playing would then be stopped and analyzed. Analyzing this scene, as well as other role-playing scenes, would require specific questions determined by what transpired in the scene itself, but we could review the questions mentioned earlier in the chapter and adapt them accordingly.

As was mentioned earlier, a major purpose of role-playing is to promote understanding and to develop skills in discussing and solving problems in human relationships, so analyzing what transpired in the role-playing experience is very important. During analysis the role-players and the observers should gain more insight regarding the feelings, pressures, and motivations of individuals involved in interpersonal relationships.

Few, if any, of us could participate in the above role-playing situation as participants or observers without thinking, "This is a complicated problem," or "I hadn't thought of that aspect." If we accept the process of role-playing seriously, we can gain greater understanding of problems and people. Many of us are eager to solve our individual problems as quickly as possible. It is necessary in a democratic society for the individual to learn to recognize the consequences of solutions to problems. When problems involve others, there may be times when the "cure" we would choose individually is worse than the "disease" as far as others are concerned!

You may want to develop scenes dealing with your personal problems. In so doing, reverse the role to see if you can see the situation from another perspective. For example, suppose you have been working and going to school. You have your own apartment and everything has been great. At mid-semester you lose your job. You have not saved any money, and you are doing so well in school that you don't want to drop out. You have asked your parents to help you either by loaning you money or by letting you move back home. They have refused your request. Set the scene, then ask someone else to play *your* role while you assume one of the parent roles.

The following problems and situations could also be developed into role-playing scenes:

> *Your sister and you have been living with your mother and sharing expenses. You both plan to move out in the near future. Your mother expects you to stay with her.*

> *Your girl friend has become a feminist. She is constantly denouncing male chauvinists, yet she is also demanding the courtesies normally extended to the "weaker sex."*

> *You are ten years old. You have just been told by your adored parents that you are an adopted child, but that your younger sister is their natural child.*

Discussion Forms and Evaluation

It is difficult to improve the discussion process and discussion skills without some type of evaluation. The standard for evaluation should be the achievement of the goals of the discussion. The evaluation involves collecting data about individual participation and group interaction, and then interpretation of the data. Evaluating may focus on the individual or on the group. In evaluating the individual the evaluator would consider the attitude of the participant, how often the person speaks, the length of the contributions, and the names of the persons in the group who interacted with the participant. The evaluator might also note whether a contribution is a question or a statement, whether the contribution was fact or opinion and so on. For these reasons, various methods have been designed (also called "forms") for both a general and a specific evaluation. The evaluation forms are quantitative and qualitative. There are forms for evaluating the individual and forms for evaluating the group. The following forms are examples.

GROUP EVALUATION FORM

GROUP _____ DATE _____

RATING SCALE   1. Poor   2. Average   3. Above Average   4. Excellent

CRITERIA   *EVALUATION*

Clarity of goals

Equal opportunity to participate

Mutual respect

Organized group thinking

Evaluation of ideas

Listening

Leadership

Positive atmosphere

Conflict resolution

Courtesy

Problem-solving

Summarizing

Final product

COMMENTS

EVALUATOR _____

Remember that the various types of group discussions, including brainstorming and role-playing, are forms of inquiry. Many groups meet to solve problems. When agreements cannot be reached, participants need to gain more information for further discussion, or they may decide to debate the issues, depending upon the individuals involved and the amount of time they have before a decision must be made. We discussed the situation where a decision must be made without the consensus of the group. When possible, this type of action should be avoided by allowing for further discussion or debate. *Discussion* in its many forms is *inquiry*. *Debate* is *advocacy*. Whichever is chosen, group discussion and debate are powerful tools in a democracy. Brainstorming and role-playing, when used as described, are most helpful learning experiences in discussion. The purpose of all human interaction should be to broaden understanding, to develop communicative

INDIVIDUAL EVALUATION FORM

Discussant's Name _____ Date _____

Rating Scale   1. Poor   2. Average   3. Above Average   4. Excellent

CRITERIA   *EVALUATION*

1. *COOPERATION:* Did the discussant
   assist in the development of ideas
   and the logical progression of group
   thinking? Did the discussant encourage
   other members, accepting, supporting,
   and adapting to their ideas?

2. *LEADERSHIP:* Did the discussant share
   responsibility for the discussion? Did
   the discussant resolve conflict? Assist
   in summarizing contributions?

3. *INFORMATION:* Did the discussant show
   evidence of knowledge of the subject and
   present documented information?

4. *REASONING:* Did the discussant show evidence
   of ability to analyze the ideas? Did the
   discussant show evidence of critical
   thinking? What were the quality and
   relevance of the contributions?

5. *COMMUNICATIVE SKILLS* Were the discussant's
   contributions clear and to the point? Was
   the discussant a critical listener? Was
   the discussant able to clarify complex
   ideas? Was the discussant able to assist
   others in their efforts to communicate?

COMMENTS

Evaluator _____

skills, and to learn more about people and problems in interpersonal relationships.

Much of what we have learned so far can be summarized by remembering and using two simple formulas. If they are applied under the proper circumstances you, the reader, will find them invaluable. If we are functioning in *social* groups, *exploratory* groups, and *laboratory* groups we can function more successfully with the formula "C + C + CR + C + C = Effective

Communication"! C stands for *Compliment* and CR means *Criticism*. Most of us find it almost impossible to associate with or work with others without disagreements and the need for criticism. When and if criticism is given it should be sandwiched between compliments. As Arnold H. Glasgow said, "Glass blowers will never produce anything as fragile as the human ego." To enjoy valuable interpersonal relationships the ego of the individual must be carefully considered.

If we want to function successfully in *task* groups we can practice the formula "C + C + C + C + C = Good Leadership and Good Followership"! These Cs stand for Character, Confidence, Cooperation, Competence, and Caring. All of them are vital to successful group discussion.

The two formulas appear to be simple. They are really profound and complex. The rewards, however, are worth every effort in putting them into practice.

FOR FURTHER INSIGHT

1. Keep a daily journal recording your experiences in the groups you belong to (social, exploratory, or other). At the end of a month evaluate your success as a communicator.
2. Choose and define an existing on- or off-campus social problem. Write a description so it can be discussed in a task group.
3. Conduct a brainstorming activity. Report the results to your instructor.
4. List five situations in which role-playing could be used advantageously.
5. How can role-playing be used effectively in other subjects such as history, English, physical education, and so on?
6. Plan a role-playing situation. Write out the problem statement, the description of the characters, and the instructions for carrying out the proper sequences of the role-playing situation.

REFERENCES

Andersen, Martin P., Wesley Lewis, and James Murray. *The Speaker and His Audience*. New York: Harper & Row, Publishers, 1964.

Applbaum, Ronald, Edward M. Bodaken, Kenneth K. Sereno. *The Process of Group Communication*. Chicago: Science Research Associates, Inc. 1979.

Baird, Craig A., Franklin H. Knower, and Samuel L. Becker. *General Speech Communication*. McGraw-Hill Book Co., 1971.

Baird, John E. and Sanford B. Weinberg. *Communication: The Essence of Group Synergy*. Dubuque, Iowa: Wm C. Brown Company Publishers 1977.

Bormann, Ernest G. *Discussion and Group Methods: Theory and Practice*. New York: Harper & Row, Publishers, 1969.

Bormann, Ernest G., and Nancy C. Bormann. *Effective Small Group Communication*. Minneapolis: Burgess Publishing Company, 1972.

Brandstatter, Hermann, James H. Davis, and Heinz Schuler. *Dynamics of Group Decisions*. Beverly Hills, Ca: Sage Publications. 1978.

Brilhart, John K. *Effective Group Discussion*. Dubuque, Iowa: William C. Brown Co., Publishers, 1967.

Bryant, Donald C., and Karl R. Wallace. *Oral Communication*, 3rd ed. New York: Appleton-Century-Crofts, 1966.

Dance, Frank E. X., and Carl E. Larson. *Speech Communication Concepts and Behavior.* New York: Holt, Rinehart & Winston, Inc., 1972.

Gruner, Charles R., Cal M. Logue, Dwight L. Freshley, and Richard C. Huseman. *Speech Communication in Society.* Boston: Allyn & Bacon, Inc., 1972.

Gulley, Halbert E. *Discussion, Conference, and Group Process.* New York: Holt, Rinehart & Winston, Inc., 1968.

Gulley, Halbert E. and Dale G. Leathers. *Communication and Group Process. Techniques for Improving the Quality of Small-Group Communication.* New York: Holt, Rinehart and Winston, 1977.

Hasling, John. *Group Discussion and Decision Making.* New York: Thomas Y. Crowell Company, 1975.

Kell, Carl L. and Paul R. Corts. *Fundamentals of Effective Group Communication.* New York: Macmillan Publishing Co., 1980.

Mabry, Edward A., and Charles M. Rossiter, Jr. "Laboratory Training and Problem-Solving Groups: Distinctions and Relationships." *Journal of the Western Speech Communication Association,* 39, No. 2 (Spring, 1975), 102–111.

Maier, Norman R. F. *Problem-Solving Discussions and Conferences.* New York: McGraw-Hill Book Co., 1963.

Martin, Howard H., and C. William Colburn. *Communication and Consensus: An Introduction to Rhetorical Discourse.* New York: Harcourt Brace Jovanovich, Inc., 1972.

Patton Bobby R. and Kim Giffin. *Decision-Making Group Interaction.* New York. Harper & Row, Publishers, 1978.

Potter, David, and Martin P. Andersen. *Discussion: A Guide to Effective Practice.* Belmont, California: Wadsworth Publishing Co., Inc., 1963.

Scheidel, Thomas M. *Speech Communication and Human Interaction,* 2nd ed. Glenview, Illinois: Scott, Foresman and Company, 1976.

Smith, William E. *Group Problem-Solving Through Discussion.* New York: Bobbs-Merrill Co., Inc., 1965.

Tubbs, Stewart L. *A Systems Approach to Small Group Interaction.* Reading, Massachusetts: Addison-Wesley Publishing Company, 1978.

Wood, Julia T. "Alternate Portraits of Leaders: A Contingency Approach to Perceptions of Leadership." *Western Journal of Speech,* Vol. 43, No. 4 (Fall 1979) 260–270.

7

Conflict Reduction

FOR PREVIEW AND REVIEW

1. Conflict is a natural part of life and may be necessary for human growth.
2. While conflict can be constructive or destructive, depending on how we manage it, all perceived conflicts produce a degree of stress, frustration, and anxiety.
3. Through better communication, awareness, study, and self-understanding, we should be able to reduce our destructive conflicts to manageable proportions.
4. Effective problem-solving discussions are kept on a clear, open, respectful level of interaction.
5. The process of fair fighting can bring about problem resolution that is mutually comfortable, foster successful patterns of behavior, and help avoid win-lose or lose-lose games.

INSTRUCTIONAL OBJECTIVES

After studying this chapter, you should be able to:
1. Explain sources and types of conflict.
2. Identify various styles and approaches in conflict reduction.
3. Recognize the psychological effects of conflict.
4. Identify and explain the steps in successful problem solving.
5. Explain various techniques for solving conflicts.
6. Recognize your personal problem-solving techniques.
7. Act more effectively in group problem-solving situations.

"I Beg to Differ . . ."

One of the major goals of communication is to establish contact and cooperation with others. But much of our social contact is filled with conflict, misunderstanding, and failures to communicate. Simply to live, and to interact with others, seems to lead inevitably to continuing differences of opinions and conflict. How many times have you been amazed at the amount of human conflict you can become involved in between the time you get up in the morning and the time you go out the door? Surprising, isn't it? Where more than one person is involved, it often seems nothing is simple.

Any thoughtful consideration of social interaction and interpersonal communications requires our thinking carefully about conflict. How and why does it develop? How does it affect us and people around us? Considering the types, causes, and effects of conflict can help us develop our individual decision-making skills and interpersonal techniques so that we can better handle conflicts and avoid or lessen potential problems. We should always be alert to techniques that could help us handle conflict and improve our personal ways of coping with problems.

Problems and conflicts involving people have existed as long as people have existed. That comes as no surprise to any of us. Through better communication, awareness, study, and self-understanding, we should be able to more adequately and creatively reduce our destructive conflicts to manageable proportions. Indeed, the success of some people can be directly related to their ability to deal effectively and diplomatically with others in conflict situations.

Let's see what we mean by "conflict." Conflict is competitive or opposing action; it can be extremely hostile or it can be relatively peaceful; it can take years or minutes to resolve; it can be destructive or constructive in outcome. Conflict exists when one, two, or more people must deal with what are, or seem to be, incompatible activities or perceptions. When two or more different and conflicting responses are demanded of one person, we call it *intrapersonal* conflict. *Interpersonal* conflict occurs when two or more individuals are in opposition. *Intragroup* conflict can arise among subgroups with incompatible goals; *intergroup* conflict may take place between established groups.

In this chapter we will concentrate on conflict between individuals and between groups. Notice that we are not talking about eliminating conflict but, rather, reducing it. Some of our most critical problems as individuals and as a nation are "people problems." The facts of mental illness, crime and violence, poverty, drug abuse, economic recessions, war, and many other problems all demand our attention. Each of us could add pressing personal problems to this list. While these problems are real in themselves, misinformation and distorted messages can make bad situations worse. Modern technology has made possible rapid, widespread dissemination of information, contributing to our knowledge but often confusing our understanding as we try to absorb efficiently the barrage of changing information.

Many checklists have been made of life events that are stressful and full of conflict. Threats to the self (see Chapter 3), life disruptions, separation from loved ones, a sense of isolation, and physical ills all represent potential conflict areas and trauma which need resolution for personal well-being. Many "positive" life events such as vacations, promotions, compliments, and so on, can also be stressful, depending upon the perceptions, memories, and feelings aroused by these events.

Present-day problems are real and the overall picture is ominous. With

An amazing amount of conflict can occur between the time we wake up and the time we walk out the door.

thoughtful use of good communication skills and effective problem-solving techniques, perhaps we can modify our problems and perceptions of issues and lead more productive, positive lives. Let us take a closer look at some of the more important aspects of conflict reduction.

Assumptions About Conflict

If we can analyze the causes and effects of problems, we should find alternatives to help us with our conflicts in this "age of anxiety." Brian Betz, a conflict management analyst, believes that conflict (1) is an inevitable part of life and may be necessary for human growth; (2) can be productive or damaging, depending upon how it is used; (3) has many meanings, arises from many causes, and assumes many forms; (4) arises from the communication process itself; (5) can increase or decrease depending upon our style of communication; (6) can be managed if we, as communicators, are skillful in analyzing the situation accurately and choosing appropriate means to deal with problems; (7) cannot always be solved, but can be managed in such a way that it can be lived with; and (8) often may be basically productive, rather than a necessary evil.[1]

Types of Conflict

There are three general sources of conflict and frustration: (1) Environmental obstacles that prevent attainment of a goal; (2) personal handicaps or deficiencies that make a goal unobtainable; and (3) motivational conflicts within an individual that deny satisfaction of one motive when attempting to satisfy another need.

Children are mostly frustrated by obstacles in the environment, but adults are also frustrated by unattainable goals and internal motivational conflicts. The internalized conflict of motives causes the most unhappiness and stress for most people and thus deserves a closer look.

Lewin[2] has listed three basic types of internal conflict situations: (1) *approach-approach conflicts* are a struggle between two positive goals—goals that are equally attractive at the same time. If you want to go to a party and to a disco dance scheduled at the same time, a conflict will arise. We try to resolve these conflicts by satisfying one goal first, then the other, if possible. We often have to choose one of the activities over the other, however; (2) *avoidance-avoidance conflicts* involve two negative goals, and are quite common. As children we may have to go to school, or get a spanking. Adults may have to work at a job they dislike or have no income. Vacillation, inability to make decisions, or, often, attempts to run away from the conflict are behaviors noted in these conflicts; (3) *approach-avoidance conflicts* are the most

---

[1] An adaptation of "Managing Conflict in Interaction" by Brian R. Betz from *Speech Communication and Human Interaction* by Thomas M. Scheidel. Copyright © 1976, 1972 by Scott, Foresman and Company. Reprinted by permission.

[2] Lewin, K. *Dynamic Theory of Personality*. New York: McGraw-Hill, 1935.

important conflicts because they are the most difficult to resolve. A person is both attracted and repelled by the same object. Many people, for example, are taught that they should not lie, steal, or cheat, but feel that they must be false in order to survive at school or work. Such people are caught between their own internalized motives, and must change or deny these motives, which can lead to serious conflict, ambivalence, and stress. In our society, sex, hostility, independence, and competition are all areas of stress, ambivalence, and frustration for many people.

As Alan C. Filley reminds us in describing kinds of conflict, not all conflicts are alike.[3] In some cases conflict may be quite patterned, following predictable rules and avoiding angry, emotional outbursts. On the other hand, some conflicts are marked by irrational behavior punctuated by violent, disruptive displays. Filley distinguishes between *competitive* and *disruptive* conflicts. In *competitive* conflicts there can be a victory only at the cost of the opponent's loss, and these interactions are governed by a set of rules. The game of baseball is such a competition. In *disruptive* conflicts the combatants do not follow mutually acceptable rules and the contestants do not negotiate with respect. Guerrilla warfare is an example of this kind of irregular contest, where the intent is to defeat, harm, or drive away the opponent. Any means are used, and the atmosphere is one of fear, tension, or hostility. These conflicts often result in irrational behavior, with any behavior being acceptable if it accomplishes the main goal—wiping out or hurting the opponent.

Both the competitive and disruptive types of conflict imply a *win-lose* outcome. When a boss threatens an employee, a win-lose method of behavior control is being used. A police officer writing out a traffic ticket for you for speeding is another win-lose situation. When an opponent refuses to respond, or runs away, the win-lose game is also operating. When a minority consistently loses to a majority rule, the majority rule can be destructive. This, too, is an example of a win-lose type of game. Force or coercion of some type or the threat of force is usually used in win-lose games.

When each side in a conflict fails to accomplish its goal or gets only a small part of what it wants, *lose-lose* strategies are operating. Unsatisfying compromises are often perceived as losses by both sides. A long, bitter strike, where labor and management lose wages and profit that can never be made up, is an example of this. Getting disagreeable jobs done by offering bribes frequently results in both parties feeling like losers. Sometimes arbitration by a third party also results in a middle-ground, wishy-washy solution which satisfies neither party.

In win-lose and lose-lose strategies, Filley says that several common characteristics emerge:

1. *There is a clear we-they distinction between the parties, rather than a we-versus-the-problem orientation.*
2. *Energies are directed toward the other party in an atmosphere of total victory or total defeat.*

[3] Adapted from *Interpersonal Conflict Resolution* by Alan C. Filley. Copyright © 1975 by Scott, Foresman and Company. Reprinted by permission.

We may use sweeping generalizations to avoid facing the real issues.

3. *Each party sees the issue only from its own point of view, rather than defining the problem in terms of mutual needs.*
4. *The emphasis in the process is upon attainment of a solution, rather than upon a definition of goals, values, or motives to be attained with the solution.*
5. *Conflicts are personalized rather than depersonalized via an objective focus on facts and issues.*
6. *There is no differentiation of conflict-resolving activities from other group processes, nor is there a planned sequence of those activities.*
7. *The parties are conflict-oriented, emphasizing the immediate disagreement, rather than relationship-oriented, emphasizing the long-term effect of their differences and how they are resolved.*[4]

With *win-win* strategies, however, a positive outcome is more likely because the possibility of shared reward is seen and accepted by both parties. The two sides emphasize seeking positive goals, avoiding unworkable alternatives, and working toward truly mutual satisfaction. Both parties in a conflict can often win when there is a lessened priority on defeating the other side, and when sharing and open problem solving are involved in the settlement of the issues. To reach this stage, obviously you are going to have to practice good interpersonal communication skills. When both parties to a conflict feel good and relatively satisfied, a win-win solution has been reached.

[4] Filley, p. 25.

Communication Styles in Conflicts

Honest communication should be the means for all of us to become more positive and open to others, but we are all aware of the negative feelings and defensiveness that go along with even the threat of a conflict. As we get more anxious and angry in a conflict, communication decreases and we thereby lessen our chances of sharing, clarifying values, and resolving stressful issues. When we feel threatened and need to be "right," we all too often try quickly to make our opponent "wrong," by rejecting or hurting that person. We end up saying "You're unreasonable," or "You can't see my side at all," or "You're a phony," and making other irresponsible, nonproductive comments. Such messages do not foster the solution of problems, but tend to deepen and polarize the issues, and eventually lead to frustration and self-defeating misperception of both the problems and the people involved.

Betz, who develops theory taken from Filley, notes that when we are under stress from conflict, our language takes on some of the following characteristics which create barriers to communication:

1. We use value statements, making them sound like facts.
2. We express our values in very simplistic right-and-wrong terms, leaving no room for the gray areas of "maybe."
3. We defend ourselves by using emotive name-calling to put down the other person.
4. We use a rigid, this-or-nothing definition of our expectancies.
5. We use sweeping generalizations to avoid a concise, clear awareness.
6. We indulge in a dialogue within ourselves as we attempt to gain control over the scene by monitoring our feelings more closely.
7. We tend to overreact and to express our overreaction both verbally and nonverbally.[5]

These practices obviously avoid the true problems, and lead to more conflict rather than to problem resolution. Once these games get going intensely, they are difficult to reverse. Our aggression and defensiveness bring out the same traits in our opponents and tend to neatly close communication channels, preventing understanding and complicating conflict reduction.

We can see, then, that a typical conflict situation is often characterized by (1) hazy definitions of problems, (2) opposition or incompatibility among two or more preferred solutions, and (3) poor discussion and defensive fighting designed to try to impose our arbitrary solution on opponents.

Individual Styles in Conflicts

Philosophers, poets, and psychologists have always been concerned with two major tasks in life which exist for all of us: (1) the development of ways to meet and satisfy our personal goals, and (2) the development and maintenance of relationships with others. Many ways have been developed to

[5] Adapted from Betz, p. 289. Also see Filley, pp. 35–47.

accomplish these two tasks, which frequently conflict with each other. We have all had the experience of being expected to attend a family function or formal gathering of some kind when we had already made plans to spend that time enjoyably with our friends. This kind of situation can cause intrapersonal and sometimes interpersonal conflict at its best (or worst). All of us learn early that the groups to which we belong often demand behavior that does not fit with our personal perceptions and values. These dilemmas can threaten our personal integrity and self-perceptions, and force us to modify our group relationships. Conscience, loyalty, and commitment to personal and group values are critical in all our lives, and we face guilt, conflict, and disequilibrium when these values are compromised or flouted.

In studying the patterns people use in handling conflict, Blake and Mouton (1970) and Hall (1969) have identified five categories of personal style in conflict communication.[6] These can furnish us with a model to analyze conflict situations.

1. *The Tough Battler.* These people enter a conflict with one thought in mind—winning at any cost. They have little regard for the opinions, feelings, or needs of others involved in the conflict. The conflict itself—and coming out on top—gives them a real psychological "high." They are the eternal gamesmen, ever out to prove themselves. In losing they see only shame, a loss of self-esteem, and personal weakness. The tough battlers are unyielding in point of view—nothing can move them. When they find opposition to their ideas, they become easily angered. For them, only winning is acceptable. They would agree with Vince Lombardi that "winning is not the most important thing, it is the only thing." These people will sacrifice others who don't go along with them. Conflict to them is often a nuisance which happens only because someone else does not see how right they are.

2. *The Friendly Helper.* These people undervalue their own goals and achievements. They place excessive emphasis on maintaining relationships with other people, and typically give in to them. They believe that someone will get hurt in conflict resolution and generally attempt at all costs to avoid trouble with others. Their goal is harmony, and they may express concern about the self-centeredness of individuals. They cannot see any constructive value in confronting other parties in a conflict. Group harmony and togetherness in goals and interests are most important in their lives.

3. *The Lose-Leave Style.* Like the friendly helpers, people adopting this style have no use for conflict. The lose-leaver avoids disagreeing with anyone, and as a result will flee the conflict scene either physically or emotionally. Typically, these people lead alienated lives, continually avoiding taking a stand on issues in conflict or in confronting anyone who is aggressive toward them.

[6] Reported in Filley, pp. 51–52, based on Jay Hall, *Conflict Management Survey* (Houston: Teleometrics, Inc.), 1969, and Robert R. Blake and J. S. Mouton, "The Fifth Achievement," in *The Journal of Applied Behavioral Science* 6 (1970).

4. *The Compromise Style.* People using this style try to find a position which lets each side feel it has gained something in the settlement of a conflict. Avoiding extremes, they are always looking for the middle ground, and the jockeying required to stay in the middle is usually pleasurable to them. Such people often will change approaches, expressing anger sometimes and at other times attempting to smooth things over. Voting and trading are tactics often used to solve the conflict and to avoid direct confrontation of real issues.

5. *The Problem Solver.* People using this approach seek to integrate the goals of all parties to the satisfaction of everyone concerned. They see no need to totally sacrifice anyone's goals, since goals need not be mutually exclusive. In their attempt to integrate the various goals which seem in conflict, problem solvers operate from five assumptions:

A. Conflict, if properly managed, is both natural and useful in channeling creative solutions.
B. The discussion of conflict issues should take place in a spirit of trust and openness which permits a display of feelings.
C. The viewpoints of all parties should be openly discussed.
D. Every party involved should feel that he or she has an equal voice in making decisions and that no one need fear being sacrificed for the sake of reaching a decision.
E. When all the parties to a conflict feel a basic, though not necessarily total, satisfaction with the decision-making process, they are more likely to accept and follow up the decision once it has been made.

For many issues, the first four styles of conflict reduction are less successful than problem solving, a fact which can lead to further problems and to frustrations which only continue the original conflicts. We should all try to become problem solvers, attempting to deal realistically and objectively with ourselves and with others. Look at your personal style of handling conflict. Practice the behavior of the problem solver, and you won't remain locked into one of the other four styles which, at best, bring only partial reduction of conflict.

Causes of Conflict Intensity

Conflict will be more severe and stress more difficult (a) the longer the conflict lasts; (b) the more important the issues being disputed are to the parties; (c) the more frustration is generated during the conflict; (d) the stronger the sides become and the more evenly matched they are; (e) the less informed the parties are regarding the issues; (f) the less competent the parties feel they are in dealing with the conflict; (g) the more ego-involved the parties become; (h) the less able the parties are to handle stress.[7]

Looking back over this list, we can begin to set up for ourselves some guidelines of do's and don't's for successful handling of conflict, which we will discuss in detail at the end of this chapter.

[7] From *Personality Dynamics and Effective Behavior* by James E. Coleman (Glenview, Ill.: Scott, Foresman and Company, 1960) p. 163.

While conflict may be potentially constructive or destructive, all perceived conflicts produce a degree of stress, frustration, and anxiety. Many studies relating to stress and anxiety have been conducted and many physical effects have been noted. The findings indicate that sustained stress overworks the endocrine and central nervous systems, with eventual serious damaging effects. Psychosomatic disorders are a result of prolonged stress—ulcers, headaches, allergies, heart disease, asthma, and many other physical problems can be helped by modifying the stress or by psychotherapy which changes perceptions and the impact of the stress. The following psychological effects are shown in conflicts: Psychological and physical energies are mobilized and heightened; anxiety and tension increase; defensiveness is shown; values are defended and rigidity is evident; trends toward aggressiveness and hostility are noted; perceptions become more polarized and distorted.

Prolonged, severe stress may initiate a general adaptation syndrome of three stages: an initial alarm reaction; a resistance stage, where a person tries to endure as best he can; and lastly, the stage of exhaustion and, possibly, death, if the stress is not alleviated.[9]

Challenge and conflict may help some people rise to great heights, as in the case of the artist or athlete who performs brilliantly under severe anxiety and stress. However, unresolved, prolonged conflicts may have agonizing consequences. Excessive stress, guilt, and feelings of self-doubt can lead to irritability, uncontrollable anxiety, indecisiveness, and eventual physical and psychological deterioration. Our adaptability and flexibility diminish as conflict continues, and our ability to cope with life eventually decreases, leading to disorganization and ultimate breakdown.

These destructive consequences are not inevitable, however. There are productive ways to resolve or manage conflicts. If we can avoid the ineffective ways to handle problems we have been describing in this chapter, and learn to be problem solvers, the result will be improvement in the overall quality of our physical, psychological, and social environments.

In conflict situations, when our self-structures and perceptions are threatened, we need to protect and defend ourselves. You may know people who use humor as a defense, hoping laughter will divert attention from what they sense are their own shortcomings. The ego defense mechanisms we use do not change or solve problems but they help us deal with the anxiety we feel about conflict. When we forget, rationalize, deny, avoid, or substitute another reward for the one we need to be concerned with, we are using ineffective problem-solving mechanisms. Needless to say, we should be aware of these unconscious mechanisms in ourselves and in others so they do not get in the way of effective problem solving and conflict reduction.

Until we become aware of our ego defense mechanisms, we are doomed to avoid reality and must defend our self-structures constantly, without change. We thus are rigidly locked into unproductive behavior, with

---

[8] Adapted from Betz, pp. 280–281.

[9] Selye, H. *The Physiology and Pathology of Exposure to Stress.* (Montreal: Acta, Inc., 1950).

little chance to explore new, more rewarding alternatives. Ego defense mechanisms are discussed more fully in Chapter 3, "Self-Awareness."

Problem Solving

In an ideally productive problem-solving situation, the conflicting parties have regard and respect for each other. They are mutually accepting and acceptable. Their main efforts are directed at handling the problem, not toward defeating each other.

Successful problem-solving discussions are kept on a clear, open, mutually acceptable level of interaction. Facts, attitudes, and personal feelings are dealt with objectively, and constant feedback is given without prejudice or disruptive accusations. Information is shared, and the areas of specific agreement and disagreement are openly discussed and clarified. Tactics which do not deal with reality and the facts are avoided, and both excessive domination and yielding behavior is out of place. The commitment of both parties to a realistic solution is the goal of true problem solving.

As a practical procedure for handling conflict we suggest Betz's adaptation of John Dewey's classic five-step method of problem solving.[10] You are already familiar with Dewey's methodology from the preceding chapter. Now let's see how we can apply it to managing conflict.

1. *Detect and analyze symptoms of the problem.* Let's say you are having trouble getting your roommates to accept the kind of music you like. They object to your playing rock music at top volume. You explain that is how the music is meant to be heard. In looking for the symptoms that reveal basic causes of a problem, we should look at the relationships between the parties involved, at how the contestants themselves define the conflict, and at the context in which the problem occurs. How do you get along with your roommates in other situations? Do they think the music issue is, indeed, a problem? Whose stereo system is it? Whose records? Often stresses exist because of misunderstanding and misperception of oneself or of others. We should examine the symptoms carefully.

2. *Assess causes of the conflict.* The success of any problem-solving technique will depend upon how well the basic causes are evaluated. Causes typically differ from symptoms. A symptom of your conflict might be that your roommates snap off the stereo the minute they enter the room. A cause might be the fact that you all prefer different types of music, or that your roommates think of their rooms as a quiet retreat while you seek noise and stimulation there. Symptoms are usually easier to detect and deal with, but basic causes must be reached and handled for effective problem resolution. We often are unaware of our own motives due to our defenses and basic needs, and this results in temporary or poor definition of causes and thus poor resolution of problems.

[10] Adapted from Betz, pp. 291–293. Also see David W. Johnson, *Reaching Out; Interpersonal Effectiveness and Self-Actualization* (Englewood Cliffs, N.J.: Prentice-Hall, Inc., 1972), pp. 203–219.

3. *Fix standards for possible solutions.* We now concentrate on types of answers available. The needs and strengths of the contestants must be assessed. Do you and your roommates agree to try to solve the problem on a friendly basis? Do you all agree that a problem exists and that you wish to solve it? Are you prepared to compromise? Or is one of you packed and ready to move out rather than give in? The common goals and actions acceptable to all must be determined at this point.

4. *Define possible courses of action.* The opposing parties should list the various options available as potential solutions. This might mean limiting record playing to certain hours of the day. Or it might mean alternating rock music with classical and with country-western. Or it might mean agreeing to play your rock music only at times your roommates are out. The degree of responsibility and sacrifice for each party must be faced. Which solution does each prefer, and which solutions are most realistic and workable? The results of possible solutions should also be discussed.

5. *Select the best solution.* The last step in this logical sequence consists of settling for a plan which seems workable to all parties. You and your roommates decide to invest in a set of headphones and to share the expense equally. The plan must be put into action at this point. Some or

Win-win outcome

all of these steps may need to be repeated, depending upon the success or failure of particular plans.

Each of these five basic steps should be monitored carefully and modified if needed. As long as respectful reciprocal relationships and positive interaction take place, a workable solution is possible.

Assertion Training

Some bold, new attempts to reduce social anxieties and improve levels of interpersonal effectiveness and communication are known as assertiveness training procedures. Assertion training usually involves four basic procedures: (1) Teaching people the differences between assertion and aggression, and between nonassertion and politeness; (2) helping people identify and accept both their own rights and the rights of others; (3) reducing existing mental and emotional obstacles to acting assertively, e.g., irrational thinking, excessive anxiety, guilt, and anger; and (4) developing assertive skills through active practice.[11]

Assertiveness training is concerned with standing up for personal rights and expressing thoughts, feelings, perceptions, and beliefs in honest, appropriate, straightforward ways, and these assertions must not violate others' rights. These techniques are especially helpful to people who are shy, timid, and relatively nonverbal. This training should be done with a psychologist or therapist who has been trained, and typically involves active role-playing and consistent practice under appropriate supervision.

George Bach and Herbert Goldberg have developed a programmed system they call *fight training,* a therapeutic way to handle aggressions creatively and to resolve interpersonal conflicts. This system relies on authentic communication, open encounter, and confrontation.

Bach and Goldberg believe that resolution of conflict and behavior changes mean acquiring new competence in the *here and now,* by using actual group stimulation, practice, and insightful programming. The specific steps in a "fair fight" that will bring about conflict reduction are:[12]

1. *The engagement:* One person with a complaint asks the other to engage in a fair fight. A time and place are agreed upon, and the discussion is conducted with mutual consent under agreed-upon conditions.

2. *Open huddle and rehearsal:* These are strategy conferences with one or more outsiders who act as coaches and observers. Huddles can be requested at any time by either partner. They are held openly, so all can listen. This helps the fight initiator define the complaint and construct a

---

[11] Lange, Arthur J. & Jakubowski, Patricia. *Responsible Assertive Behavior.* (Champaign, Ill.: Research Press, 1978).

[12] Adaptation from *Creative Aggression: The Art of Assertive Living* by George Bach and Herbert Goldberg. Copyright © 1974 by George R. Bach and Herbert Goldberg. Reprinted by permission of Doubleday & Company, Inc.

"demand for change" and assists the "fight partner" to express resistance to the demand in clear, simple terms.

3. *Statement of the "beef" and its hurtful impact:* The initiator now states his or her "beef." It includes a statement of how the complaint hurts or bothers the initiator.

4. *Feedback:* Feedback operates from this point on. Neither partner may express himself or herself without first repeating what the other has just said, to that person's satisfaction. This slows down the fight, forces careful listening, and is crucial in the fair-fight process. Feedback is difficult, often requires training, and does not mean mere rote parroting. It means grasping the sense of what the other person has just said, and it must be accurate.

5. *The demand for change:* Now the initiator is ready to make a specific demand for change. These demands must relate to actions, not attitudes. Once agreed to, the changes can then be measured in specific, concrete terms.

6. *Comeback of the fight partner:* After the demand for change has been correctly fed back, the fighting begins. The partner has a chance to respond to the demand and to the complaint with his or her side of the picture.

7. *Fair-fight interplay:* The fair fight now moves back and forth, each person expressing himself or herself in direct, simple statements. Each statement is fed back before the other person responds.

8. *Closure:* After mutual interchange, closure is required. The fight partner has agreed to the demand for change, rejected it, or made specific conditions for partial change. Closure is a restatement of the agreement just made. If fatigue sets in first, a later date acceptable to both can be set for continuing the fight.

9. *Follow-up engagement:* At this later meeting, the success or failure of the agreement is discussed. Any changes made should be recognized and reinforced. This means thanking the person who has successfully made a change. The closure agreement may either be reaffirmed or renegotiated. Commitments are kept fluid.

Describing this exchange in terms of a fight may seem overly dramatic, but when you think about it, this can be a helpful approach. The *process* of fair fighting is more important than the *content,* and in the give and take, the fighting is never over. If you can learn the process of fair fighting, you will have a method of handling future problems. This procedure can sensitize you to your own unique style of interaction and help cut down on evasions and distortions that frustrate problem solving. It can bring about problem resolution that is mutually comfortable, foster successful patterns of behavior, and help avoid win-lose or lose-lose games. The emphasis in fair fighting is upon both partners winning. If one person loses, then both have lost in terms of handling future conflicts and in terms of burdening and hurting the personal relationship. It is important to constantly clarify the ground rules, to be honest and open, and to respect your opponent and his or her rights.

Guidelines for Managing Conflict

Many professional techniques and strategies for coping with stress and managing conflict have been designed, including biofeedback, assertiveness training, chemotherapy, group therapy, meditation, behavior modification, and various types of psychotherapy. These procedures are beyond the scope of this chapter, but if unhappiness and stress persist, the wise person will seek medical and psychological help for persistent stress-related problems. Because effective problem solving is so important in our lives and because our skillful handling of communication determines our effectiveness as a problem solver, we would do well to consider the following communication guidelines for managing conflict:

1. *Accept the other party as a person, even though we may disagree with many of his or her values and beliefs.*
2. *Be convinced that we have enough in common to make communication possible.*
3. *Focus on the problem which is to be dealt with. Avoid threats, name-calling, ego-involvement.*
4. *Be descriptive, using nonjudgmental terms, and avoiding the strongly emotion-laden words.*
5. *Choose the specific rather than the general focus.*
6. *Discuss the issues that are most open to change rather than those which offer little hope of alteration.*
7. *Foster spontaneity of giving feedback when it is appropriate and at the time it is called for. This avoids the confusion that results when we react now to something that happened in an earlier encounter. The other party may possibly misinterpret our behavior.*
8. *As nearly as possible fit our words to our experience of reality. Remember, reality is what things do to us and for us.*
9. *When we respond to persons or situations we should make sure that the other party or parties accurately interpret our meaning.*
10. *Project an expectancy of success and acceptance.*[13]

While not a magic cure or panacea, if we will conscientiously and consistently apply the basic steps of problem solving along with these guidelines, we can learn to deal more effectively with our conflicts. The resulting workable decisions, reduced hostilities, and happier life-styles will be their own reward. Genuine interpersonal dialogue and win-win attitudes and behaviors are undoubtedly worth the effort. If these techniques are not tried, then we as individuals and society will be losers. It is no exaggeration to suggest that the many problems facing society today, if left unresolved, mean disaster for us and for future generations.

Court and lawyers now decide how major conflict is resolved in our

[13] Betz, p. 290.

culture. Hopefully they will continue to learn the basic principles of "waging peace" discussed in this chapter. It would, indeed, be a welcome change for the world if people and countries would actively wage peace, using the skills and resources which are now used to wage war.

1. Discuss with a friend you trust a real problem between yourselves.
   a. How did you feel about the discussion?
   b. How did your friend feel about the discussion?
   c. What problem-solving techniques did you use?
   d. What problem-solving techniques did your friend use?
   e. How was the issue resolved?
   f. If not resolved, how will you approach the problem in future discussions?
2. Repeat the preceding exercise but have a third person present as an arbitrator. Did this help you reach a solution? If not, why not? What factors blocked discussion?
3. Discuss a mutually interesting topic with a friend. After five minutes, each of you can talk only after you have summarized what the other has just said, to his/her satisfaction.
   a. Did this exercise clarify the topic?
   b. Did you listen more carefully? Did your friend?
   c. Did you understand your attitudes and feelings, or your friend's, more fully?
   d. Was it difficult to summarize what your friend said?
4. In a group discussion, note if any decisions were made, and when conflicts arose.
   a. Did any group member (including the leader) force decisions?
   b. Did any member try to block or prevent decisions?
   c. Did any group member give in to group pressure?
   d. How were conflicts handled by the group?
   e. How were facts treated? Feelings? Attitudes?
   f. Were trades used?
   g. Was a group consensus reached? How?
   h. What else could have been done to facilitate group interactions and decisions?
5. Read a letter from an advice column. Analyze the problem and answer for effective problem solving and clear communication in terms of:
   a. Clarification of real problems.
   b. Value judgments or factual statements.
   c. Over-generalizing.
   d. Simplistic, either/or solutions.
   e. Name calling.
   f. Interfering or blocking tactics.
   g. Practical, realistic problem-solving methods.
   h. Problems in long-distance techniques.
6. Try these steps the next time you must deal with a conflict situation.
   a. Isolate and specify the problem, then look at the alternatives.
   b. Draft, then let both sides criticize and edit a statement of the problem.
   c. Cast out inflexible doctrines.
   d. Deal with any differences in manageable units.
   e. Keep stakes limited and contained.
   f. Keep open the option of having third-party intervention.
   g. Be responsive and willing to take risks.

FOR FURTHER INSIGHT

REFERENCES

Bach, George, and Herbert Goldberg. *Creative Aggression; The Art of Assertive Living.* New York: Avon Books, 1975.

Beier, Ernst G., and Evans G. Valens. *People Reading.* New York: Stein and Day, 1975.

Coleman, James C. *Personality Dynamics and Effective Behavior.* Glenview, Illinois: Scott, Foresman and Company, 1960.

Filley, Alan C. *Interpersonal Conflict Resolution.* Glenview, Illinois: Scott, Foresman and Company, 1975.

Hall, Jay. *Conflict Management Survey.* Houston: Teleometrics, Inc., 1969.

Kell, Bill L., and William J. Mueller. *Impact and Change; A Study of Counseling Relationships.* New York: Appleton-Century-Crofts, 1966.

Lange, Arthur J. and Jakubowski, Patricia. *Responsible Assertive Behavior.* Champaign, Ill.: Research Press, 1978.

Lewin, K. *Dynamic Theory of Personality.* New York: McGraw-Hill, 1935.

Postman, Neil, and Charles Weingartner. *Teaching as a Subversive Activity.* New York: Dell Publishing Co., Inc., 1969.

Scheidel, Thomas M. *Speech Communication and Human Interaction,* 2nd ed. Glenview, Illinois: Scott, Foresman and Company, 1976.

Selye, H. *The Physiology and Pathology of Exposure to Stress.* Montreal: ACTA, Inc., 1950.

Toffler, Alvin. *Future Shock.* New York: Bantam Books, 1970.

Persuasion and Attitude Change

FOR PREVIEW AND REVIEW

1. An examination of our attitudes, beliefs, and opinions can help us resist such inaccurate belief systems as stereotypes, prejudices, superstitions, and delusions.

2. Persuasion is an honest, ethical attempt to influence others. It is motivated by the persuader's sincere conviction that the view he or she holds or the action he or she advocates is the right one.

3. We can be persuaded by appeals to personal needs, to logic, and to emotion, as well as by the appeal of the speaker.

4. Propaganda is any systematic scheme or concerted effort to persuade others to a certain action or point of view. We need to be aware of various propaganda techniques and logical fallacies.

5. In analyzing persuasive communications, we should examine the speaker's reliability and authority, the wording of the argument, and the meaning of the argument.

INSTRUCTIONAL OBJECTIVES

After studying this chapter, you should be able to:

1. Explain the significance of attitudes, beliefs, and opinions in interactions with others.

2. Explain Maslow's "Hierarchy of Personal Needs."

3. Analyze basic propaganda techniques of the mass media.

4. Identify and demonstrate the three basic types of persuasive appeals: ethical, emotional, and logical.

5. Recognize fallacies in the process of reasoning.

6. Explain the theories of persuasion and how they function in attitude change.

"Would You Believe. . . ?"

We do very few things in our day-to-day living that do not relate to our beliefs and attitudes toward ourselves, friends and acquaintances, and environment. Each of us tries to create favorable, predictable attitudes in others, and we also try to eliminate or change unfavorable attitudes toward us. Many of our interpersonal behaviors are designed to influence our friends, teachers, relatives, and others. Most of us have seen the socially adept "apple-polishers" who get their own way, and we are often surprised when we are not so adept, or when others misunderstand us. How do minds and attitudes change? Why do they change? These are very old, important questions, and many people, including politicians, reformers, teachers, philosophers, business executives, and con artists, have been very much concerned with the conditions which influence people to accept new ideas. An understanding of these conditions may help us change for the better, communicate more effectively, and resist the unwanted propaganda and manipulative promotions of others.

Persuasion, debate, and attitude change are all used at times in the resolution of conflict (see Chapter 7), and the artful use of these techniques can help improve our relationships with others and prevent useless, unwanted battles.

Belief Systems

Attitudes are tendencies to respond positively or negatively to persons, situations, or objects. Social attitudes are related to issues and concerns of our groups and our society. Most of us have strong attitudes about taxes, cars, religion, wars, and people, among other things. Group leaders, politicians, and business people are particularly concerned about these attitudes and possible ways to change them. The manipulation of public opinion through

We often maintain beliefs that have little basis in reality.

persuasive techniques is an expensive and intricate science; an understanding of such techniques is a necessity for successful modern living.

It is of much practical value to know about our attitudes and preferences; for example, we buy most products in a fairly predictable way. Even the color of the wrapper on a can of soup is important because the seller can use our preferred colors and designs to sell more soup to us. Many of us will buy more groceries when lively, cheerful music is being played, and supermarkets use this knowledge in their attempts to sell their products.

We also have individual personal attitudes toward our families, our friends, our pets, and so on, which may be different from the more general group attitudes. These personal attitudes are very important in our adjustment to life, and have considerable impact on our happiness. Many of our attitudes were picked up quite early in life, almost automatically. We learned rather quickly to avoid unpleasant experiences and to accept what was pleasant and rewarding. If our parents preferred sports cars, we may also have adopted a positive attitude toward sports cars, although we might believe that we independently arrived at this conclusion.

Attitudes are closely related to beliefs and opinions. A *belief* is the acceptance of a statement as true. Our beliefs involve thinking, and we thus feel that there is good evidence for them. Often we believe what some authority has led us to believe, even if the authority is questionable or quite faulty. Some students may believe that a teacher is fair, while others may believe that the same teacher is prejudiced and unfair. To consistently maintain a belief, we often will ignore evidence which does not support our belief and rigidly insist that it is correct. We may also withdraw physically so that we do not have to listen to contrary evidence.

Between attitudes and beliefs are *opinions*. An opinion implies the acceptance or rejection of a statement, but it is often vague. We are not so sure that our opinions are provable. Generally opinions are either for or against something, as in the statement "I don't know, but I think that Ms. Smith is a good teacher."

It is difficult in practice to distinguish among opinions, attitudes, and beliefs. Sometimes our beliefs about an issue differ from our attitudes; we may believe that minority groups should have equal opportunities, while expressing unfavorable, prejudiced, attitudes toward them. More often, however, if we have an unfavorable *attitude,* we are also likely to *believe* unfavorable things. For example, if we have an unfavorable attitude toward members of a particular ethnic group, we will also more than likely believe that they are irresponsible, lazy, or sloppy. The same process holds true for most prejudices and stereotypes. Our beliefs and attitudes ordinarily go hand-in-hand—what affects one is usually going to influence the other. It is possible that by changing an attitude we may also change a belief, although the belief is typically of longer standing and more firmly held.

Strong feelings play a vital part in the formation of our beliefs, and many of our beliefs are distorted or false because of our intense emotions. Often our beliefs are not logical because we see only some of the facts. At times it is not possible to get all the facts before we have to make some decisions, and this lack of information may prevent the development of accurate beliefs and perceptions.

Several types of inaccurate belief systems exist, and a brief look at them may help in our search for truth, accurate communication, and objectivity.

The *stereotype* is a belief that is widely held and tends to oversimplify or distort reality. The belief that geniuses are peculiar, that college teachers are "long hairs," or that blondes are less intelligent than brunettes are simply stereotyped distortions which are not supported by research data.

Prejudices are judgments made about someone or something before the facts are known. Prejudices usually put their objects at a disadvantage. Racial and religious prejudice generally contradict the relevant facts, and often deeply held prejudices contradict each other. A black person seen as "working like a slave" is sometimes also seen by the same person (contradictorily) as lazy and shiftless.

Superstitions are widely held beliefs that differ from known laws of science or from what society generally considers true or rational. Seeing a black cat cross one's path, breaking a mirror, and walking under a ladder are events which are sometimes believed to bring bad luck, but most sophisticated people recognize these beliefs as baseless.

Delusions are another kind of false belief. Fortunately, delusions are not held by many people, but some deluded leaders have had a great impact on the world. People who believe that other people are following them and spying on them, or who think that they are the victims of a conspiracy, are most often badly misperceiving reality and need professional psychological help.

While the attempts of professional psychotherapy to change perceptions, attitudes, and defenses are beyond the scope of this discussion, most therapists try to effect positive changes by the systematic use of warm, honest, trusting, genuine relationships and communications. These same principles can also enhance the quality of our day-to-day attitudes toward, and interactions with, others. Needless to say, we should try to be aware of all our attitudes and beliefs, including our prejudices and our inaccurate, illogical beliefs.

Persuasion

In its broadest sense, *persuasion* is any attempt to change another person's attitudes or beliefs and to influence his or her decisions. For our purposes here we shall consider it an honest, ethical attempt to influence others. It is motivated by the persuader's sincere conviction that the view held or the action advocated is the right one. Persuasion is a nonviolent way of resolving issues and influencing others. Most reasonable people agree that differences should be resolved, and change should be accomplished, by persuasion rather than by physical force. An American once expressed surprise that no blows were being struck in a heated argument he was watching between two Orientals. A Chinese observer said, "The man who hits first is admitting that he has no more ideas." A genuine acceptance of this wisdom could go a long way toward uniting people and settling controversy without the use of physical power.

Persuasion is the dominant decision-making process in modern, free societies. It is a democratic technique for influencing others and resolving differences through the expression of majority opinion after consideration of all views. Persuasion involves the total communication process, with consideration given to individual personalities as well as to broader social factors.

Analysis of the process of persuasion indicates that there are four general steps which usually occur, roughly in this order:
1. Gaining and maintaining attention;
2. Arousing needs and issues useful to the persuader's purpose;
3. Showing how these needs can be satisfied by the persuader's arguments; and
4. Producing the desired response.[1]

In practice, these steps usually overlap. A car salesperson will often get our attention by an amusing story, or by noting our intelligence in admiring the cars for sale. We will then be assured of our increased status and prestige gained by driving a particular car, and impressed with the money we will

[1] For further development, see Alan H. Monroe and Douglas Ehninger, *Principles of Speech Communication*, 7th brief ed. (Glenview, Ill.: Scott, Foresman and Co., 1975), pp. 41–53.

save by buying it now. The final step will be to get us to sign a long-term contract at high rates of interest, thus "proving" our high status, intelligence, sound economy, and overall worth!

To persuade people successfully, you should try to analyze the existing beliefs and attitudes of your audience which can serve as a basis for the new attitudes you wish to develop. You will also analyze their basic existing needs and try to appeal to these needs.

According to A. H. Maslow, we all have a hierarchy of needs, each of which must be fulfilled before we are concerned about the next, and so on. First are our *physiological* needs, which include food, shelter, protection from the elements, rest, and exercise. When these needs are fulfilled, we are more concerned with *safety* needs, such as protection against danger or deprivation. Next are the *social* needs, the needs to belong, to associate with and be accepted by others, to give and receive friendship and love. Fourth are our *ego* needs, the needs for self-esteem (self-confidence, independence, achievement, competence, knowledge) and for reputation (status, recognition, appreciation, the deserved respect of associates). Last in our hierarchy of needs are the *self-fulfillment* needs, or the needs to realize our potentialities, to continue self-development, to be creative.[2]

Maslow's theory states that our physiological needs have precedence over other needs. When the physiological needs are fairly well satisfied, the higher-level needs will operate as prime motivators. However, until our physiological and safety needs are reasonably well handled, we will have relatively little time and energy to develop our higher-level needs of love, self-esteem, and self-actualization.

Jurgen Ruesch and Gregory Bateson identify five important emphases in American value systems:

1. *Puritan and pioneer morality;*
2. *Equality;*
3. *Sociality;*
4. *Success;*
5. *Change.*[3]

According to these authors, American life centers around these values and the communications designed to deal with these values. Value systems affect persuaders and listeners alike and are of critical importance to our thought processes and to all our communications.

Some further ideas about our needs and how those needs are satisfied are described by psychological consistency theories.[4] Psychological consistency theories suggest that we are motivated to keep harmony or a balance in all of our thinking processes, beliefs, and judgments about our environments and ourselves. If things happen to create an imbalance in our perceptions and beliefs, we have to adjust our thinking to achieve a new harmony

---

[2] *Motivation and Personality* (New York: Harper & Row, Publishers, 1954).

[3] *Communication: The Social Matrix of Psychiatry* (New York: W. W. Norton & Co., Inc., 1951).

[4] For further development, see Roger Brown, *Social Psychology* (New York: The Free Press, 1965).

or inner balance. If we thus feel positively about a person, we will be positive about what he or she says or does. If a conflict develops, we would have to achieve a new balance between what this person says or does, and our positive perception of him or her.

Bandler and Grinder[5] have formulated a communication theory which states that everyone has a "primary representational system," which is the sensory mode in which one is most sensitive, and can make the first distinctions. Most people see the world in visual, auditory, or kinesthetic (tactile) ways. A primarily visual person translates information into images and relies on vision and verbal responses related to statements like "I see," "that looks clear," and so on. Auditory people respond with "I hear you," "that sounds right," while kinesthetic people say "that feels good," "I'll touch bases with you," and so on. To communicate well, we should use the sensory modality of the speaker. Ideally, a person should be adept in all senses, selecting whichever is appropriate to the moment. This new theory could be useful in helping people become more sensitive to all dormant senses, and to live more fully. These theories we have been discussing are important in helping us understand our audience's needs and ways we can ethically appeal to those needs.

Propaganda

Propaganda is any systematic scheme or concerted effort to persuade others to believe in a particular practice, doctrine, or point of view. The rather common use of propaganda techniques makes them a type of persuasive communication that merits our attention. There is nothing necessarily bad or underhanded about propaganda; the same techniques are used, in varying degrees, in advertising, politics, education, religion, public relations, and even most group discussions. Nearly all information-giving and persuasive activities involve some propaganda. If we can learn to examine these techniques and logically evaluate information and issues for ourselves, we will be able to examine the issues critically, and not naively accept persuasive arguments.

Propaganda techniques may be used by the sincere persuader, but they may also be used by the self-serving manipulator. Manipulation is the attempt to influence others, by any means possible, to think or do what the manipulator desires them to do, as he or she seeks to achieve some selfish end or purpose. The manipulator has only his or her own interests at heart. Obviously, at times our own motives are mixed, and the line between honest persuasion and selfish manipulation becomes very thin indeed.

Often propagandists appeal to group standards. They also try to block or avoid any critical examination of their main points so that arguments against them will not arise and hinder or halt their persuasive effectiveness. The following are seven of the most commonly used techniques of propaganda.

[5] Grinder, John and Bandler, Richard. *The Structure of Magic.*, Vols. I and II. Science and Behavior Books, 1976.

1. *Name Calling.* Calling someone a "pinko," "fascist," "kike," or "war-monger" arouses such strong emotions that the "loaded" word often blocks rational thought about the issue or person under discussion. It may also brand the person called such a name as bad, leading to his or her rejection.

2. *Glittering Generalities.* Superpatriots who say, "Our God-fearing, dedicated, sincere, and patriotic leader . . ." are loading the dice with vague and noble-sounding generalities. If examined critically, these generalities are often blatantly inconsistent and false.

3. *Transfer.* Sometimes a tone of strong positive feeling is created and then transferred to the topic under discussion or to the speaker. For instance, many rallies start with the national anthem and presentation of the flag, after which the speaker attempts to pick up the good feeling and bask in the unquestioned borrowed glory. Thus the authority, sanction, and prestige of something we respect is carried over to something or someone else.

4. *Testimonials.* Testimonials are endorsements of a person, idea, or product by prestigious, well-known people. Movie stars who use Brand X, or athletes who eat Brand Z cereals, are used in testimonials, but the logic behind such endorsements is questionable. Nevertheless, this technique is quite effective in selling products.

5. *Plain Folks.* Most politicians have their picture taken with assembly-line workers and farmers, suggesting that they also are just average, ordinary, plain people. After posing for these pictures, the politician often gets into a million-dollar airplane and goes back to a luxurious home, which should indicate to any thinking person that the suggested similarities have serious limitations!

6. *Card Stacking.* Some propagandists use the clever selection of some facts and figures, ignoring others, to present either the best or the worst side of an issue. Many car manufacturers list the large number of cars they have built, but they seldom publicize the number of cars that have been recalled due to defective parts.

7. *The Bandwagon.* "Why not join us now? Everybody's doing it!" The aim of this approach is to make us follow the crowd. It is often successful with impulsive people who are anxious to be on the right or winning side, and who do not pause for more careful consideration of products, issues, or candidates.

Propagandists are often successful because many of us need to be given the "right" answers. Most of us do not like ambiguous situations and thus are susceptible to easy solutions from friends, television, newspapers, and other authorities. The passive, quiet person is many times exploited by the expert. We are vulnerable to propaganda when we tolerate one-way communication rather than talking back and critically evaluating the issues.

Many expert book reviewers "talk back" to books by writing their reactions to the book in the margins as they read it. This is an effective, active way of being critically involved with the book, provided that the reader owns the book!

Persuasive Appeals

"The *person* who says something is as important as *what* is said." This state-ment reflects a basic persuasive principle, that of *ethos,* or source credibility. How we perceive the speaker determines how easily we may be influenced. The speaker's status and prestige, personality, expertise, and role in the issue are all important. The persuasive effectiveness of the message is deter-mined by our attitude toward the speaker—our perception of the speaker as trustworthy, credible, fair, and honest.

Another basic type of appeal is *logos,* or the appeal to logic and reason. This appeal involves the use of a logical progression of facts to back up an argument. "It only seems sensible . . ." or some such comment often pref-aces this appeal to rational thought.

A third basic type of appeal is *pathos,* or the use of emotional appeals in the attempt to persuade us. Such appeals must be examined very carefully, as they may be legitimate or fallacious, and we are usually more vulnerable where our emotions are concerned.

As we listen to others, we should try to determine what it is the speaker appeals to in trying to influence us. Sometimes the appeal is explicit, some-times more implicit; sometimes legitimate, sometimes fallacious. It is the

Source credibility af-fects audience re-ceptivity.

listener's job to sense what the speaker implies, and to evaluate the legitimacy of the appeals used. This is most important in evaluating arguments.

There are many kinds of *logical fallacies*. If a speaker attempts to persuade by threats or physical force, or attacks the person rather than the relevant issues ("Of course Smith won't make a good President: he is Catholic"), he or she is using *nonrational* arguments.

The student who says, "That grade you gave me on the test wasn't justified. Besides working all night, I take care of my two children . . . ," is appealing to the teacher's *pity*. This is not a legitimate use of emotion.

An appeal to *authority* is fallacious:

1. When a person is used as an authority in a field other than his or her specialty;
2. When the authority is biased;
3. When it is assumed that, because the authority's judgment was good under certain conditions or at a certain time, it will be good at other times or under different conditions; or
4. When arguments are based upon tradition, are pseudoscientific, or use questionable statistics and procedures.

People vary in their degree of persuasibility. Those who have strong, extreme views of issues, who have a high degree of ego-involvement, typically are difficult to persuade. Individuals with high self-esteem and those who are hostile and aggressive are also hard to influence. Some studies show that hostile, aggressive people are not open to suggestions or new ideas of any type.[6] There also is evidence that men, traditionally, are not as easily persuaded as women. Women often seem to follow instructions more closely and generally accept authority more willingly than men. With more people reexamining traditional sex-roles, this difference will likely change. Other variables—age, for instance—influence acceptance and persuasibility, and we should constantly try to understand these variables in ourselves and in others.

Recent brain research has shown that the two hemispheres of our brains store and process different information and function quite differently: In the right-handed person, the left hemisphere is the dominant one, and it mainly communicates with the world in a verbal, logical, step-by-step, rational fashion. Damage to this hemisphere leads to handicaps in speech, writing, counting, and reasoning. Being involved with details, the left hemisphere often does not see the forest for the trees, but it is responsible for our verbal communications.

The function of the right hemisphere is quite different. It is involved with grasping complex patterns and relationships, and deals with dreams, images, colors, music, learned sequential processes, and relatively primitive percepts. Damage to the right hemisphere leads to poor perceptions of images and patterns. This hemisphere also deals with creativity and emotional experience and generally mediates our nonverbal behavior.

It now appears that we have, in essence, *two* brains that can function

[6] W. J. McGuire, in *The Handbook of Social Psychology*, 2nd ed. Gardner Lindzey and Elliot Aronson, eds. (Reading, Mass.: Addison-Wesley Publishing Co., Inc., 1969).

independently of each other. Each reacts to different external stimuli, and is receptive to different influences and "languages." These facts account for the difficulty we all have in translating a musical or emotional (right hemisphere) experience into words (left hemisphere). The potentials for conflict and confusion are tremendous, considering the different, possibly antagonistic, functions of the two brain hemispheres.

At the present time, much effort is going into ways of influencing and persuading people, based upon this information. Insight and understanding of these brain dimensions can help resist such influencing attempts and also can aid our communications by understanding the hemispheric "language" of others. Goethe and other philosophers have sadly stated that two souls dwell within all of us, but this new research may help us understand and thus more successfully use these two different inner capabilities.[7]

Suggestibility

Many psychologists believe that there is a general tendency in some people to respond positively, and thus to be highly suggestible. High suggestibility appears to be related to people who have low self-esteem, show anxiety, have social inhibitions, and feel inadequate. Such people are often very sensitive to their environment and especially vulnerable to the impact of external events. Persons with high self-esteem appear to be more able to ignore, challenge, or question environmental experiences and do not need to conform to get social approval. People who easily respect and obey authority and admire power and aggression also tend to accept persuasion from authorities.

The advisability of using direct or indirect suggestion depends on the circumstances.

Direct Suggestion

1. Use when the audience feels inferior to the speaker.
2. Use when the audience is polarized.
3. Use when the speaker's prestige is high.
4. Use when addressing young listeners.
5. Use when an immediate, precise, definite form of action is required.
6. Use when the speaker is the master of the speaking situation.

Indirect Suggestion

1. Use when the audience feels equal or superior to the speaker.
2. Use when the audience is mentally alert.
3. Use when the speaker's prestige is low.
4. Use when addressing adults.
5. Use when the aim is to create an attitude or belief which may lead to future action.
6. Use when the speaker is relatively unskilled.[8]

[7] Kinsbourne, Marcel (Ed.). *Asymmetrical Function of the Brain*. Cambridge, England: Cambridge University Press, 1978.

[8] From Winston Lamont Brembeck and William Smiley Howell, *Persuasion: A Means of Social Control*, p. 169. Copyright © 1952 by Prentice-Hall, Inc. Reprinted by permission of Prentice-Hall, Inc., Englewood Cliffs, N.J.

It is generally a good policy to use positive suggestion and to state issues affirmatively. The positive is usually more rewarding and influential than the negative, because negative messages invite resistance and rebellion, and their influence may not last as long or be as persuasive as positive messages. A positive approach used by salespeople consists of deliberately getting you, the client, to agree with the salesperson about anything at all. After a series of positive responses are obtained, the salesperson says, "Wouldn't you like to buy a . . . ," and you have been carefully led to say *yes* to this pitch. By the time you become aware of the series of "yes" responses you have been led to give, it is often too late to back out, as the purchase has been made. Awareness of this sales technique could aid us in developing better sales resistance.

Most of us are aware of the influence that group attitudes and opinions have on our behavior. We need the social approval of our friends, families, and teachers. We all have to conform to at least some group pressures, and we feel anxious and tense when strong conflicts and the possibility of rejection exist in groups that are important to us. One way to resolve our feelings and attitudes is to conform to the group position and thereby avoid criticism and rejection.

Many studies have shown that radio messages, as well as newspapers, leaflets, and other printed materials, have comparatively slight influence on us. What usually influences us most is direct contact with other people, especially family, friends, and prestigious people. These highly valued people interpret mass media information for us. Generally ideas flow from television, radio, and the printed page to these important people, and through them eventually to us. These personal influences generally help shape our attitudes in conjunction with, and filtered through, our individual personalities and perceptions.

Sex, age, and physical characteristics are also important influences. Status characteristics such as education, vocational position, past experience, or civic reputation can be important in influencing group behavior. Nonverbal cues such as angrily pounding a table, being silent, or using sex appeal also influence discussions and persuasive attempts.

It is important to note that we do not all get our attitudes and beliefs about the world in the same way. Some of us adopt and change our beliefs in response to logic and reason. Others of us accept or reject beliefs mainly because of the social impact upon us, while some of us are motivated by our emotions and our self-esteem, defensiveness, and expectancies. This variability, and the unique individuality of each person, needs to be recognized when we attempt to influence and persuade others.

In general, we respond to persuasive communications which have value and use for us, and which promise to help us get something we need and want. We also respond strongly when we are very much involved and deeply committed to a position. It is difficult to change an attitude of this sort; generally, the greater our ego-involvement, the more difficult it is to persuade us to a different view.

Persuasive communications must pass through our perceptual filters, and we may reject or distort ideas which do not fit in with our own motives, needs, and goals. This perceptual defensiveness occurs because ideas relevant to our needs are usually easily accepted, but ideas that are antagonistic or unrelated to our goals are often seen as threatening or unimportant, and so are rejected or distorted.

A persuasive message should first gain attention, and then support and confirm ideas which are consistent, understandable, and acceptable. If the message relates to ideas and feelings already held by the recipient, it will generally be successful. If the ideas presented are supported by people and groups which are trusted and admired, the ideas will be more readily accepted.

Theories of Persuasion

The *immunization theory* of communication holds that both sides of an argument should be presented so that the listener can be prepared for subsequent counterarguments and counterinfluence. If only one side of an issue is presented, there often is little resistance later to counterarguments. Thus, presenting both (or all) sides of an issue is usually successful in immunizing the listener against subsequent counterarguments.

The *cognitive-dissonance theory* states that conflict occurs when we are confronted with two incompatible responses. Once a commitment has been made to one of two choices, subsequent information-gathering and -evaluating are biased in defense of the commitment. When we experience dissonance and discomfort after being exposed to discrepancies or incongruities, we try to reestablish balance and reduce tension by:
1. Criticizing and derogating the source of information;
2. Seeking new information to support our choice;
3. Reinterpreting or selectively reevaluating old information;
4. Avoiding discrepant information;
5. Changing our attitude or conduct to achieve consistency with the new information.

Persuaders must try to influence people who have various degrees of commitment or ego-involvement. The attitudes which we strongly endorse compose our *latitudes of acceptance,* and the positions which are objectionable and unacceptable compose our *latitudes of rejection.* Between these two are areas of relative noncommitment. One factor which determines the likelihood of attitude change is the closeness of a communication to our latitude position. The closer the advocated position is to our position, the more likely it is that we will change our attitude. The more deeply involved we are, the less likely it is that we will change. A degree of ambiguity in our own thinking, or a lack of sharp definition, seems to prompt a shift in our attitude toward that of the persuader. Finally, if explicit, objective standards can be used in communications, prospects for attitude change are improved.

The *balance* or *congruity theory* can be summarized as follows:
1. We develop attitudes that are often all positive or all negative.
2. When incongruous information is communicated, our carefully bal-

anced attitude is upset and tension and dissonance develop, which motivate us to restore the balance.

3. Balance can be restored by reaffirming or restructuring the attitude.
4. Whether or not we change our attitude depends on several factors, including where we place the communication we have received on our personal acceptance/rejection latitude scale (how strongly we hold the attitude).

To move us toward accepting his or her own attitude, a persuader must create imbalance or incongruity in an acceptable way, and then show that this imbalance can be helped or alleviated if we accept his or her position. The persuader in this case is using the psychological consistency theory discussed earlier in this chapter to influence and change our position.

Evaluating Persuasive Communications

A very useful series of steps can help us evaluate the influence of persuasive communications:

1. *Who* said it? Was "They said . . ." or "I heard . . ." used? Evaluate the source.
2. What was *said?* Listen carefully, as distortions and misperceptions are common.

Look at the motivations for the message.

3. What was *meant?* Do you understand what the speaker means by the words used? Ask questions and try to get clear, unmistakable meanings.

These steps can help you get at the facts and avoid misunderstandings.

We are often persuaded to our disadvantage if we do not weigh alternatives. Patience and careful thought are necessary if we are to make decisions successfully and avoid being persuaded against our better judgment. Sometimes there are only two solutions to a problem in persuasive communication, but often there are many possible courses of action if we are not persuaded too quickly or illogically.

A logical approach would be to:
1. Analyze the persuasive message;
2. Look at the motivations for the message;
3. Develop alternatives;
4. Select the best solution; and
5. Continue the process.

We should always check our judgments with those of others to avoid accepting false or distorted communications. Sound reasoning, honesty, and systematic inquiry are essential to ensuring good communications and evaluating persuasive messages accurately. We should reject fraud, deception, and illogical arguments. Understanding and accepting our own values, feelings, and expectancies will help in our attempts to communicate, persuade, and honestly relate with others.

Accurate perception and understanding of others' motivations also is critical in effectively evaluating persuasive communications. No one ever achieves perfect self-perception or complete understanding of others, but the goal is worth the attempt!

FOR FURTHER INSIGHT

1. Attempt to persuade someone to your point of view on a controversial issue. Obtain verbal feedback to determine how successful you were.
2. Observe a salesperson who is attempting to sell you something. What techniques did he or she use? Were they successful?
3. What medium of communication influences you most—radio, television, newspapers, magazines, speeches, conversation? Why is it so influential?
4. Clip some advertisements from magazines and newspapers and analyze the techniques and appeals they use. Which influence you most? Why?
5. List your most important needs and values. How might someone use these to get your attention and persuade you? Analyze a friend's needs and values in the same way.
6. In which stores do you buy your food and clothing? Why were you persuaded to buy there? Do you have the option and freedom to buy in other stores?
7. Try to persuade a friend to go to a show with you. What arguments did you find to be the most effective? Why were they persuasive?
8. What type of candidates do you vote for? Which behaviors and/or arguments persuaded you?

REFERENCES

Brown, James A. C. *Techniques of Persuasion*. Baltimore: Penguin Books, Inc., 1963.

Brown, Roger. *Social Psychology*. New York: The Free Press, 1965.

Cohen, Arthur R. *Attitude Change and Social Influence*. New York: Basic Books, Inc., 1964.

Dobb, Leonard W. *Propaganda: Its Psychology and Technique*. New York: Holt, Rinehart & Winston, Inc., 1935.

Festinger, Leon. *Conflict, Decision and Dissonance*. Stanford: Stanford University Press, 1964.

Grinder, John and Bandler, Richard. *The Structure of Magic*, Vol. I and II. Palo Alto: Science and Behaviour Books, 1976

Hovland, Carl I., Irving L. Janis, and H. H. Kelley. *Communication and Persuasion*. New Haven: Yale University Press, 1953.

Kinsbourne, Marcel, ed. *Asymmetrical Function of the Brain*. Cambridge: Cambridge University Press, 1978.

Lindzey, Gardner, and Elliott Aronson, eds. *The Handbook of Social Psychology*, 2nd ed. Reading, Mass.: Addison-Wesley Publishing Co., Inc., 1969.

Maslow, Abraham, H. *Motivation and Personality*. New York: Harper & Row, Publishers, 1954.

Minnick, Wayne C. *The Art of Persuasion*. Boston: Houghton Mifflin Co., 1968.

Oliver, Robert T. *The Psychology of Persuasive Speech*. London: Longmans, Green & Co., Ltd., 1942.

Restak, R. M. *The Brain: The Last Frontier*. N.Y.: Doubleday, 1979.

Ruesch, Jurgen, and Gregory Bateson. *Communication: The Social Matrix of Psychiatry*. New York: W. W. Norton & Co., Inc., 1951.

Scheidel, Thomas M. *Persuasive Speaking*. Glenview, Ill.: Scott, Foresman and Co., 1967.

Schwartz, Gary E., and Beatty, Jackson (Eds.) *Biofeedback: Theory and Research*. New York: Academic Press, 1977.

Watzlawick, Paul. *The Language of Change: Elements of Therapeutic Communication*. New York: Basic Books, 1978.

The Job Interview

FOR PREVIEW AND REVIEW

1. Preparation for a vocation or profession begins with a self-inventory of talents, skills, and qualifications.
2. Knowing our talents and abilities, we can decide on a suitable career.
3. We can become aware of important qualifications by interviewing leaders in various fields of employment.
4. Necessary written materials include a resumé, letters of application, and personal identification.
5. Practice in filling out forms is helpful in job hunting.
6. Acceptable dress for an interview is dictated by the times, the environment, and the accepted style.
7. Businesses are seeking individuals with good writing and speaking skills.
8. Preparation for an interview includes becoming familiar with typical interview questions.
9. Knowing why people don't get jobs can help us to improve our opportunities.

INSTRUCTIONAL OBJECTIVES

After studying this chapter, you should be able to:
1. Identify and record your talents, skills and qualifications for employment.
2. Match your talents, skills and qualifications with a desired career.
3. Identify your needs for additional knowledge and training.
4. Prepare a resumé, write a letter of application, obtain letters of recommendation and organize personal identification.
5. Fill out application forms accurately and neatly.
6. Identify and work to eliminate any negative characteristics which may hinder you in finding employment.
7. Continue learning and practicing human relation skills, decision making skills, technical skills and social skills to assure you of success in the career of your choice.

"Communicating You"

In previous chapters in this book, learning about interpersonal communication has involved you in a process of self-discovery and personal development. But developing our ability to communicate with others is an important practical skill as well. Leading business executives consistently indicate that the ability to communicate is the most important skill an employee can have.

When one is considered for advancement on the job—or for a salary increase—communication skills are among the criteria that are evaluated. In fact, good communication skills are usually necessary for getting a job in the first place. Being interviewed by a prospective employer involves the same kinds of skills and techniques described throughout this book; the major difference is that "interviewing is a conversation directed to a definite purpose other than satisfaction in the conversation itself."[1]

Preparing for an interview involves several tasks, including some, or all, of the following:

1. Self-analysis and job-analysis.
2. Gathering personal information.
3. Writing a resume.
4. Gathering references.
5. Writing a letter of application.

Self-Analysis and Job-Analysis

Self-analysis includes a written self-inventory of our talents and of our human relations skills. Once we have identified and recorded our talents and skills we can match them with a desired career. Those involved in hiring in the business and professional worlds have identified a consistent set of skills needed for most jobs. They suggest the following:

[1] Walter Van Dyke Bingham, Bruce V. Moore, and John W. Gustad, *How to Interview* (New York: Harper and Row, 1959), p. 3.

1. Aim at jobs in a field that has captured your interest.

2. Prepare yourself personally and professionally for the job.

3. Know the companies in your field of interest. Know what they do, and what their needs are.

4. Keep a file on each company. Find out any and all information from annual reports, bulletins, personnel directors, and employment offices.

5. Know the guidelines each company uses in screening applicants. People in personnel are professional.

6. Know if a company is looking for "generalists" or "specialists."

7. Be honest and straightforward.

8. Start a good relationship. Convey openhandedness. Business relationships are the same as other interpersonal relationships. They are built on trust.

9. Know your communicative and investigative skills and continue developing them. Skills in speaking, writing, and research are essential. The more polished one becomes in these areas, the more likely the possibility of success in any vocation or profession.

Matching your talents, skills and qualifications is a challenge. One way to begin is to interview individuals working in your chosen field. They can help you identify and specify requirements for "generalists" and for "specialists" in their fields. You could then make yourself a chart, keeping a record of your talents, skills, and qualifications—*and* noting your progress in the area of needs.

If you have not yet chosen a particular profession or vocation a variety of sources can help you narrow down your areas of interest. One excellent pamphlet provided by the U.S. Department of Labor's Bureau of Labor Statistics is *Matching Personal and Job Characteristics.* The pamphlet, which lists close to 300 occupations and identifies both personal and job characteristics, can be obtained at most libraries or by writing the Government Printing Office.[2]

Gather Personal Information

Collecting, organizing, and certifying personal identification is another important part of preparing for an interview. Information that may be needed includes health records, school records, driver's license, social security card or number, union card, work records, and so on. If you're applying for a job in the fields of art, design, etc., prepare a portfolio of your work. In these lines of work your prospective employer may ask to *see* what you *say* you can do!

[2] Public Documents Distribution Center, Pueblo, Colorado 81009.

Dress properly for the occasion.

Write a Resumé

One of the most important pieces of information you have, as a job applicant, is your resumé. A resumé is, literally, a summary—a brief description of your work experience and educational background that you feel qualifies you for a particular position. It should be written specifically to present the "best you," the "unique you," to your prospective employer. It is evidence that you have taken time to prepare carefully. Too many individuals think a resumé is something you compile "after you finish school" or "when you are older." Actually, most if not all prospective employers are impressed with even a limited resumé. The important thing is to start where you are, then re-do the resumé periodically.

In preparing the resumé, brainstorming with friends and relatives can provide the information you need. Also, it will help you see yourself in the most positive way (see Chapter 6 on brainstorming). You then can sift and refine the information until it says exactly what you want it to say in the best way. The resumé should be brief and direct, not wordy. It should be set up to be easily read and reviewed by a prospective employer. The simple one-page functional resumé will serve very well if you have limited work experience to cite. It should state, on one page, an objective and describe your experience.

The following are examples of ways you can do a one-page functional resumé.

Cora Faye Nelson
1132 River Lane
Anaheim Hills, CA. 92807
734 798-2323

JOB OBJECTIVE

Coordinating Supervisor for a Pre-School Nursery

QUALIFICATIONS

Leadership skills: President, Interclub Council. Vice-President Music
Club
Technical skills: Awards and trophies in arts and crafts
typing ability

WORK EXPERIENCE

1976–present   *Educational Assistant* at an elementary school.
Create and coordinate student activities
Prepare instructional material for math and reading
Evaluate student materials
Office duties

1974–1976   *Receptionist—Secretary*   Collected and prepared
property tax returns. Did checkbook and ledger
entries and balances. Handled delinquent
payments. File maintenance

1972–1974   *Receptionist-Secretary*   Compiled advertising
material
Handled direct sales. Delivered work to customers.

EDUCATION

Work in progress—Child Development courses
A.A. Child Development, Youngtown Community College 1976
Relevant courses outside major fields: speech communication,
Spanish, creative arts and crafts, theatre arts, typing, business
management, math

PERSONAL INFORMATION

Born July 6, 1952
Excellent health
Member of Honor Society
Outside interests: gardening, bowling, jewelry making, photography

REFERENCES

References available on request

Name
Address
Phone Number

Job Objective	Be specific about the field or position you are seeking. Identify any career requirements you feel are important.
Qualifications	Summarize and emphasize your key talents and skills (technical and interpersonal). Give examples of major accomplishments.

Employment

Past and present in chronological order; present job first.

Dates, job title(s), names and addresses of employers.

Briefly describe your job duties.

Educational Background

If your work experience is more impressive than your education, list it first. If your educational experience is more impressive, list it first.

Dates (month/year), name and address of institution (city/state). If you have degrees, give the dates they were granted. List major and minor emphasis areas. Describe scholarships, honors, special training, extra-curricular activities. Indicate if you paid for or contributed to the costs of your education.

possible additions:
Special Skills
Voluntary Community Service
Professional Memberships
Special Awards
Hobbies/Interests
Other Personal Information

References

List with telephone numbers and addresses (or indicate they will be furnished upon request).

Gather References

Gathering letters of recommendation are important because they verify our qualities and experience. Letters of recommendation are generally obtained from former teachers and professors for evidence of scholastic ability, and from former employers who know of your ability and dependability. Letters from close associates and friends, providing character references, may also be appropriate. When you request that someone write such a letter for you, it's a good idea to provide several questions for them to answer, to direct their comments. Never list someone as a reference if you haven't first checked it out with him or her. Letters of recommendation usually are not included with your resumé, but should be available if the interviewer asks for them.

Write a Letter of Application

A letter of application, like a resume, is also your introduction to a prospective employer. It too can "open doors" or "close doors," so it should be carefully written. Its purpose is to capture attention and create interest, so it must be brief and concise. The letter of application should provide the opportunity for an interview where you can "sell yourself." In writing your letter of application ask yourself:

"What is the situation and the need?"

"What can I do to gain attention and create interest?"

"What can I honestly claim about myself that will result in an interview?"

There is no "best way" to write the letter, but it should reflect your personality. It is important to:

1. Use a good grade of letter-size white bond paper.
2. Type neatly, checking sentence structure, spelling, and punctuation.
3. Address your letter to a specific person if possible. (Call the personnel departments of companies you're interested in, to find out to whom you should direct your letter).
4. State the kind of position you are seeking and why you are applying to the particular firm.
5. Be clear and brief.

Writing a letter of application is the customary way to ask for a personal interview. This is especially true in the following situations:

1. As a cover letter when you are mailing resumés.
2. When you are answering a want ad.
3. When the employer you wish to contact lives in another city.

The following letter may be helpful to you in preparing your letter of application.

1275 Carol Street
Santa Paula, Ca. 12345
January 15, 1981

George H. Wilson, Ed.D.
Director, San Luis Pre-School Nurseries
604 Berkley
San Luis, Ca. 54321

Dear Dr. Wilson

For the past four years I have served as an Educational Assistant at the Youngtown Elementary School. I have worked with grades one through four in order to gain experience with, and an understanding of, the different age groups.

Contributions I have made as an Educational Assistant include:

I created and coordinated social activities for each grade.

I prepared instructional materials for reading and math. These materials are now being used by other educational assistants.

I evaluated student materials in a satisfactory way for each of the instructors.

I did office duties to learn procedures and techniques of office management.

My career objective is to put my professional skills, human relation skills, and management skills to work as a Coordinating Supervisor in a pre-school nursery.

I am confident that I can make a positive contribution to one of the nursery schools in your area. I would appreciate the opportunity to personally discuss this with you. I will call your office next week to arrange a mutually convenient appointment.

Sincerely,

Cora Faye Nelson

Prepare for the Interview

With all of the previous preparation for the interview there are still other important areas to consider. You have learned the need for congruence in your verbal and nonverbal communication and that most of your communication is nonverbal so how can you extend your personality in the most positive way? The answer lies in considering the following preliminaries.

Preliminaries

"How should I act?" and "How do I look?" are important questions for the job applicant. The answers are relatively simple. Good manners are universal. Dressing appropriately for the interview is also important. However, acceptable dress style is determined by the times, the job requirements, and the environment.

From time to time, studies are done to provide suggestions or answers to these questions. Two Stanford University graduates, Jane Anton and Michael Russell, completed a study for Hayward State University and the Western College Placement Association. They sampled more than 100 personnel recruiters from 17 different industry groups. The recruiters had hired more than 75% of college graduates for their firms during 1972. What the study discovered about appearance and manners should be of interest:

Success in a job interview depends on careful preparation and planning.

1. A job applicant should dress neatly and act friendly when reporting for an interview.

2. While a young man creates a mildly positive impression if he wears a sport coat, shirt, tie, and slacks, he makes a stronger impression if he wears a suit.

3. To make a favorable impression you should not wear jeans, shorts, and sandals.

4. Failure to maintain eye contact with the recruiter, fiddling with objects on the desk, dirty fingernails, or speech larded with jargon create "mildly to strongly negative" impressions also.

5. Trimmed hair and beards on males made a more positive impression.

6. If the interviewer felt that an applicant was composed, cordial, cooperative, enthusiastic, and sincere, there was a strong positive influence.

7. Being assertive, intelligent, independent, and inquisitive created a mildly positive impression. Being grateful or jocular were considered neutral.

8. Applicants who appeared to be nervous, defensive, tense, quiet, skeptical, or shy earned negative ratings. Strong positive ratings were given if the interviewee seemed relaxed, balanced, and professional.

9. Casual interviews got a mildly positive rating, while those which seemed tense or dominated by either party were rated negatively.

Of special interest to liberal arts students is the fact that only communication majors received an overall positive rating from the majority of employer groups.[3] Of further interest—the results of a questionnaire sent to 142 business schools and 94 businesses (industrial corporations, utility, financial, retail, and life insurance industries), showed that businesses are seeking individuals with well-rounded communicative skills! The five most important communication skills were:
1. clear writing principles
2. how to listen and understand others
3. writing correctness
4. correct speaking techniques
5. report writing

The report further states that businesses want employees to know the techniques of *group problem solving* and persuasion. They also want them to know how to *resolve conflict.*[4]

Having prepared yourself to the best of your ability, according to the previous suggestions, and having determined how to act and how to dress, you can now search the want ads in newspapers and ask relatives, friends, and associates for help in seeking employment. Then write or call for appointments.

Being organized is important and will help you maintain poise and con-

---

[3] Employer Attitude and Opinions Regarding Potential College Graduate Employers.
[4] Journal of Organizational Communication, 7 (1978) p. 22.

fidence. Carry a sheet of paper or a notebook to keep a record of your appointments. Write down the date of the interview, the name of the company, the name of the employer, and the name of the person who will interview you. Then, if you want to make a second contact, the information you need is readily available.

Learning to fill out application forms is another important step in the application procedure. In almost all fields of employment the job applicant is asked to fill out an application form. College students are somewhat familiar with forms, having filled out registration forms, IRS forms, and so on. Since this is a part of the employment process you may want to obtain forms and become familiar with the standard procedures. Read the application form in its entirety before filling it out, then fill out the form neatly. Most of the information you will need for the application form will be contained in your resumé or your personal identification. Transferring the information is easier than trying to remember details. Carrying a pocket dictionary may be useful. Misspelled words could cost you an interview. A typed application form looks neater than a handwritten one so try to obtain an application form ahead of time from the personnel departments of the companies you are interested in. If this isn't possible, carry a couple of pens with you. As Murphy's Law says, "If anything can go wrong, it will," and pens have a nasty habit of going dry at the most inopportune times!

The Opening

If you have prepared yourself for the interview your written achievements have gotten you the interview. Now you have the opportunity to sell yourself personally. Because you have received training in speech, it should be somewhat easier for you to be enthusiastic and relaxed. Remember, you have been "invited" to an interview; but realize also that interviews are structured. The interviewer knows what he or she wants to know and how much time he or she can take to get the information. You will hopefully assist them in every way possible.

Once again, let's remind ourselves of the importance of, and need for, congruence in our verbal and nonverbal messages. If you apply this to the interview situation you should remember that from the moment you walk into the building your nonverbal behavior is vital! We impress before we even speak. We have already discussed the need for appropriate attire for the occasion. Being on time is another important nonverbal message. Courtesy and consideration of others must not be overlooked. Often there is a general receptionist to direct you to the appropriate office. Then a secretary will perhaps take you to the person doing the interviewing. If you do not know the name of the person doing the interviewing, ask the secretary for the name. Know how to pronounce and spell the name. Write it down. The secretary will probably introduce you to the interviewer. If the interviewer makes the first move, shake hands but remain standing until you are asked to sit down. (Do not smoke or chew gum!) After the social amenities are completed, usually the interviewer will begin the interview with an open-ended question. (Open-ended questions allow considerable freedom for you to determine the amount of information you give. An example of an open-ended question is, "Tell me about yourself." Closed questions may be answered with a "yes" or "no").

The Interview

Pretend you are the interviewee in the following dialogue. Identify the best answers.

Interviewer   "Why are you interested in this company?"

Interviewee   a. "The pay scale and benefits are good."
b. "I want to find a job close to where I live."
c. "I have learned a lot about your company. My training and goals qualify me for the job."

Obviously, there are numerous answers to such a question. Out of the choices given above, answer "c" represents the best response. It indicates that you have prepared for the interview and that you have goals; and it allows you the opportunity to "guide" the interviewer, since it leads to a discussion of your background. If you chose answer "c" the next two questions would probably be about your training and your goals. The interviewer would possibly continue as follows:

Interviewer   "What qualifications do you have for the job?"

Interviewee   a. "I have an AA degree in Business Administration."
b. "I have both theoretical and practical training."
c. "In addition to a degree in Business Administration I have training in speech communication. I've also been working since I was 12—my first job was delivering papers, which gave me a lot of experience working with people."

Remember, if the interviewer has access to your resumé he or she already knows about your degree, so answer "a" is not appropriate. Answer "b" is too general. Answer "c" elaborates and encourages the interviewer to continue with the next question. You told the interviewer you had goals so the interview could continue as follows:

Interviewer   "Tell me about your goals."

Interviewee   a. "I want to get a job and start my professional career."
b. "I'd like to be the president of the company."
c. "I have both long-range and short-range goals. They include gaining practical experience with theoretical training. I want to be an asset to my employer. My long-range goals are to keep myself balanced in all areas of my life."

Again, answer "c" allows the interviewer an opportunity to ask another typical question:

Interviewer   "You mention other areas of your life. What are your interests and hobbies?"

And so it goes! The interviewer should be given as much positive information as possible in the shortest possible time. Speak to the point. Don't ramble. Be honest. Anticipate the interviewer's questions if possible. By doing this you are making a good impression. You are assisting the interviewer. The interviewee who has assisted the interviewer by providing the information he or she wants to know has an edge over other applicants. This technique shows that you have qualities that are being sought in every vocation and profession: preparation, honesty, integrity, depth, and breadth.

You and your interviewer will want to cover your accomplishments with respect to human relations skills, leadership skills, decision–making skills, and technical skills. Since you have learned these skills in previous chapters, make "claims" about them. Claims can be made in either of two ways:

a. Begin with a general statement and move to a specific example.

b. Begin with a specific example and move to a general statement.

Let's return to our mock interview to see how it works. The interviewer has just asked about your interests and hobbies. The interviewee chooses to begin with a general statement and move to a specific example. He or she could say:

"I am a volunteer coach in my community."	*which leads to*	"It helps me develop empathy for and understanding of people of all ages."

or

"I enjoy people."	*which leads to*	"I serve as a volunteer P.E. coach in my community. It gives me a chance to work with and enjoy people from all walks of life."

If you wish to start with a specific and move to a general statement you could say:

"My job as a volunteer athletic coach gives me experience in recruiting and planning activities with people of all ages."	*which leads to*	"This shows I have learned to work successfully with people."

or

"As a volunteer athletic coach I train individuals and conduct activities for people of all ages."	*which leads to*	"This demonstrates my ability to cope with problems. I have learned how to deal with winners and losers."

"While doing volunteer   *which leads to*   I have developed a repu-
work in the community,   tation for being fair, de-
                                                         pendable, and honest."

    With either of these approaches, general or specific, you have provided
the interviewer with valuable information concerning your human relations
skills. If you have not had sufficient job experience to exhibit your leadership
skills, it is possible to convey these skills through a discussion of interests
and hobbies, as you have noted. If you have interests and hobbies, get that
information across as quickly as possible.

    Decision–making skills are vital in all areas of life. Our ability to make
decisions is directly related to emotional and intellectual stability. In the
business and professional world, "time is money." Do you have interests
and hobbies in areas which provide examples of effective decision–making
skills? If so, you could say:

"My job as a volunteer athletic coach helped me get a job in a sporting
goods store."

The interviewer could then ask:

"What were your responsibilities in that position?" Your reply could be:

Your prospective employer needs to have insight into your technical skills.

"I was a salesperson. I also assisted in ordering equipment and supplies. This job helped me develop the ability to make decisions. I had to anticipate what buyers would need and want, then balance those needs and wants with quality equipment at the lowest prices to benefit both the buyer and my employer."

Along with human relation skills, leadership skills, and decision–making skills, your prospective employer needs to have insight with respect to your technical skills. He or she needs to know that you are qualified for and capable of doing the specific job for which you are applying. Most companies consider the selection of an employee to be only a beginning. They plan to keep and continually train the person they hire; thus they need to know if you are "trainable." How can you expose or display conceptual and technical skills? You could express interest in a specific position or type of work. Then, if you are interested in and willing to consider other possibilities, watch for and listen to hints from the interviewer—but be honest. For instance, if the interviewer asks: "As a salesperson were you ever responsible for handling or repairing damaged equipment?" your answer could be:

"No, I did not do repairs. I could have, but my employer felt I was more valuable as a salesperson."

or

"No. I am not capable in technical areas. I believe I could be trained to do technical work but my real strength is in sales work."

Both of the answers are positive. The important thing to remember is to avoid pretense, at all times, during the interview.

There are other things your prospective employer wants to know about you. They can be categorized under the following areas:

1. Is this the right kind of work and environment for you?
2. Are you cooperative and do you get along well with people?
3. Do you plan to stay with this company or do you consider this a temporary job?
4. Do you have family responsibilities that will interfere with the job?
5. Are you dependable and reliable?
6. Can you accept constructive criticism?
7. How much, if any, of your personal time will benefit the company?
8. What motivates you? Are you motivated by salary, fringe benefits, opportunities to display creativity, or flexibility in hours?

Most of the interview questions are geared to gain this information. Provide as much of it as you want to and can in the most effective way possible. The following interview questions are ones that *may* or *may not* be asked prior to hiring. (The law forbids some questions. Others, while not barred by law might, at a later time, be the basis for legal action.) You may want to write out your answers to these questions and practice role-playing. Ask a family member, a friend, or classmate to participate with you. They, in asking the questions and listening to your answers, could provide some insightful feedback.

In verbalizing your answers you can also practice enunciation, pronunciation, vocal variety, and projection. Use your voice, your "musical instrument," to convey your personality at its best. Your voice can convey enthusiasm. Thus you will be able to project a more confident and knowledgeable image.

Even though some of the following questions cannot be asked, you can, through role-playing, become familiar with them. You can also develop courteous answers to the questions that will probably be asked.

Questions that should not be asked

What is your age?
What is your date of birth?
Are you married, divorced, separated, widowed, or single?
Do you have children? How old are they?
What church do you attend?
What is your race?
What sort of military discharge do you have?
Have you ever been arrested?
What organizations or clubs do you belong to?
Do you own or rent your home?
What does your wife/husband do?
Who lives in your household?
Have your wages ever been attached or garnisheed?

Questions that can be asked

How many years of experience do you have?
Why do you want to return to work? (to anyone who has been out of the job market for some time).
What are your career goals?
Who have been your prior employers?
Why did you leave your previous job?
Are you a veteran? Did the military provide you with job-related experience?
If you have no phone, where can we reach you?
Can you do extensive traveling?
Who recommended you to us?
What did you like, or dislike, about previous jobs?
What is your educational background? What schools did you attend?
What do you think are your strong points? Weak spots?
Do you have any objection if we check your former employer for a reference?
What specific skills do you have (writing, speaking, typing, etc.)?
Would you feel comfortable supervising other people?
What are your interests outside of work?
What previous experience have you obtained that would apply to this job?
What compensation are you looking for? *or* What motivates you?

Where do you want to be and what do you want to be doing ten years from now?

What do you want to be remembered for?

Are you applying to other companies?

When would you be available if we did have a position for you?

Communicate You

As an interviewee you should be aware that your interviewer is probably evaluating your personality while listening to your answers to the questions. Many interviewers use a checklist to determine their response to your hand-shake, disposition, and manner of dress. They make note of your voice and eye contact, and observe whether you are nervous or poised. Your command of grammar, your enthusiasm, and your initiative during the interview is also noted. It's important, however, not to try to evaluate how you are doing during the interview nor estimate the length of it. Maintain confidence throughout the entire interview, even if the interviewer is discouraging. Some interviewers may attempt to discourage you simply to test your reactions. Keep remembering you are "selling yourself," so you must be convincing. Prospective employers should not be expected to search for your assets. You must display them. If you can measure up to the job requirements—prove it!

The Closing

You don't have to wonder about when the interview is over. A skilled interviewer has the technique of terminating the conversation. You can recognize the nonverbal indications: Tone of voice and physical movement emphasize the verbal message. Be ready to thank the interviewer, and ask for permission to follow up in a few days with a telephone call. Say goodbye to the secretary and the receptionist.

After the Interview

You should not take notes during the interview; but, immediately after, write down pertinent information. It is a courtesy to write a thank you letter. Write the letter, then wait a few days to mail it. This gives you a chance to "polish" it.

Also, at this stage you may want to analyze the entire process of the interview. In so doing you will be able to improve your performance in a future interview.

Final Pointers

Finding the job and getting the job is both a scientific and a human process. In seeking employment, you need to analyze your talents, skills, and needs, then match them with the job opportunities; but you must also make the prospective employer aware of your value. We need also to consider, among all of the things suggested, a very human ingredient. Prospective employers prefer to hire people they already know have proven their value in another company or circumstance; people they know and like; and people who have been recommended by their friends and acquaintances. For these reasons, all of our communicative skills can, and should be, put to practice in a social way. Now perhaps more than ever we can appreciate our understanding of the communication process and the skills we have learned. Hopefully we have realized that interpersonal relationship skills and interview skills are really much more similar than different. The following list of suggestions will help us remember the key concepts as we enter or progress in our vocations and professions.

1. Prepare a portfolio to carry with you which contains: *a.* copies of your resumé; *b.* your letter of application; *c.* letters of recommendation; *d.* names, addresses, and telephone numbers of references; *e.* all personal identification; *f.* a sample application form you have filled out; *g.* a pocket dictionary; *h.* a couple of pens.

2. Dress properly for the occasion—in clothes you feel at ease in.

3. Go alone to the interview.

4. Know the exact location of your destination. Know how to get there. (Carry a map with you.) If using public transportation check schedules and allow for emergency situations. If driving your own car, allow extra time for possible traffic problems.

5. Write down the name, address, area code and telephone number of the organization. Also the name of the person you are to see.

6. Write down the time and date of your appointment. Be there ahead of time. Allow yourself time to relax after reaching your destination. Carry something with you to read for a few minutes. Be as relaxed as possible.

7. As you wait in the office, look around to see if there is any company literature available for reading. You may learn something important that will assist you in the interview.

8. Review the materials in your portfolio to refresh your memory. Be prepared to answer questions about the information on your resumé.

9. If you are given an application form, read it in its entirety before filling it out. Fill it out completely and neatly. Remember, it will represent you. Content and appearance are important. Check your portfolio for information and use your dictionary to check your spelling. Do not forget to sign the application.

10. Assist the interviewer by giving as much information as you can in the shortest amount of time.

11. Don't take notes during the interview. Write down the points you want to remember immediately after the interview.

12. Do not make negative comments about a former employer, teacher, or associate, even if criticism is justified.

13. If you have been fired, and are asked about it, tell the truth. Be as brief as possible, then move on to another subject.

14. Show you are interested in the company. Ask the questions you prepared when you researched the company.

15. Be careful about creating an unfavorable impression if you have left one or more previous positions. If it was to accept a position with a higher salary, or to go to school, your decisions will not be questioned.

16. Let the interviewer control the direction and pace of the interview, but provide a possible direction. Maintain good eye contact. Clearly pronounce your words and project your voice. Remember, speech is an extension of your personality. Watch the interviewer for nonverbal indications that your answers have been satisfactory.

17. Be prepared to ask some questions. Talk and listen. Balance the two. When the interviewer decides he wants you he or she will begin to discuss fringe benefits. Wait for the information.

18. Be honest, open, cooperative, and courteous. Admit any limitations, but be prepared to state why you are the best candidate for the job; why they should hire you instead of someone else. Know the key points you want to make about yourself and look for the right moment to introduce them. Be enthusiastic.

19. Be alert to signs indicating the interview is almost over. Sum up your interest in the job briefly and restate your strong points. Thank the interviewer for the time and consideration given to you.

20. It is possible that you may be offered the job at the close of the interview. Be courteous and tactful but ask for time to consider the offer. Set a definite time to give them your answer. Never accept a job offer if you have lined up other interviews. You may find a better one.

21. Write a brief thank you letter to the interviewer. Express appreciation. Restate your continuing interest and your qualifications.

Even with all of the preparation we'll usually experience some rejections. We may wonder why we didn't get the job. Bruce Bennett Associates Inc. (a West Coast organization which assists individuals in obtaining employment), has provided some important information you may want to review periodically:

Why Didn't I Get the Job?

What are the reasons why you as an applicant sometimes receive only a thundering silence from prospective employers after your interview has been completed? Frank S. Endicott, a well-known placement director at Northwestern University, recently made an interesting survey of 405 of the top, well-known firms to find these reasons.

1. Poor personality and manner: lack of poise; poor presentation of self; lack of self confidence; timid; hesitant approach; arrogance, conceit.

2. Lack of goals and ambitions, does not show interest, uncertain, and indecisive about the job in question.

3. Lack of enthusiasm and interest, no evidence of initiative.

4. Poor personal appearance and careless dress.

5. Unrealistic salary demands, more interest in salary than opportunity, unrealistic about promotion to top jobs.

6. Poor scholastic record without reasonable explanation for low grades.

7. Inability to express yourself well, poor speech habits.

8. Lack of maturity, no leadership potential.

9. Lack of preparation for the interview—failure to get information about the company and therefore unable to ask intelligent questions.

10. Lack of interest in the company and the type of job they have to offer.

11. Lack of extra-curricular activities without good reason.

12. Attitude of "What can you do for me," etc.

13. Objection to travel. Unwilling to relocate to branch offices or plants.

14. No vacation jobs or other work experience, and did not help finance his or her own education.[5]

Fortunately, most of these "reasons" emphasize the need for understanding and practicing the concepts, skills, and techniques you have been introduced to throughout this text!

FOR FURTHER INSIGHT

1. Write your "Life Story." Recording places, people and events will help you identify skills, techniques and qualifications you may have forgotten to list.
2. Take three sheets of paper. Write on them "Things I Have Done," "Things I Want To Do," and "Things I Need to Do." Refer to them regularly and reward yourself for accomplishments and progress.
3. Investigate organizations that use standard evaluations of employees and merit rating systems. Determine which system would be best for you.
4. Collect rating forms and screening forms that are used in the interviewing process. Evaluate yourself and ask others to evaluate you. Classify the results in categories of Strengths and Limitations. Reinforce the strengths and work to eliminate the limitations in part-time jobs and volunteer services.
5. Plan a role-playing interview situation. Ask leaders in business and industry to be guest evaluators. Showing interest in their needs and wants may cause them to be interested in you and your abilities.
6. Watch interviews on television. Observe the verbal and nonverbal strengths and limitations of those involved. Make a list of Do's and Don'ts. Role-play them with classmates, friends and relatives. Give and take positive criticisms.

[5] Bruce Bennett Associates Inc., 500 S. Main, Orange, Ca. 92665.

REFERENCES

Bachhuber, Thomas D., and Richard K, Harwood. *Directions: A Guide to Career Planning.* Boston, MA. Houghton, Mifflin Co., 1978

Bolles, Richard Nelson. *What Color Is Your Parachute?* Berkeley, Ca: Ten Speed Press, 1979.

Crystal, John and Richard N. Bolles, *Where Do I Go From Here With My Life?* The Crystal Life Planning Manual. Berkeley, Ca: Ten Speed Press, 1974.

Holland, John L., *Making Vocational Choices: A Theory of Careers.* Englewood Cliffs, New Jersey: Prentice-Hall Inc., 1973.

Lathrop, Richard, *Who's Hiring Who?* Berkeley, Ca: Ten Speed Press, 1977.

Miller, Donald B., *Personal Vitality Workbook: A Personal Inventory and Planning Guide.* Reading, MA. Addison-Wesley Publishing Co. 1977.

Occupational Outlook Handbook, 1978-79. Bulletin 1955. (Available from: Superintendent of Documents, U.S. Government Printing Office, Washington, D.C. 20402).

Standard Occupational Classification Manual. 1977. (Available from: Superintendent of Documents, U.S. Government Office, Washington, D.C. 20402).

Personal Interviews and Information from:

MacHale, Richard M. Western Regional Manager, Topflight Corporation.

Matkin, C. A., President of Soil Plant Laboratories.

Swenerton, Henry K. Manager of Executive Development for Southern California Edison Co.

Swenerton, Stephen K., Director of Marketing for Norris Industries, Thermador Waste King.

Millard, Frank., Manager for Walker and Lee Real Estate Co.

10 Communication in Organizations

FOR PREVIEW AND REVIEW

1. Organizations are human structures deliberately constructed to seek goals. Their two basic components are staff, or management, and line, or production.

2. The formal structure of an organization follows the chain of command by which authority is delegated from one person to another. The informal structure is based on the formal, but is influenced by such things as family ties, common interests, and congenial temperaments.

3. Downward communication in an organization usually discourages a high level of feedback, while upward communication helps employers understand their employees and gives employees a feeling of self-worth.

4. Managers who underrate the importance of expressing their appreciation of employees' efforts, listening sympathetically to employees' problems, and helping employees feel "in on things" damage employee morale.

5. By building feedback into communication situations, members of organizations can help avoid communication breakdowns.

INSTRUCTIONAL OBJECTIVES

After studying this chapter, you should be able to:

1. Explain the different characteristics of organizations.

2. Graphically describe organizations, including the components of staff and line, tall and flat organizations, formal and informal structures, and types of communications.

3. Analyze the communication flow in organizations, whether vertical, horizontal, or diagonal, and compare the advantages and disadvantages of each.

4. Provide examples of factors which influence employee morale and communication.

5. Define the different theories of management in terms of how they utilize the full potential of employees.

"Nobody Understands My Problems!"

We are all increasingly involved in the activities of many different groups and organizations, from the basic family group to local voluntary social or service clubs to highly complex national corporations or government agencies. We are continually being challenged to become effective participants and/or leaders in these varied groups. To do so, we need to understand the structures and purposes of organizations, as well as the ways in which people work and play together. We must learn to fit comfortably and productively into a culture composed of interrelated, competitive organizations.

Organizational Structures

Organizations are human groupings deliberately constructed to seek goals. Members of organizations vary in their authority, status, prestige, and friendships. *Authority* is reflected in the degree to which an individual is expected to direct the activities of certain other people. *Status* is determined by the relative rights and privileges an individual possesses. *Prestige* can be measured by whether or not others behave deferentially toward an individual. *Friendships* are the trust relationships individuals within an organization develop with each other. Each of these factors has an important effect upon communication in the organization by influencing the expectations that people have of who should communicate to whom, about what, and in what manner. We will find that these factors are prevalent in *any* type of organization, whether it be the family, a service club, fraternity, corporation, or government.

In most formal business organizations there are two basic components: the *staff,* or management (both upper and middle), and the *line,* or workers on the operative or production level. Upper management includes the board of directors, the president or general manager, and the vice-president(s). Middle management, which usually makes no major decisions, includes divi-

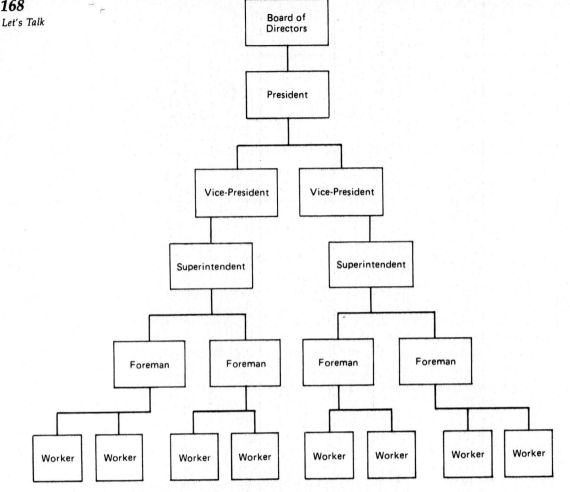

Figure 1. *Tall organizations have several levels of authority.*

sion and department heads. The line includes the operative supervisors and operative workers, which is where most of us are in our work positions.

Organizations can be classified as tall or flat. *Tall* organizations have several levels of authority from top-level management down to the bench-worker (Figure 1). Some problems with tall organizations are:

1. There are more distortions of communication as it travels from one level to the next;
2. Communication is generally slower;
3. More people are out of touch with what is going on outside their own unit;
4. Such organizations are usually "boss"-oriented;
5. There are usually more problems with staff groups (and wasted time with meetings).

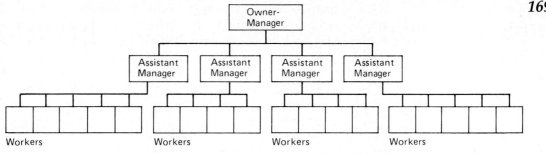

Figure 2. *Flat organizations have relatively few levels.*

Flat organizations have relatively few levels from top management down to the benchworker (Figure 2). Some problems with flat organizations are:

1. Each supervisor usually has more workers under him or her, and thus has less time for direct communication with any individual;
2. Because of the smaller number of management positions, there is less opportunity for advancement;
3. Supervisors, with a greater number of workers to handle, must be more skillful;
4. As the size of the organization increases, communication generally decreases and worker morale goes down.

Formal and Informal Organizations

Typically a business is divided into two large organizational systems—formal and informal. The *formal* organization is the one usually shown on organizational charts, and it is structured by means of a chain of command in which authority is delegated successively from one person to another. Organizations, then, have a formal division of labor, authority, and responsibility. Associated with the division of labor they also have a formal division of status and prestige.

When the formal structure of an organization is activated by a given group of people, a new dimension becomes evident. When individuals are placed in formal positions they begin to exercise their authority and thereby exert power, which is the effective use of authority. Esteem and prestige are also associated with persons in formal structures. Prestige is influenced by the individual's *position* in the formal structure, but esteem is *earned* by the person who occupies the position. It is possible that a person in a position of authority may have more prestige than esteem.

The formal channels of communication influence the nature of messages in several important ways. Organizations generally specify the nature of the messages that flow through formal channels. If they are spoken messages, they may be expected on certain set occasions, they may be restricted as to time, and they may take a certain form.

When the static structure of an organization is set in motion with a given complement of workers and managers, *informal* channels of communication (broken lines) develop. These channels may stem from a host of factors, such as previous acquaintance, family ties, common hobbies and interests, shared irritations, sexual attraction, and congenial temperaments. If the individual in position D is the son-in-law of the member in position A, an important informal communication channel between the two may be established. If the persons in positions B, F, G, and H frequently play golf together, they may establish another informal communication network. In any work situation, people find that they develop friendships or share common interests with some, but not all, of the others in the organization.

Another important factor in communication channels is the formal position of executive secretary. The executive secretary can act as a valve, turning off or on the flow of messages through the formal channels. Obviously, such gatekeepers, or persons who receive and control communication, are very important to any organization.

Often the messages that flow through informal channels (the *grapevine*), since they have no official sanction, are less carefully drafted and more loosely interpreted. Frequently they contain a high proportion of scuttlebutt. Properly guided, the informal organization can help build teamwork, company loyalty, and the kind of motivations that make people want to do their best. It may weld the group together more effectively than can

The grapevine is often faster than formal communication.

company policy and other formal tools of the organization. To try to do away with the informal organization is not only impossible, but also dangerous. Robbing employees of legitimate social satisfactions on the job leaves a vacuum that is usually filled by resentment and low morale.

The *grapevine* in any organization is variable, dynamic, and arbitrary, running back and forth across organizational lines and rapidly changing its course. Its characteristics include the following:

1. It cannot be eliminated or suppressed. (It cannot be fired, and if held down in one place, it crops out in another.)
2. It is fast, often faster than formal communication. (Company news, for example, may be disseminated by the grapevine, sometimes long before any *formal* announcement is made.)
3. It is influential. (It can make or break an employee, undermine a manager, or decrease morale.)
4. There is no way of holding it accountable for its mistakes.
5. It can be useful where formal communication is inappropriate.
6. It can bypass managers in the chain of command without difficulty because it is not confined by formal procedures.
7. It is often incorrect. (It is difficult for the participants in the grapevine to distinguish fact from myth or distorted information.)

Since most researchers agree that the grapevine cannot be uprooted, and since it is very effective for fast communication, management levels of organizations often try to feed it with accurate information. Many managers consciously use informal organizations as channels of communication and molders of employee morale.

The modern organization, then, is a message-processing system. Intertwined in the formal organizational structure is a complicated and ever-changing network of informal communication channels, through which flows the information that achieves a community of understanding to provide objectives, divide the work, develop morale, evaluate performance, and mobilize the resources of the organization. If the circulation of messages is good and the level of understanding high, the organization will be effective.

If the formal structure always matched the informal structure, most organizations would be highly productive and cohesive, and enjoy considerably more communication efficiency than they do now. Problems arise from the fact that the informal structure is changing, fluctuating, and dynamic, whereas the formal structure is static. Frequently the power and esteem that members earn in the informal organization differ from those in the formal organization. When this happens, communication problems often follow.

Communication and Communication Flow

There are several different types of communication in an organization: information received and disseminated, instructions given or received, approval given or received, problem-solving activities, and nonbusiness-related

Downward communication often does a poor job.

communications, or scuttlebutt. Except for the last, the purposes of these forms of communication are to inform, to evaluate, to instruct, and to motivate or persuade. Companies relying heavily upon formal written statements to spell out company policy find that such statements:

1. Do not get the job done.

2. Raise more questions than are answered.

3. Discourage individual initiative in carrying out policy.

4. Stifle upward communication.

5. Build resistance to new ways of doing things.

6. Cause dissatisfaction and serious misunderstanding among 75 percent of the managers affected.

7. Are no substitute for face-to-face discussion.[1]

Good speech communication has several important advantages as a medium of business discourse, in addition to speed and economy. It permits give-and-take, which, if properly used, results in more accuracy and less confusion. A spoken message can be more precisely timed than a written message, and its effect can be more immediately and accurately gauged. If the listener does not understand something, or disagrees, the speaker can deal with this problem on the spot. In addition, a spoken plea can add to the words the persuasive power of gestures, facial expressions, tone of voice, and so on. We seldom ignore a personal, spoken message, as we sometimes ignore a written memo.

The communication flow in an organization may be *vertical* (downward or upward), *horizontal,* or *diagonal.* The forces which determine how communication flows are:

1. The structure of the organization itself;

2. The policy set by top management;

3. The reasons that people communicate (to achieve a goal, to satisfy a need, or to improve a situation);

4. The subgroups in an organization (members of these talk to others in their own group the most); and

5. The fact that most people prefer to talk to higher-status rather than lower-status people.

In *downward communication* management has at its disposal a multitude of elaborate techniques and skilled staff assistance, yet with all this help it many times does a poor job. Fancy booklets, expensive films, and noisy public-address systems often fail to achieve employee understanding, affect attitudes, or increase productivity, which are basic tests of communication effectiveness. Sometimes these devices become ends in themselves; they are made prettier, fancier, or more expensive, without any evidence that this approach improves employee understanding. These downward communications may be technically efficient, but they are inefficient in improving human relations.

Interpersonal communication among people with different organizational status is inhibited by that difference. Good communication among equals is usually characterized by honesty, ease, consideration of all relevant information, and a high level of feedback. But when a supervisor has a conference with subordinates, honest, complete, easy communication with

[1] E. G. Bormann et al., *Interpersonal Communication in the Organization,* pp. 13–14. Copyright © 1969 by Prentice-Hall, Inc. Adapted by permission of Prentice-Hall, Inc., Englewood Cliffs, N.J.

adequate feedback is difficult to achieve simply because he or she has authority over the others and is in a position to control their fate.

According to Ralph Nichols,[2] if the chairman of the board calls in a vice-president and tells him or her something, on the average only 63 percent of the message is assimilated by the latter. If the vice-president relays the same message to a general supervisor, 56 percent of it arrives. If the supervisor gives it to a plant manager, 40 percent arrives. If the plant manager passes it along to a foreman, 30 percent is received. And if the foreman gives it to the group of workers who are his or her responsibility, only 20 percent of the original message will have passed down through the five levels of authority to reach its ultimate receivers! This declining efficiency in downward communication is illustrated in the following story:

> *A colonel issued the following directive to his executive officer: "Tomorrow evening at approximately twenty-hundred hours Halley's Comet will be visible in this area, an event which occurs only once every seventy-five years. Have the men fall out in the battalion area in utilities, and I will explain this rare phenomenon to them. In the event of rain, we will not be able to see anything, so assemble the men in the theater and I will show them films of it."*
>
> *Executive officer to company commander: "By order of the colonel, tomorrow at twenty-hundred hours Halley's Comet will appear above the battalion area. If it rains, fall the men out in utilities, then march to the theater where the rare phenomenon will take place, something which occurs only once every seventy-five years."*
>
> *Company commander to lieutenant: "By order of the colonel in utilities at twenty-hundred hours tomorrow evening, the phenomenal Halley's Comet will appear in the theater. In case of rain in the battalion area, the colonel will then give another order, something which occurs once every seventy-five years."*
>
> *Lieutenant to sergeant: "Tomorrow at twenty-hundred hours the phenomenal colonel will appear in the theater with Halley's Comet, something which happens every seventy-five years; if it rains, the colonel will order the comet into the battalion area."*
>
> *Sergeant to squad: "When it rains tomorrow at twenty-hundred hours, the phenomenal seventy-five-year-old General Halley, accompanied by the colonel, will drive his comet through the battalion area theater in utilities."* [3]

Recently, some major companies with a more integrated type of management have realized the advantages of *upward communication*. They have found that a two-way system of communication provides the feedback loop necessary for understanding employee attitudes. In a report by Earl Planty and William Machaver, several values of effective upward communication were listed:

Values to Superiors

1. *It is through unobstructed communication upward that we learn how fertile and receptive the soil is for communication downward.*
2. *If we are to gain understanding and full acceptance of our decisions, subordinates*

[2] Bormann et al., pp. 188–89.

[3] Adapted from Paul H. Dunn, *The Ten Most Wanted Men* (Salt Lake City: Bookcraft, Inc., 1967), p. 64.

*must be given the opportunity to participate in their making, or at least to discuss
the merits and defects of proposed actions.*

3. *From upward communication we discover whether subordinates get the meaning
from downward communication that is intended by their superiors.*

4. *Effective upward communication encourages subordinates to offer ideas of value to
themselves and the business.*

Values to Subordinates

1. *Upward communication helps satisfy basic human needs.*

2. *Employees who are encouraged to talk directly and frankly with their superiors get
a release of emotional tensions and pressures which otherwise might find outlet in
complaining to other members of the company and the community, or in a loss of
interest or efficiency.*

3. *Unlike the organizational structure of a church, school, or other similar organization, industry is essentially authoritarian, which makes it even more necessary that
every opportunity be given subordinates to express their views freely and to make
their influence felt.* [4]

Although management may realize the benefits of upward communication, there are several barriers to be overcome. Some of these barriers are:

1. The physical distance between superior and subordinate;
2. Time and complexity;
3. Dilution and/or distortion;
4. The superior's attitudes;
5. Lack of rewards; and
6. Apprehension.

An open-door policy, participation in social groups, and letters from employees should be encouraged. The main advantage of the employee letter,
or some sort of suggestion box, is that it encourages employees to make
their ideas known. The same effect is achieved, to a lesser extent, by the
open-door policy and social groups. The family relationship is also important; the employer should make an effort to establish a good relationship
between employees' families and the organization. It is also important that
the employer actually make use of the communications from the workers, or
they will stop taking the time to communicate.

Horizontal communication also plays an important role in organizational
communication flow. All enterprises depend on voluntary horizontal channels of communication at all levels to speed information and improve understanding. Horizontal and diagonal relationships exist between personnel of
varying status in different divisions, and direct communication between
them substitutes for making a message follow the chain of command up
through one or more superiors, horizontally across a level of organization,
and then down to the particular recipient. Enterprises simply cannot operate
in such a stilted fashion because the communication time would be excessively long and the quality of information inferior.

---

[4] Adapted from Earl Planty and William Machaver, "Upward Communications: A Project in Executive
Development," *Personnel*, January 1952, (New York: American Management Association, Inc.,
1952), (304–18). Adapted by permission of the publisher.

Inevitably, the effectiveness and the communication climate of any organization depend to a great extent upon the management of the organization. According to Lawrence Appley of the American Management Association, "Management is simply the business of getting other people to do the things that must be done."[5] And to get others to do the things that must be done, it is imperative that managers keep in communication with them. Every manager must see that objectives are set, work clarified, performance reviewed, and problems solved. Almost everyone today has management responsibilities of one kind or another, and all depend heavily upon speech communication in even their routine functions. Each day is filled with appointments, interviews, conferences, and meetings.

How does the leader do this complicated job? Leaders do not "handle" people. They persuade and guide them, and organize their tasks, to accomplish results. They develop and maintain a system of communication. A number of their critical functions depend on their ability to communicate. The leader in a modern organization must plan, organize, direct, control, delegate duties and responsibilities, and develop subordinates. In order to accomplish these tasks, the effective manager uses a process that involves setting up objectives; clarifying the steps to reach the objectives (including communication of functions, responsibilities, and authority for decision making to appropriate subordinates); and reviewing the work in the light of the established objectives.[6] Speech communication plays a key role in each of the steps, from the discussion and establishment of overall goals to the final evaluation and review.

The higher one goes in the chain of command, the more concerned he or she will be with human relations problems, simply because people are all one has to work with. The minute a person is taken from the bench and made a supervisor he or she is removed from the basic production of goods and must begin relating to individuals instead of nuts and bolts. People are different from things, and the supervisor is called upon for a completely different line of skills. The new tasks require him or her to become a special kind of a person, and the first step in this development is to become a good listener.

Dr. Earl Planty of Johnson and Johnson states that, "By far the most effective method by which executives can tap ideas of subordinates is sympathetic listening in the many day-to-day informal contacts within and outside the work place. There is no full-blown system that will do the job in an easier manner. . . . Nothing can equal an executive's willingness to hear."[7]

Unfortunately, many executives seem unaware of the importance of

[5] Bormann et al., p. 14.

[6] Bormann et al., p. 49.

[7] From Alfred G. Clarke, "How to Learn by Listening," *Dun's Review and Modern Industry*, 65 (April 1965), 46.

[8] Chart entitled "Morphological Synthesis" from *Psycho-Dynamic Synthesis: The Key to Total Mind Power* by Dr. Myron S. Allen. Published by Astara's Library of Mystical Classics, 1979. Reprinted by permission of the author.

Figure 3 — Morphological synthesis

Each of the vertical strips, if separate and movable, may be adjusted to any position in relationship to the other strips, enabling us to gain a greater perspective of and better insight into what is involved in any communication situation within the organization.

Areas of Communication	Functions of Management	Purposes of Communication	Interests Inherent in Communications	Marks of Effective Communications	Elements of an Information System	Management-Labor Relations
		Instruction				
	Leadership	Acquisition of Knowledge				Management-Labor Understanding
Areas of Communication	Problem Solving	Develop Understanding	How the Receiver Will Benefit			Management Wants to Know
Intra-Management	Decision Making	To Help Management Do Its Job	Opportunity to Participate	Founded on Mutual Interests	Everybody Profits if Followed	Supervision Wants to Know
In-Plant Operations	Control	Humanizing Management	Raise Level of Self Respect	Gains Immediate Attention	Clearly Reflects Visual Objectives	Foremen Want to Know
Sales	Authority	Coordination	People Are More Interested in People	Makes use of Standard Terms	Utilizes Two-way Communication	Employees Want to Know
Customers	Responsibility (Profit)	Develop Confidence	Elimination of Doubt	Language Level Is Appropriate	Prepares for Action	Morale Is Based on Communication
Suppliers	Load Distribution		Freedom from Resentment	Educational Level Recognized	Is Sensitive to Entire Community Affected	Economic Security Information Given
Financial			Occupational Social Status	Uses Time Well, Says Something	Acquires and Handles Ideas	
Competitors				Can Not Be Misunderstood	Ties in With Responsibilities	

Figure 3. Morphological synthesis.[8]

listening to their workers, making sure they feel "in on things," and expressing appreciation for the work they do. Managers ranked these three factors *lowest* in importance to employee morale. When hourly workers were asked to rank ten morale factors in the order of actual importance to them, their ranking was: (1) feeling their work was fully appreciated, (2) feeling "in on things," (3) receiving sympathetic help from superiors on personal problems.[9] Management must recognize its responsibility to listen as well as to speak. As an ancient philosopher once remarked, "Nature has given us two ears and one mouth, so we may *hear* twice as much as we speak."

Communication Problems

Several characteristics of organizations create communication problems. An organization is a series of interrelated groups, and people tend to communicate with those close to themselves. Group alliances form, each with its own goals, sanctions, rewards, and punishments. Built into the organization are various divisions, such as management, marketing, finance, production, data processing, each of which develops its own value system, specialized sets of meanings, jargon, etc. Employees are structured into different systems of relationships, and this sets up expectancies, based on structure, of what another group or part of the organization is supposed to do. It also requires that the persons involved know to whom they should communicate various kinds of information.

Among other factors, the effectiveness of communication depends on the prior feelings and attitudes that the people concerned have about each other, the preexisting expectations and motives of the communicators, how the subordinate's needs are satisfied, and the reaction of the subordinate to communication from the superior.

At every step in the communication process, poor communication may result in the failure to define objectives and responsibilities clearly. When this happens, people are unsure of what they are to do, and accurate, meaningful performance becomes difficult, if not impossible. How many times have problems occurred because we expected someone to communicate with us, and they didn't (and *we* didn't check it out!). An illustration of the possible results of such a breakdown in communication may be seen in Figure 4.

If we are realistic about the workings of an organization, we will not expect to avoid completely the communication breakdowns stemming from misunderstanding, disagreement, and misinformation. We can, however, do a great deal to dissipate their destructive potential by consciously building *feedback* into our communication situations, by distinguishing between disruptive and productive disagreements, and by discriminating between statements of fact and statements of inference. (See Chapter 5.)

[9] From Ralph Nichols' recording "Listening Is Good Business," distributed by Edward M. Miller and Associates, Inc., Grand Rapids, Mich.

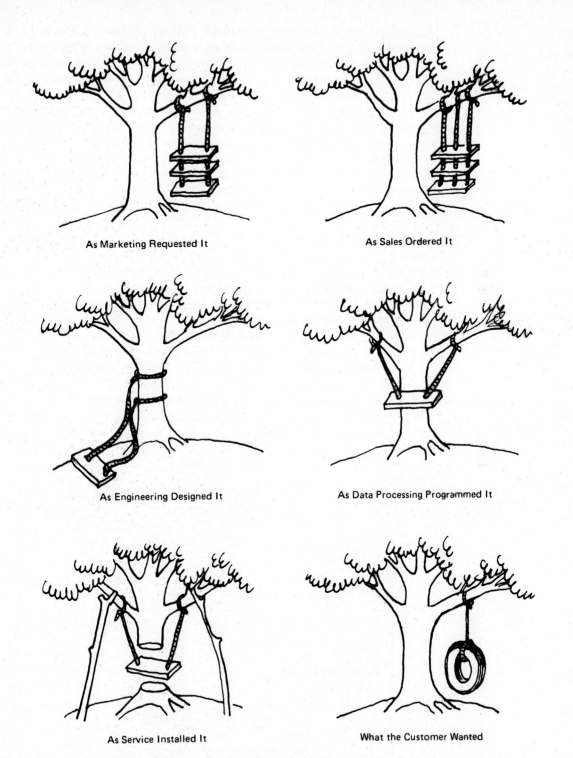

Figure 4. *Communication breakdowns make performance difficult.*

Communications problems are really human problems. Recognizing and understanding human individuality are the keys to effective communication. In an organizational setting, this means taking into consideration not only passing information up, down, and across the line, but also such subtle factors as emotional reactions, attitudes, and feelings.

Most people are relatively good communicators. When they aren't communicating as well as could be expected, it is usually the working climate that is putting up barriers which freeze reliable exchanges. The values of honesty, sincerity, and trust are vital in creating a climate in which communications grow. Where they do not exist, communications will be faulty, no matter how many methods or techniques are used.

A vital prerequisite for effective communication, then, is a proper climate. This must begin with the initial willingness of the chief executive to take a fresh look at his or her own communication activities and attitudes. This person is the pacesetter in building a favorable climate. He or she must first be honest with himself or herself, and must not merely give lip service to the idea of communication.

One of the first recommendations for establishing effective communication in any organization is for the top managers to go out into the plant and offices regularly and often to talk to the employees about problems. Then, over a period of time, subordinates will begin to place more trust and confidence in the communications being passed on from top management. It is

Effective upward communication encourages subordinates to offer ideas of value.

important that such communications also keep the employees well informed concerning their mutual interests in company success.

Management must recognize its responsibility to listen as well as to speak. If the boss is not a good listener, those who report to him or her will soon stop trying to communicate.

Improving communications involves building a relationship between superiors and subordinates in which disclosure is encouraged and rewarded. It must be a supportive relationship—one in which subordinates feel that the superior will not take advantage of them if they fully speak their minds. For full disclosure to occur, subordinates must know that they can express their feelings, difficulties, and opinions without fear of reprisal. They must look upon the superior as a source of help rather than as an all-powerful judge.

If management is successful in establishing a favorable climate, this attitude will then radiate downward throughout the entire organization. In order to sustain this climate, management must be employee-centered, keep an open door, listen actively, and allow time for communication. If these things are done, there will be big dividends in the way of increased efficiency and production, more effective communication, and higher employee morale. Most employees desire to help their company, and communication is the key to tapping this great potential.

Theories of Management

Two theories of management—called "Theory X" and "Theory Y" by Douglas M. McGregor—have important implications for organizational communication.[10] Theory X assumes people are inherently opposed to working and must be coerced by any means before they will put forth any effort. Theory Y suggests that people will naturally expend effort in work as well as in pleasure, and do so because of the rewards associated with their efforts.

The basic assumptions of both theories are as follows:

Theory X

1. The average human being dislikes work and will avoid it if possible.
2. Because of this characteristic, most people must be coerced, controlled, directed, and threatened with punishment to get them to put forth adequate effort toward the achievement of organizational objectives.

Theory Y

1. The expenditure of physical and mental effort in work is as natural as play or rest.
2. External control and the threat of punishment are not the only means for trying to achieve organizational objectives. People exercise self-direction and self-control in service of objectives to which they are committed.
3. Commitment to objectives is a function of the rewards associated with their achievement.

[10] From "The Human Side of Enterprise," *Management Review*, November 1957, pp. 22–29, 88–92. Copyright © 1957 by the American Management Associations, Inc. Adapted by permission of the publisher.

Theory X

3. The average human being prefers to be directed, wishes to avoid responsibility, has relatively little ambition, and wants security above all.

Theory Y

4. The average human being learns, under proper conditions, not only to accept, but to seek responsibility.
5. The capacity to exercise a relatively high degree of imagination, ingenuity, and creativity in the solution of organizational problems is quite common.
6. In modern industrial life, the intellectual potentialities of the average human being are only partially utilized.

Theory X is the set of assumptions about human nature and human behavior upon which traditional organizations are based. These assumptions are behind every managerial decision or action, and are inadequate for the full utilization of human potentialities. Assumptions of Theory X reflect an underlying belief that management must counteract an inherent human tendency to avoid work, that the dislike of work is so strong that even the promise of rewards is not generally enough to overcome it, and that paternalism is necessary for the masses.

The relatively new knowledge concerning motivation which tells us that humans are wanting animals, with a hierarchy of needs, helps point out some of the glaring inadequacies of Theory X. A fact of great significance that Theory X ignores is that a *satisfied* need is *not* a motivator of behavior. If we accept Maslow's description of the hierarchy of needs (physiological, safety, social, egoistic, self-fulfillment, intellectual, and aesthetic), and if we accept the belief that one need has to be satisfied before the next can be a motivator, it is easy to see how Theory X prevents attainment of higher needs. Traditional management can and does use the first two needs to motivate and control as long as the individual is struggling for subsistence. Theory X managers, however, cannot use social, egoistic, self-fulfillment, intellectual, and aesthetic needs as effective motivators. Management cannot provide a person with self-respect, nor can it satisfy a need for self-fulfillment. Management *can* create conditions whereby one is stimulated to satisfy these needs for oneself, or it can thwart one's endeavors—but neither of these is control. Direction and control are essentially useless in motivating people whose important needs are beyond the physiological and safety levels. Thus, people who are deprived of satisfaction of certain needs are similar to people who are nutritionally deprived. Both exhibit abnormal behavior, behavior that is in harmony with the assumptions of Theory X: indolence, passivity, resistance to change, lack of responsibility, willingness to follow the demagogue, incessant demands for economic benefits.

Many human problems in organizations arise because relatively healthy people are asked to participate in work situations which force them to be dependent, subordinate, and submissive, and which do not require them to reach their full potential. Healthy human beings tend to find dependence, subordination, and submission frustrating. They prefer to be independent, and aspire to positions equal to or higher than those of their peers. They wish to be active and to develop their abilities. Frustrations resulting from the pressures of modern organizations can lead to regression, aggressiveness, tension, and the restriction of creativity. These, in turn, often lead to conflict and make for major breakdowns in communication.

Adherence to Theory X assumptions prohibits clear communication— whether it be between father and son or manager and subordinate. Most of the communicative interactions are downward and take the form of commands; in this situation there is a much greater chance that ego-involvement or a defensive climate will cause misunderstandings.

Theory Y is more consistent with current research knowledge in human behavior. This theory can lead to higher motivation and greater realization of both individual and organizational goals. The assumptions of Theory Y are dynamic rather than static; they indicate the possibility of human growth and development, and they stress the necessity for selective adaptation rather than a single absolute form of control. Most important, these assumptions point up the fact that the limits on human collaboration in the organizational setting are not the limits of human nature, but of management's ingenuity in discovering how to realize the potential represented by its human resources. If employees are lazy, indifferent, unwilling to take responsibility, etc., Theory Y implies that the causes lie in management's methods of organization and control.

People are more effectively motivated when they are given some degree of freedom in the way they do their work than when every action is prescribed in advance. They do better when they are allowed some degree of decision making about their jobs than when all decisions are made for them. They respond more adequately when they are treated as personalities rather than as cogs in a machine. In short, if the ego-motivations of self-determination, self-expression, and a sense of personal worth can be tapped, the individual can be more effectively energized. The use of external sanctions or pressuring for production may work to some extent, but not as well as more internalized motives do. When the individual comes to identify with the job and with the work of the group, his or her human resources are much more fully utilized in the production process.

Adherence to Theory Y assumptions in any type of organizational setting will provide for an easier flow of communication upward, downward, and horizontally, and will result in more effective, less threatening interactions and communications among people.

Two other approaches to management are the systems approach and the contingency approach. The systems approach focuses on the interdependence of the parts inside an organization and on the interdependence of the organization and its environment. This systems concept alerts managers to these interdependencies. The contingency approach stresses the need for managers to tailor their practices to specific situations, recognizing that no *single* style will be effective in different structures and for different purposes.

Management by objectives, or MBO, emphasizes the initiative of the subordinate in setting goals within the framework provided by the superior.

The superior and subordinate, in discussion, agree upon a set of goals. Then, after a specified period of time, the subordinate reviews his or her progress and reports to the superior. MBO helps to clarify goals and expectations, leading to improved planning, clear standards for control, improved motivation, more objective appraisal, and better morale. These results are consistent with the motivational theory that most people bring unsatisfied higher-level needs for affiliation, power, achievement, esteem, and self-fulfillment to their jobs and respond to the opportunities to satisfy them that MBO seems to provide.[11]

FOR FURTHER INSIGHT

1. Evaluate yourself in terms of your capacity for hard work, your ability to work with and through people, your ability to accept responsibility and make decisions, and your ability to communicate.
2. Agree or disagree with the following: "One must be a follower to be a leader."
3. Ask two people you know who are in leadership positions to react to the following: "One cannot really listen to a person toward whom one feels fundamentally superior."
4. Think of a situation in which you played (or might play) a managerial role. Discuss the differences in how you might approach your management activities of planning, organizing, leading, and controlling if you applied each of the following perspectives: getting the task done, being concerned about people, and being concerned about administrative duties.
5. Make a list of occupations you feel are important and worthwhile. Do they have anything in common? Does society in general rate these occupations as highly as you do? If not, why not?
6. Prepare a list of objectives for your job if you presently have one. If not, prepare a list of objectives for any job you have held in the past. If your list is for your current job, show it to your supervisor and ask how well it matches his or her expectations for the job.
7. Review any job experiences you have had. Did your supervisors seem to accept the assumptions of Theory X or of Theory Y? Did their attitudes affect your production on, or enjoyment of, your job?

REFERENCES

Argyris, Chris. *Integrating the Individual and the Organization*. New York: John Wiley & Sons, Inc., 1964.

Barnard, Chester I. *The Functions of the Executive*. 30th Anniversary Edition. Cambridge: Harvard University Press, 1968.

Bormann, Ernest G., W. S. Howell, R. G. Nichols, and G. L. Shapiro. *Interpersonal Communication in the Modern Organization*. Englewood Cliffs, N.J.: Prentice-Hall, Inc., 1969.

Buzzotta, V. Ralph, R. E. Lefton, and Manuel Sherberg. *Effective Selling Through Psychology: Dimensional Sales and Sales Management Strategies*. St. Louis: Psychological Associates, Inc., 1972.

Dessler, Gary. *Organization Theory: Integrating Structure and Behavior*. Englewood Cliffs, New Jersey: Prentice-Hall, Inc., 1979.

[11] From *Contemporary Management* by David R. Hampton, copyright 1977 by McGraw-Hill, Inc., pp. 136, 137.

Dunnette, Marvin, and W. K. Kirchner. *Psychology Applied to Industry*. New York: Appleton-Century-Crofts, 1965.

Guetzkow, Harold. "Communications in Organizations." In *Handbook of Organizations*, ed. J. G. March. Chicago: Rand McNally & Company, 1965. pp. 534–73.

Hampton, David R. *Contemporary Management*. New York: McGraw-Hill Book Company, 1977.

Holwerda, Tom. "Communication Flow in the Organization." Orange Coast College, unpublished syllabus, 1971.

Hunt, Gary T. *Communication Skills in the Organization*. Englewood Cliffs, New Jersey: Prentice-Hall, Inc., 1979.

Huseman, Richard C., Cal M. Logue, and Dwight L. Freshley. *Readings in Interpersonal and Organizational Communication*, 3rd edition. Boston: Holbrook Press, Inc., 1977.

Katz, D., and R. Kahn. *The Social Psychology of Organizations*, 2nd edition. New York: John Wiley & Sons, Inc., 1978.

Koontz, Harold, and Cyril O'Donnell, *Essentials of Management*, 2nd edition. New York: McGraw-Hill Book Company, 1977.

McGregor, Douglas M. "The Human Side of Enterprise." *The Management Review*, November 1957, pp. 22–29, 88–92.

——. *The Human Side of Enterprise*. New York: McGraw-Hill Book Company, 1960.

Morse, J. J., and J. W. Lorsch, "Beyond Theory Y." *Harvard Business Review*, May-June 1970, pp. 61–68.

Schein, Edgar H. *Organizational Psychology*. Englewood Cliffs, New Jersey: Prentice-Hall, Inc., 1980.

11 Communication with Other Cultures

FOR PREVIEW AND REVIEW

1. Communicating with other cultures involves interpersonal interactions with people from backgrounds differing widely from our own.
2. It is important for us to understand and allow for cultural differences if we are to communicate effectively.
3. Our attitudes (social perceptions, world view, ethnocentrism, values, stereotypes, and prejudices) are a major factor influencing our interactions with those from other cultures.
4. Both the structure of language and vocabulary, including denotative and connotative word meanings, can be a barrier to intercultural communication.
5. Nonverbal factors that are particularly significant in communication with other cultures are space and territoriality (proxemics), time, and kinesics (body language, movement, gestures, facial expressions).
6. Recognition of our common humanity, the ability to see each person as an individual, and a genuine desire to understand each other are necessary if we are to have successful communication with other cultures.

INSTRUCTIONAL OBJECTIVES

After studying this chapter, you should be able to:
1. Define culture and intercultural communication in more than one sense.
2. Explain the significance of thought patterns in communications with persons from other cultures.
3. Identify and illustrate the influence on communication of perception, world view, ethnocentrism, values, stereotypes, and prejudices.
4. Discuss the significance of the Sapir-Whorf hypothesis in communication with those from other cultures.
5. Analyze the effect of language differences on communication, including vocabulary, denotation/connotation, and structure.
6. Recognize and discuss the differences in nonverbal cues from culture to culture, including space/territoriality, time, and kinesics.
7. Explain the qualities of a good intercultural communicator, identifying those that you already have, and those that you need to develop.

"What Do You Mean When You . . . ?"

. . . as one comes to understand people who live by institutions and values different from one's own, at the same time one comes to see that these people are, nevertheless, at bottom quite like one's own people. The alien culture at first appears to us as a mask, enigmatic or repugnant. On closer acquaintance we see it as a garment for the spirit; we understand its harmonies and appreciate them. Finally, as acquaintance goes deeper still, we do not see, or for a time forget, the culture, but look only to the common humanity of the men and women beneath.[1]

The above quotation serves as a keynote for our discussion of some of the elements of communication with other cultures. As we know, effective communication does not occur automatically, simply because you and I speak the same language and both of us hear what is said. Many of the problems discussed in previous chapters will also apply to intercultural communication, because it involves interpersonal interaction. But there are some other problems involved here. We need to discuss (1) barriers to communicating with a person from another culture, and (2) what we can do to become more effective communicators with those from other cultures.

First of all, what do we mean by "communication with other cultures"? Second, why is it important to us? There are as many definitions of culture as there are of communication. Most of us have some idea of what is meant when we talk of cultural differences. We can distinguish different cultures in several ways: racial (Black, Oriental, Caucasian); ethnic or national (English, French, German, Polish, Jewish, Greek); socioeconomic (wealthy, middle class, or poor; rural or urban). Cultures also develop around ways of life and value systems, such as age/youth, the drug culture, and others. Most of these cultural differences we can find here in our own country. For what is the United States if not a cultural mix? Most of us come in contact with those

[1] From "The Study of Culture in General Education" by Robert Redfield from *Social Education* (October 1947) p. 262. Reprinted with permission of the National Council for the Social Studies and Robert Redfield.

It is important that we accept and understand cultural diversity.

from other cultures every day. This makes our study in this chapter especially important and relevant.

In the traditional anthropological sense, culture is "the sum deposit of experiences, beliefs, values, attitudes, perceptions, ways of doing things, ways of living, religion, habits, modes of dress, uses of space, conceptualization of time, and social organization shared by a geographically bound group of people over generations."[2]

This definition was true as long as cultures were highly stable and changed slowly. Before World War II this was generally true. Many people never traveled very far from home, and had little opportunity to learn about other ways of life. Often they lived, essentially, in isolation.

Then there were wars which brought many people in contact with other cultures (Europe, Korea, Viet Nam), and television and jet travel contributed to the end of cultural isolation. Now we are not only a highly mobile society, but we are also exposed every day to other cultures, either in person, on television, or both. The fact that we live in a "shrinking" world is one reason for us to discuss communication with other cultures. A more important

[2] From "Intercultural Communication in the Group Setting" by Richard E. Porter from *Speech Communication: A Basic Anthology* by Ronald J. Applbaum, Owen O. Jenson and Richard Carroll. New York: Macmillan Publishing Co., Inc., 1975.

reason is that we encounter culturally caused problems in communication within our own nation, between ethnic and racial groups, and educational, economic, and age groups. More and more we are working, interacting, and communicating with culturally different people. This exposure to different ideas and ways of life *can* broaden our understanding and enrich our experience, *if we let it*. Cultural diversity adds interest—and also presents a challenge to our abilities as communicators. It is important that we accept and understand this diversity if we are to communicate successfully with those from other cultures, whether at home or in other countries.

We know that

. if we choose to venture beyond our national boundaries, we will find even greater differences in cultures. Religious, philosophical, political, economic, and social-role views may be greatly different from our own, as may be communities, modes of life, forms of work, degrees of industrialization, and social organizations. In these cases, people are noticeably different from ourselves in their ways of life, customs, and traditions.[3]

An awareness of ourselves and of others as *culture-bearers* will help us better understand and interact more effectively with each other. It is commonly agreed that difficulties in human relationships mount as people try to talk with other people across barriers caused by cultural differences. We see every day—locally, nationally, and internationally—the complex problems that arise as people from one culture try to communicate their knowledge, questions, feelings, and preferences to people from another culture. Among the many variables in the communication process, there are four we will discuss as they relate to or are influenced by culture: thought patterns, attitudes, language, and nonverbal communication.

Thought Patterns

One of the major difficulties in communicating with someone from a different culture occurs if that person has been trained in thought processes or ways of reasoning different from ours.[4] A major difference in thought patterns becomes evident if we contrast Western cultures with Eastern cultures. Most Western cultures, including our own, view humans as rational, capable of factual, sound reasoning; people are presumed to be free, having the right to decide things for themselves. This is called the Aristotelian mode of reasoning. In contrast, many cultures of Asia and the Orient have non-Aristotelian views. For instance, the Taoists believe that people are *not* rational, that truth is not to be conceived in terms of reason and logic, that human life is not free, that we achieve success only when we recognize this limitation and make ourselves dependent on the harmonious and beneficent

[3] Ibid., p. 244.

[4] Much of the material on "Thought Patterns," "Attitudes," "Language," and "Nonverbal Factors" is based on *Intercultural Communication: A Reader* by Larry A. Samovar and Richard E. Porter (Belmont, Cal.: Wadsworth Publishing Co., Inc., 1976).

*Communication with
Other Cultures*

forces of the universe. They believe in the wisdom of being foolish, the success of failure, the strength of weakness, the futility of contending for power. Their basic philosophy is the need to achieve harmony with the universe. A Taoist believes one waits for truth to appear, while it is the Western tradition to actively seek the truth. If we are aware of these differences in thinking, we are more likely to understand the frame of reference from which someone is communicating, and we are more likely to interpret their communications accurately.

Another stumbling block in communication among cultures is the varying focus of thought patterns. People from some cultures tend to think in terms of the concrete, tangible world; if they can't experience it with their senses, they can't understand it. People from other cultures can also deal with the concrete, but are just as likely to think and communicate in terms of abstractions and symbols. If we don't recognize and allow for this difference in some cultures, we will encounter difficulties in communicating.

Another problem is the tendency of many Americans to think and speak in terms of either/or statements. (See discussion of two-valued orientation, Chapter 5.) We often look for absolute distinctions and neglect fine shadings of difference. While Americans seem to consistently try to sharpen the differences, the Japanese pattern of thinking, for example, strives to assimilate such differences.[5]

Attitudes

Attitudes, as we learned in Chapter 8, are *tendencies to respond* positively or negatively to persons, situations, or objects. As we discuss intercultural communication, we will consider our attitudes as they involve social perception, world view, ethnocentrism, values, stereotypes, and prejudices.

Perception

Social perception, the process by which we attach meaning to the objects and events we encounter in our environment, is an extremely important aspect of any communication. It is the means by which we assign meanings to the messages we receive. As we discussed in Chapter 5, we tend to perceive only those stimuli in any given situation that are meaningful to us at the moment. This selective perception is universal; but each culture values certain things more than others, so tends to "see" or emphasize those things, often to the exclusion of others. Our culture guides or determines our social perceptions and is responsible in large measure for conditioning and structuring our perceptual processes.

Much of our sense of reality comes from our culture and from perceptions we share with other members of our cultural group. These culturally determined perceptions influence not only which stimuli reach our aware-

---

[5] Adapted from *Intercultural Communication: Proceedings of the Speech Communication Association Summer Conference X*, edited by Nemi C. Jain, et al. (New York: Speech Communication Association, 1974).

The way that we view our world is a function of our culture.

ness, but also the meanings we attach to them. Such meanings are internal, often below our level of awareness. When we encounter a social stimulus, we dip into our reservoir of prior experiences and, using our own unique thought process, extract the meaning we consider appropriate, usually in keeping with our cultural conditioning experiences. Cultural groups may differ from one another in behavior because of fundamental differences in their ways of perceiving social situations. Funerals are an example of a universal event with different social meanings in different societies. In some cultures a funeral is a dignified solemn occasion; in others it can be almost festive. These perceptual differences become quite evident in the various cultures within our own country, once we are aware of them, and could cause communication problems unless we understand and allow for such differences.

World View

The way we view our world is a function of our culture, and it affects our social perception. If we would be successful communicators with people from other cultures, we must understand their world view. Do they see human nature as basically good, evil, or a combination of both? What is humanity's place in the universe? Do they emphasize the past, present, or future? Does the culture believe in humanity's mastery over, submission to, or harmony with nature? Americans tend to have a human-centered view. We are likely to see the world as something we can use to carry out our desires. We build what we wish, we control nature as we can, and when we are not pleased with it, we tear it all down and start again.

In other cultures, humanity's relationship to the world is viewed differently. An Oriental world view is apt to be one of balanced relationships in which people share a place with heaven and earth. Each thing we do has some effect on the balance of that relationship. Consequently, we must act carefully so as not to upset the balance because the universe naturally tends toward harmony.

Ethnocentrism

Ethnocentrism is a predisposition to judge others (often unconsciously) by using our own group and our own customs as the standard for all judgments. It is a very easy attitude to slip into, and a *very dangerous one*. We put our racial, ethnic, or social group at the center of the universe and rate all others accordingly. Those closest to our own views we rate higher than those who are further away. We tend to see our own groups, our own country, our own culture as the best, the most moral, and so on. It has been said that ethnocentrism is "strongest in moral and religious contexts, where emotionalism may overshadow rationality and cause hostility to a degree that communication ceases."[6] Ethnocentrism can rob us of the desire to communicate interculturally, if we do not temper it with tolerance and acceptance of those who are different from us.

Values

One definition of "values" describes them as "culturally derived notions we have of right and wrong, good and bad, beautiful and ugly, true and false, positive and negative, and so on. They influence our social perception by providing us with a set of basic precepts from which we judge the behavior and beliefs of others."[7] We take these culturally derived values to be absolute, to be truth, and often fail to recognize that people from other cultures feel the same way about their cultural values. Our own socially influenced perception of cultural value systems can lead us to inaccurate judgments about the social reality of other cultures, causing conflict with members of the culture and seriously hindering our communication efforts.

Since an awareness of our own cultural values is important, we will touch on a few of them here, and more later on. Two values commonly associated with American culture are practicality and individualism. If you consider these two values carefully, you may discover how deeply embedded they are in American culture and how deeply influenced you are by them, whether or not you accept them as your own personal values. From

[6] Samovar and Porter, p. 7.

[7] Ibid.

the early days of our country, many Americans have stressed doing and accomplishing—practicality—over theory and principles alone. Americans traditionally take pride in the actions, accomplishments, and qualities of the individual person, glorifying those people whose success is "self-made"— the millionaire who started in the mail room, the super sport star. In connection with this, a high value is placed on individual freedoms, our right to choose for ourselves just about anything relevant in our lives.

The American concern with the individual is not shared by all cultures. Many Japanese, for example, do not place the individual on a pedestal; they stress the group and its norms. Some of the strain in relations between white Americans and Native Americans comes from a failure to understand that Indian cultures historically subordinated the individual to the group, much as do the Japanese.

Experience with another culture often increases our understanding of our own culture more than of the other. Recognizing our own assumptions and values should help us to understand someone else's responses in that person's culture, and hence contribute to our ability to work with people from other societies. An important objective for us is to identify similarities.

Any time we deal with values, whether our own or those of others, we are likely to make value judgments or evaluations. Such evaluations may interfere with understanding. We need to remind ourselves of the information in Chapter 5 on statements of observation, inference, and judgment. Inferential reasoning is based on conclusions we draw about others from our *own* frame of reference. Such inferences may not even be valid about people from our own culture, let alone those from another culture. We must not assume or infer *anything* in intercultural communication without checking it out! Obviously, if inferences can cause trouble, making judgments or evaluations can be even more of a problem. We would do well to qualify our statements and unspoken thoughts with: "This is how the world looks to *me,* from *my* frame of reference, *today.*"

Stereotypes and Prejudices

Although we looked at stereotypes and prejudice in Chapter 5, they are particularly important in the context of intercultural communication and require further discussion. Both prejudices and stereotypes can often be below our level of conscious awareness, particularly if they have been ingrained in us as children. For this reason we should try to become consciously aware of anything that influences our attitudes toward and treatment of people from other cultures.

Prejudices are those attitudes or feelings that may predispose us to behave in certain ways toward people solely on the basis of their membership in some group. For instance, denying some people membership in clubs or organizations, forcing some to live in ghettos or barrios, restricting others to low-paying jobs or menial tasks—all are results of prejudice. Another example would be refusing to talk to or associate with someone simply because she or he belongs to some group we are prejudiced about.

Stereotypes are those attitudes by which we *assign attributes or qualities* to others solely on the basis of the class or category to which they belong. Stereotypes would be useful if they held true for all members of a culture, but this isn't the case. People cannot be pigeonholed. By using stereotypes, we try to reduce the threat of the unknown by making the world predictable. We often identify people from different nations by certain qualities we feel reflect their national character—the stuffy British, the romantic French, for example. Unfortunately, the idea of a national character can degenerate into the stereotypes (often unflattering) which one nation has of another, and makes no allowance for individual differences. Stereotypes, of course, apply to any group, not just to nations. Some examples are of Americans as materialistic, Japanese as inscrutable, the Irish as quick-tempered, Arabs as excitable, Jews as shrewd and grasping, and blacks as superstitious and lazy.

Once established, stereotypes tend to persist. We sustain and feed our stereotypes by *selective perception*. New facts and experiences which support the stereotype are accepted as reassuring and familiar; those which would contradict it are subject to doubt and easy rejection. Stereotypes persist because they help us rationalize our prejudices; also, they may be firmly established as truisms by our own culture. Asian or African visitors who are accustomed to privation and the values of denial and self-help cannot fail to perceive American culture as materialistic. For them, the stereotype is a concrete reality.

Clearly our expectations or predispositions have an effect on our interactions with others. If we expect certain traits or behaviors from certain individuals or groups, we will, in effect, see only those things that reinforce our expectations, ignoring (unconsciously or otherwise) any contradictions. This process tends to make us behave in such a way (again, often unconsciously) as to *bring about* the behavior in others that we expect! (See discussion of self-fulfilling prophecy, Chapter 5.) What self-defeating behavior this is! We can never be successful communicators as long as we let prejudices and stereotypes interfere with understanding. Perhaps we need to learn to communicate in terms of the expectations and predispositions of the person from the *other* culture, as he or she interacts with *us*. And ever and always, there are individual differences to be taken into consideration. The uniqueness of all people, regardless of culture, cannot be suppressed.

Language

One of the most obvious differences in culture—and one of the most obvious barriers to communication—is language. When traveling to foreign countries, one of the first things many of us do is to learn a few basic words and phrases in the language of the countries to be visited. These words and phrases may help us to get by in our travels, but obviously they are grossly inadequate if we truly wish to learn about and experience other cultures, for language is much more than merely having names for things. Even if we are fluent in the foreign language, it is only the beginning.

In the narrowest sense, language can be described as

a set of symbols (vocabulary) which evoke more or less uniform meanings among a particular population and a set of rules (syntax or grammar) for using the symbols. In the broadest sense, language is the symbolic representation of a people, and it includes their historical and cultural backgrounds as well as their approach to life and their ways of living and thinking.[8]

So a book of foreign phrases hardly gives us access to the language of another culture.

The Sapir-Whorf Hypothesis

Culture has a great deal of influence on our use of language. In fact, some people think it strongly determines just what our language is and how we use it. The central idea of the Sapir-Whorf hypothesis (developed by Edward Sapir and Benjamin Lee Whorf) is that language is more than just a mental experience, that language functions not simply as a device for *reporting* experience but also as a way of *defining* experience for its speakers. Far from being simply a means of communication, language is a way of directing the perceptions of speakers, providing ways of analyzing experience into significant categories. Every language, according to Sapir and Whorf, has an effect upon what the people who use it see, what they feel, how they think, what they can talk about. Concealed in the structure of each language is a whole set of unconscious assumptions about the world and life in it.

In effect, language influences the way people of a particular culture perceive and evaluate their world. Conversely, the realities and demands of the culture help to shape the language. Let's explore our *perceptions* of reality—what we see. What word can be made from the following letters?

A C O T

Many will say "coat." Those from the Southwestern United States might see the word "taco." This is an example of selective perception. As culture and perception are interdependent, so are culture and language, and language and perception.

Languages also *conceptualize* realities in ways that correspond to distinctions important within the culture. For instance, English verbs are conjugated for time—past, present, future. However, in American Indian languages verbs are conjugated for validity—who did it, who observed it being done, if it is hearsay, and so on. These two language differences express vastly different views of the world.

Language expresses or implies an *evaluation* of what is talked about. In English, "snow" is a total concept, and the word itself gives no evaluation of snow. In contrast, Eskimos have numerous words for snow, which evaluate the type and condition of snow being talked about.

Language also influences *motivation and behavior.* Since there is no word for "germ" in Navajo, it might be difficult persuading a Navajo mother to get

---

[8] Ibid., pp. 97–98.

her children vaccinated against polio or any other disease. In English we say, "I missed the bus," and "I dropped the dish." The nature of our sentence structure makes us take personal responsibility for what we do. In contrast, Spanish sentence structure places the responsibility elsewhere: "The bus left me." "The dish dropped itself."

Each language, then, guides its users in observing, reacting, and expressing themselves in a particular way. There are truly as many worlds as there are languages. And to the extent that languages differ markedly from each other, so should we expect to find significant barriers to intercultural communication and understanding.

Vocabulary

The vocabulary of any language reflects to some extent what that culture values, or the emphases of the culture, as well as cultural history. For instance, camels obviously have been of great importance in the Arab world; this is affirmed by the fact that in Arabic there are more than six thousand different words for the camel, its parts, and equipment. To most of us, snow is snow; however, skiers are interested in differentiating the conditions and kinds of snow to be found on the ski slopes, so they want to know whether it is hard-pack, powder, and so on. For the Eskimos snow is a daily fact of life and has a relationship to survival; as we just mentioned, its importance is seen in the fact that Eskimos have words for seventeen different kinds of snow. The Spanish cultures value paternalism; just a few words reflecting this are *papá* (father), *compadre* (buddy), *patron* (employer), *padre* (priest), *papa* (pope), and *padrino* (godfather). How many words can you think of for automobiles of various makes, sizes, and types, not to mention all the words related to equipment, extras, maintenance, and so on? Need we say that our culture values the automobile? What one culture may regard as unimportant or even nonexistent because it cannot be expressed in words, another culture, by the same criterion, may regard as supremely important. Many times, though there are no directly equivalent *words* from culture to culture, there are equivalent *concepts*. Also, what calls for a verbal response in one culture may evoke a nonverbal response in another.[9]

People who translate from one language to another work closely with the intercultural situation.

> *Anyone who has struggled with translation is made to realize that there is more to a language than its dictionary. . . . I asked a Japanese with a fair knowledge of English to translate back from the Japanese that phrase in the new Japanese constitution that represents our "life, liberty, and the pursuit of happiness." He rendered, "license to commit lustful pleasure." English to Russian and Russian back to English transmuted a cablegram "Genevieve suspended for prank" into "Genevieve hanged for juvenile delinquency."*[10]

[9] Adapted from *An Introduction to Intercultural Communication* by John C. Condon and Fathi Yousef (New York: The Bobbs-Merrill Company, Inc., 1975) p. 189.

[10] Kluckholm, Clyde. Cited in *Intercultural Communication: A Reader* by Larry A. Samovar and Richard E. Porter. Belmont, California: Wadsworth Publishing Company, Inc., 1976.

In Chapter 5 we discussed the fact that words have literal, dictionary definitions (denotations), which are usually what we learn first as we add words to our vocabulary or learn the vocabulary of another language or culture. We have also seen that words have connotative meanings, which are the individual, subjective, often emotional interpretations each of us has for words. Thus, words refer not only to events, but to the attitudes and feelings we have toward those events. We know that communication can break down if two people even from the *same* culture use words for which each has a different connotation, if they don't clarify what the words mean to them. In addition, the same words often don't mean the same thing to people of different generations within the same culture. Interpretations of words also vary from group to group in the same culture, as each group uses particular words in its own way. A related problem occurs when two people have different words for the *same thing*. (A nice restaurant to you may be a gyp joint to someone else.)

Living in the same country, then, is no guarantee that those involved in a communication situation speak a common language. Within a country as large and diversified as the United States, it is inevitable that certain groups—the drug culture, the black street subculture—develop and use their own particular and specialized languages. Groups may emphasize their unity by a special jargon or language. Criminals, various businesses and professions, and social or recreational groups are examples of such groups. The use of speech forms in common implies other experiences in common as well. "He talks like one of us" indicates acceptance; whereas the person who talks differently or "wrong" is often treated as an outsider who is strange or open to suspicion.

What we have been saying here should illustrate that, if word meanings are a problem in our own culture, they are most certainly an area for concern and caution in communicating with people from different cultures. While many persons may feel that "capitalism" implies a good economic system, the word may have negative connotations of exploitation to a Latin American. Many of us have generally negative connotations for the term "socialism," while it may have positive connotations of social justice and welfare for a Latin American. We must remember to allow for such differences if we are interested in communicating with those from another culture.

Structure

Anyone who has ever studied a foreign language knows how difficult it is to learn a new word order for sentences, a new grammar, when we may not even have mastered our own! It takes some time before we can even *begin* to "think" in the new language. Some languages have verbs, adjectives, and pronouns which discriminate between animate and inanimate things. In the Hopi language there is no substantive noun for time, and no tense system of past, present, and future as in English. It might be difficult to try to get a

Hopi to do something for some future reward or benefit, as what is meaningful to the Hopis is *now*. Many languages have both a formal "you" and a friendly or intimate "you," and we could give offense or cause embarrassment if we used them improperly.

Navajo language forms and patterns are much more specific than English. We may say we went somewhere, and let it go at that. The Navajo, however, "never fails to specify whether it was afoot, astride, by wagon, auto, train, airplane, or boat. If it be a boat, it must be specified whether the boat floats off with the current, is propelled by the speaker, or is made to move by an indefinite or unstated agency."[11]

The Chinese tend to give priority to "How?" and to nonexclusive categories. European languages are likely to give priority to "What?" and to exclusive categories. English has both real (tangible) plurals, such as "ten children," and imaginary (abstract) plurals, such as "ten weeks." We could go on and on with such structural and linguistic differences. The point is, an understanding of such differences and a willingness to accommodate ourselves to them are essential if we are to communicate successfully.

Nonverbal Factors

The discussion of nonverbal communication in Chapter 4 should serve as the basis for a general understanding of the significance of nonverbal cues in our interactions with others.[12] Here, we will more fully discuss only those nonverbal cues which are of particular importance in intercultural communication: space/territoriality (proxemics), time, and kinesics (body language).

Space

Proxemics, or the study of space and territory relating to people, includes *types* of space and *relational* space in human contact (intimate distance, personal distance, social distance, and public distance).

For many Germans, there is no such thing as sharing a room with someone without being inside the zone of intrusion, particularly if one *looks* at the other person, no matter how far away (visual intrusion into personal space). Most Germans have a need for visual privacy and will go to almost any length to preserve their private sphere. They may keep their doors closed when others would leave them open. Edward T. Hall has noted that "the open-door policy of American business and the closed-door patterns of German business culture cause clashes in the branches and subsidiaries of American firms in Germany."[13]

Many English people have no need for or expectation of rooms of their own (as children) or private office space (as adults). In that culture many

---

[11] Ibid., p. 111.

[12] Much of the material on "Nonverbal Factors" is based on *The Hidden Dimension* by Edward T. Hall. Copyright © 1969 by Edward T. Hall. New York: Doubleday & Company, Inc.

[13] Hall, p. 135.

never developed the practice of using space as a refuge from others. Instead, they have *internalized* cues or barriers to indicate when they want to be left alone, which others are supposed to recognize. The more an English person withdraws when with an American, the more likely the American is to break in to be assured that all is well, and this can cause friction.

Japanese spatial patterns generally emphasize centers; for them, psychologically, there is positive reinforcement toward the center of the room and negative reinforcement toward the edges. To most Westerners space means the distance between objects; we think of space as "empty." The Japanese, however, give *meaning* to spaces; they perceive the shape and arrangement of spaces, or *ma* (meaning the interval), which is a basic building block in all Japanese spatial experience. These spatial orientations may have some bearing on the contrast in behavior between us: a Japanese may be indirect, moving *around* the point, where an American might insist on coming *to* the point.

In the Arab world, public space is often compressed, crowded, and noisy. The Arab way to be alone, like the English, is to stop talking. In the Western world, the person is synonymous with an individual inside a skin, and even clothes are often considered part of that "personhood." In the Arab world, the person is somewhere down inside the body; there is a total separation of the body and the ego, and no concept of a private zone outside the body. Consequently, pushing and shoving are often characteristic of Middle Eastern culture. Americans may consider this behavior rude, but many Arabs don't look at it this way. For an Arab there is no such thing as personal space (either body or territory) when one is in a *public* place; one cannot be intruded upon in public. In our culture, we give up rights to space as we move, but when standing still we claim our "territory." The reverse is true with the Arabs, who take on rights to space as they move. It is infuriating to many Arabs to have someone else cut in front of them on the highway. (Of course we all know Americans who feel that way too.) Our use of moving space might make the Arab call *us* aggressive and pushy.

The Arab's distance-setting mechanism is a sense of smell; the American's is sight. Arabs generally consider it impolite to look at or talk with another person side to side; they must be face to face. To talk to someone with one's back turned is usually considered very rude. In Arab communications, the noise level is very high and involves piercing looks, touching, and close, face-to-face proximity—all of which most Americans would find intolerably intense. To the Arab, smells are pleasing, a way of being involved. To smell one's friend is not only nice, but desirable; to deny your breath is to act ashamed. In contrast, consider the American advertising and purchase of deodorants and mouthwashes.

Time

Another important nonverbal factor in intercultural communications is that of time, and the different ways various cultures have of dealing with it.[14] For

---

[14] The material on "Time" is based on *The Silent Language* by Edward T. Hall (New York: Doubleday & Company, Inc., 1973).

most of us in the United States, time can be compared to a road stretching into the future, along which we progress. We may handle time like a material; we can earn it, spend it, save it. We generally feel that time is valuable, and should not be wasted; time should be planned and future events fitted into a schedule. Many of us feel we should look forward to the future and not dwell too much on the past.

The Middle Eastern Arabs have three discernible points in dealing with time: *no* time at all; *now* (or present time), which is of varying duration; and *forever*, which is too long. In the Middle East it is often pointless to make an appointment too far in advance because everything beyond a week away may be put into the single category of "future," in which plans tend to slip out of mind. In Iran, present appointments are usually treated rather lightly but the past has very great importance. The Navajo Indians have no word for the future. Only immediate time has reality for them; future events are generally not even worth thinking about. Also, Navajos have no words in their language for "late" or "waiting," a further indication of how they handle time.

In the United States we show respect by arriving a little before the appointed time. Americans usually don't mind waiting five to fifteen minutes, but get irritated if it is longer; forty-five minutes is the insult period! However, with most Latin Americans, forty-five minutes may be only the *beginning* of the waiting scale. By our standards, Latin Americans treat time rather lightly; they feel we take it too seriously.

In the United States we generally feel that once the time is scheduled, we should use it as planned. Many Arabs do not feel it improper to meet without ever touching on the topic of the meeting. The latter is also often true of the Japanese. In the United States and Northern Europe, just plain sitting is not considered to be doing anything. In the Middle East, Japan, India, and the Navajo cultures, just plain sitting *is* doing something.

Kinesics

Perhaps the most obvious nonverbal factor in communication with other cultures is that of kinesics: body language, gestures, facial expressions, movement.[15] The examples are endless, but a few should serve to illustrate that we need to be careful of our own kinesic cues when interacting with those from different cultures, and in particular that we should not jump to quick interpretations of others' kinesic behaviors.

In American and Northern European cultures we point to things with an extended forefinger, the other fingers curled. The Mongoloid peoples and the Indians of both North and South America point with their lips. Americans indicate agreement by an up-and-down nod of the head; the Bulgarians do so by shaking their head side-to-side, which is our indication of disagreement.

Friendly greeting is shown among the Copper Eskimos by a buffet on the

---

[15] Some of the material on "Kinesics" is based on "Face Muscles Talk Every Language" by Paul Ekman in *Psychology Today* (September 1975).

head or shoulder with the fist. Polynesian men embrace and rub each other's backs; Tibetans stick out their tongues. Among Spanish-American males there is a traditional embrace of greeting: head over right shoulder, three pats on the back; head over left shoulder, three more pats.

Americans show surprise with a gaping mouth and raised eyebrows, as do most Europeans. Eskimos and Brazilians show surprise by slapping their hips; Tibetans, by pinching their cheek. Europeans and Americans show affection by embracing and kissing. Eskimos and Polynesians show affection by rubbing noses; Mongols, by smelling heads. One American gesture of farewell is waving goodbye with the palm forward and moving the hand from side to side. The same gesture in Greece means something equivalent to "A curse on you and your family for five generations!"

Many Chinese hate to be touched, slapped on the back, or even to shake hands. We could easily avoid offense merely by omitting these intended gestures of friendliness. Americans who smile are usually showing happiness, pleasure, or amusement. The Japanese smile is a law of etiquette and not necessarily a spontaneous expression of amusement. It is said that "the Japanese child is taught to smile as a social duty, so he will always show an appearance of happiness and avoid inflicting sorrow upon his friends."[16] In our American black subculture, stress or conflict, especially with authority figures, may be indicated by rolling the eyes and assuming a limp stance; trust and friendship might be shown by turning one's back on a person, which says, in effect, "I trust you enough to turn my back on you, leaving myself vulnerable."[16]

Despite the many cultural differences in kinesics, there are similarities in facial expressions among various cultures. In tests made in nine cultures there was agreement on both the identity and the intensity of emotion being expressed in pictures of different facial expressions. The emotions portrayed in the pictures (which showed a range of intensity) were: interest-excitement; enjoyment-joy; surprise-startle; distress-anguish; disgust-contempt; anger-rage; shame-humiliation; and fear-terror. Apparently there is a universality of some felt emotions, and of some facial expressions reflecting these emotions. However, the specific events that *activate* an emotion and the *rules* of managing the *display* of emotion are learned and culturally variable. Americans and Japanese both show disgust and delight, but when they express them and with whom varies in and is determined by each culture.

Becoming a Better Intercultural Communicator

There are several approaches we can take as we interact with persons from other cultures.[17] We can ride roughshod over them, insisting that things must be done our way, that we are right and they are wrong. This approach causes hostility and antagonism, with no positive benefits to be gained in

---

[16] Porter, p. 248.

[17] From *Speech Communication and Human Interaction* by Thomas M. Scheidel. Copyright © 1976, 1972 by Scott, Foresman and Company. Reprinted by permission.

We should learn from other cultures rather than insisting on our own ways.

human relations or communication. Needless to say, wars have been fought where such an attitude was held on a large scale by one or more groups. Another approach is to manipulate those of other cultures. Although a little more subtle, this approach is likely to cause resentment as it is not honest, and people usually know or can sense when they are being used. Again, little or nothing is gained in human relationships or in communication. A third approach is to go native, adopting every possible facet of the new culture (language, dress, behaviors, etc.) and rejecting one's own culture. This approach may be fun for a while, but it does not ultimately succeed. Others cannot respect and learn to like us if we do not respect and like ourselves— like who and what we are, which is inextricably interwoven with our culture. The best approach seems to be that of seeing ourselves as culture-bearers, aware and accepting of our own culture, but susceptible to change by contact with other cultures. This approach fosters the mutual respect, understanding, and appreciation that are essential for effective intercultural communication.

Human differences are often considered to be obstacles to communication, but we could profitably reverse the thought and consider cultural differences as human resources. When we find another society which appears to have greater knowledge, skill, or understanding in a given area, we should try to learn from them rather than insist on our own thinking and ways. Another objective for intercultural communicators is "to create an appreciation of the common human qualities underlying cultural differences to aid an understanding of the central values of other cultures, and to instill a realization that the different value systems of the world's peoples are each compatible with the universal human qualities, even when not compatible with each other."[18]

If we are to achieve our goals in communicating with those from different cultures, whether the goals be social, educational, business, or whatever, we will need certain skills and qualities. Many of these have been indicated throughout this chapter; indeed, to a great extent they reiterate the skills we have discussed throughout the book as important for effective interpersonal communication.

Following is a list of qualities desirable for a good intercultural communicator:[19]

1. *Above all, a genuine liking for people, sincerely enjoying and caring about them.*
2. *Language ability, for gaining self-confidence in a culture other than one's own.*
3. *Openness to taking risks, including the ability to overcome the fear of making mistakes.*
4. *Being an empathic listener and observer, sensitive, perceptive, compassionate, appreciative.*
5. *Being nonjudgmental and being careful about drawing inferences.*
6. *The ability to ask questions, generate feedback, and test possible interpretations.*
7. *Being a good communicator on the verbal and nonverbal levels, perceiving others' nonverbal behavior and being aware of one's own.*
8. *A sense of humor, especially the ability to laugh at oneself.*
9. *An awareness of the culturally based aspects of one's own attitudes and behavior.*
10. *The ability to come up with good hunches, good explanations, good references about what things mean and count for.*
11. *An awareness of one's own psychological needs, strengths, and weaknesses to help us know when the problem is within us, or related to some other aspect of the communication situation.*
12. *The ability to recognize the symptoms of miscommunication, and to know when to seek guidance from those who know the culture as natives.*
13. *A sensitivity to answers by indirection.*
14. *A respect for the cultural differences in values and life-styles, and a liking for diversity.*

A fitting conclusion for our discussion of intercultural communication is from Julius K. Nyerere, Prime Minister of Tanzania. "We believe that all mankind is one, that the . . . differences between us are unimportant in comparison with our common humanity. . . . Each one of us is part of the human species and has a part to play in the development of mankind."[20]

---

[18] From "International Communication and the World" by Robert C. Angell in *Reader in Public Opinion and Communication,* edited by Bernard Berelson and Morris Janowitz. New York: The Free Press, 1950, p. 374.

[19] Adapted from Scheidel, pp. 36–39.

[20] From "All Mankind Is One" by Julius K. Nyerere in *Sow the Wind, Reap the Whirlwind: Heads of State Address the U.N.,* edited by Michael H. Prosser. New York: William Morrow & Co., Inc., 1970, pp. 823–824.

FOR FURTHER INSIGHT

1. Study the attitudes of some culture other than your own. Pay particular attention to the attitudes toward materialism, sex, youth, age, the future, the past, and how these attitudes are communicated in that culture. Compare these attitudes with those of your own culture.
2. Study basic communication patterns from another culture regarding greetings, food, transportation, social occasions, business transactions, celebrations. How do they differ from such patterns in your own culture?
3. Analyze political and humorous cartoons or posters from different cultures for the communication assumptions that the symbols reflect.
4. Read at least one novel that focuses on life in another culture and analyze the communication variables that reflect the intercultural situation.
5. Collect and compile as many as possible of the statements which stereotype and/or indicate prejudice or discrimination with respect to various races, nationalities, groups. (Examples: "the luck of the Irish," "stingy as a Scotsman," etc.) What effect do such statements have on our attitudes toward and communication with members of these groups?
6. Study at least one American subculture (black, Latin, Native American, Jewish, Asiatic, etc.) and observe their rituals, linguistics, nonverbal behaviors, and other behaviors. Write a report on your study. Comment on what effect the study had on your own attitudes, feelings, etc., about the subculture.

REFERENCES Bem, Daryl. *Beliefs, Attitudes and Human Affairs.* Belmont, Cal.: Brooks/Cole Publishing Company, 1970.

Brown, Ina Corinne. *Understanding Other Cultures.* Englewood Cliffs, N.J.: Prentice-Hall, Inc., 1963.

Condon, John C. and Fathi Yousef. *An Introduction to Intercultural Communication.* New York: The Bobbs-Merrill Company, Inc., 1975.

Davis, Flora. *Inside Intuition.* New York: New American Library, 1975.

Ekman, Paul. "Face Muscles Talk Every Language," *Psychology Today.* September 1975, pp. 35–39.

Hall, Edward T. *The Hidden Dimension.* New York: Doubleday & Company, Inc., 1969.

——. *The Silent Language.* New York: Doubleday & Company, Inc., 1973.

Harms, L. S. *Intercultural Communication.* New York: Harper & Row, Publishers, 1973.

Jain, Nemi C., Michael H. Prosser, and Melvin H. Miller, eds. *Intercultural Communication: Proceedings of the Speech Communication Association Summary Conference X.* New York: Speech Communication Association, 1974.

Mehrabian, Albert. *Silent Messages.* Belmont, Cal.: Wadsworth Publishing Company, 1971.

Pettersen, Duane D. *Language: An Approach to International and Intercultural Communication.* (Paper presented at WSCA Convention at Seattle, Washington, November 1975).

Prosser, Michael H. *The Cultural Dialogue: An Introduction to Intercultural Communication.* Boston: Houghton Mifflin Company, 1978.

——, ed. *Syllabi in Intercultural Communication: 1974.* Charlottesville, Va.: University of Virginia Speech Communication Department, 1974.

Rich, Andrea. *Interracial Communication.* New York: Harper & Row, Publishers, 1974.

Samovar, Larry A., and Richard E. Porter. *Intercultural Communication: A Reader.* 2nd ed. Belmont, Cal.: Wadsworth Publishing Company, Inc., 1976.

Scheidel, Thomas M. *Speech Communication and Human Interaction,* 2nd ed. Glenview, Ill.: Scott, Foresman and Company, 1976.

Index